To Rob

With best wish

from all at

Barrington Street

JACKIE MILBURN
IN BLACK AND WHITE

— JACKIE MILBURN — IN BLACK AND WHITE

A Biography

MIKE KIRKUP

STANLEY PAUL

London Sydney Auckland Johannesburg

Dedicated to my three sons, Nathan, Aaron and Adam:
all potential Newcastle United centre-forwards

Stanley Paul & Co Ltd
An imprint of Random Century

Random Century House
20 Vauxhall Bridge Road, London SW1V 2SA

Random Century Australia Pty Ltd
20 Alfred Street, Milsons Point, Sydney, NSW 2061

Random Century New Zealand Limited
PO Box 40–086, Glenfield, Auckland 10

Century Hutchinson South Africa (Pty) Ltd
PO Box 337, Bergvlei 2012, South Africa

First published 1990

Phototypeset in 10/12pt Baskerville by
Input Typesetting Ltd, London

Printed and bound in Great Britain by
Richard Clay Ltd, Bungay, Suffolk

British Library Cataloguing-in-Publication
Data for this title is available
upon request from the British Library

ISBN 0 09 174483 0

CONTENTS

Acknowledgements

The author is grateful for the help and support given by the Milburn family, both in producing the play and with this book

Thanks are also due to ex-Magpies: Charlie Crowe, Frank Brennan, Bob Cowell, Bob Stokoe, Albert Stubbins and English international Tom Finney, for providing anecdotes and photographs; and to Jack Charlton for giving a rare insight into the management of Newcastle United

Additional material and photographs by: Neil Atkinson; Carmel College; Colorsport; Belfast Telegraph; Daily Mail; Hulton-Deutsch Collection; Lancashire Evening Post; Newcastle City Library – Local Studies; Newcastle Journal, Chronicle and Sunday Sun; News of the World; Palmer Photographics Newcastle; Weekly News

Personal photographs provided by: Norman Brotherton, John Courtney, Bill Harrison, Edna Ralph, Joe Smith, Jack Wallace, and family of the late Jackie Milburn

Painting by Oliver Kilbourn

Front cover of Woodorn Colliery Museum by Reuben Daglish

Foreword

In the days when Jackie Milburn grew up, and then, a decade or so later, me and our kid, the only way you could get away from Ashington was to play football. Or like some of my pals, you could go away to London to find a job and sort something out for yourself. Out of the lads that I knocked around with, maybe half of them left home, the rest are still at Ashington, and have been there all their lives.

One of the things about going away to play football was that you were worried that you might not make it, and get sent home again . . . then you went back as a failure. This was probably why we worked so hard when we went away from Ashington. In the first two years I was at Leeds I only played about once in the Central League before I went into the army.

Me and our kid played for Ashington YMCA. The pitch was at Reyrolles factory and it was like kicking a ball up one hill and down another. We played in the under-18 League at the time. I was only about fifteen, and our kid would be thirteen. We got murdered every week – in one season all we managed was one draw.

We had a football, which was through having uncles who played the game, and we took it over to Hirst Park on a Sunday, and got kicked to bits. If you wanted to go home for your dinner, they would talk you into leaving your ball, and they promised you would get it back, which you very rarely did. I've run around half-a-dozen houses trying to borrow a football so that we could start a game. And that one game would go on all day! Strangely enough, I could get a game in the morning when there weren't many there, but in the afternoon, if me and our kid had gone home for dinner, when we came back they'd probably give him a game, and I wouldn't get to play at all.

I worked at the pit for a short while. It was on 'bank' in the weigh-cabin at Linton colliery with a lad called Jackie Summers. I enjoyed it there. On the screens and spirals, which every young'un had to go on, you were sat in a little cubby hole all day, watching little bits of coal drifting by . . . and the noise! It didn't work all the time, and sometimes there was a quiet period when no coal was coming down and that was great. You used to draw pictures with a piece of stone. It was an artist's paradise! There were footballers, goals, nudes . . . everything. Some men worked in the screens and spirals for ever!

It was a worrying time. I didn't particularly want to leave home, and I didn't mind going into the pit or doing something within the mining industry. It was just that you were glad to leave school and go and get a job. And obviously at Ashington at that time there was only the pits – there was very little else.

Jackie Milburn lived and worked at Ashington at that time. My other uncle, Stan Milburn, played as well, and he used to be an 'oil-boy' at the pit, going around oiling all the machinery. Footballers in those days working at the pit were pretty well looked after. And with Jackie playing for Newcastle United, the gaffers used to turn a blind eye while he went off training.

In those days for me and our kid it was just football all the time. We used to go and queue at Portland Park, Ashington, to get behind the goals. The first laddies through the gates got to act as ballboys, and sometimes we used to get one end each – other times we had to share behind the same goal. When Stan Milburn played for Ashington, he used to let us into the dressing-rooms, and we used to clean up and carry the bucket out for the trainer. We thought that was great!

We didn't see Jackie all that much during that period, but sometimes called in to see him when he had the Fireplace shop on Station Road. He lived at the top-end of the town, and we were at the Hirst end. I used to visit my aunt Nance, Jackie's mother, quite a lot when they lived in one of the colliery rows. And I used to bump into Jackie there and at my aunt Ciss's – he was fond of her. We didn't bother him very much. It was in the days when you were told not to bother people.

Me and our kid would go to Newcastle to see him play. My father put us on the bus, and we'd get off at the Haymarket and go for something to eat at the British Home Stores restaurant. Then we'd go and queue at St James's Park. We'd always leave it to the last minute so that we could get passed over everybody's heads in the crowd, ending up right at the front.

Whatever match you saw, there would always be some great stars on the field. We used to go and see Charlton Athletic, because they had Sam Bartram in goal. And Manchester City had Frank Swift. We used to see Stan Matthews and Len Shackleton. We all had our heroes, and if a famous player came to Newcastle, you became that player for the rest of the week during your own little kickarounds in the backstreet or the park: 'OK! I'm Sam Bartram, and you can be Len Shackleton.'

Jackie Milburn became my idol, but he wasn't in the first place. When he first started to play he wasn't all that well received. He was an outside-right, and not the best in the world. It was only when they moved him to centre-forward and he started to score goals, that he took off. And our kid and me went through that period when sometimes you were a bit . . . although you had a relative playing on the field, you didn't tell anyone. It was only when he became popular that we started to say that Jackie was related.

After I went to Leeds, me and our kid used to meet up on a Saturday on the train coming back from Manchester. Newcastle United had their own special carriage attached to the train when they travelled. We didn't go into the Newcastle section, but Jackie would come out into the corridor and talk about the game he'd just played, and ask us how we'd got on. When the train arrived at Newcastle Central, we had invariably missed the last bus, and Jackie used to shove us in a taxi and tell the driver to charge it to Newcastle United! Great!

Jackie went through probably the greatest era for Newcastle United, playing in all three Cup Finals and he scored great goals. I played against him at the end of his career when I played for Leeds. I remember racing him for a ball to the touchline and I got there first. As he went to cross the ball, I blocked it with a tackle, and I remember thinking to myself: 'I didn't think I was as quick as him,' but by then Jackie was about thirty-three, and obviously not as fast as he had been.

My most vivid memory is of Jackie scoring a goal against Ted Ditchburn of Spurs. He got this ball on the half-way line and hit it, and it just flew, I can see Ditchburn diving and the ball going away into the far corner of the net. He had this sliding tackle as well, chasing a defender and hooking it away from him. And when Jackie was running, he always looked around him, looking to see where people were so that he could lay on a pass. That was unusual in those days: to run with the ball keeping your head up.

Jackie was never one to get involved in putting in a personal appearance. I was at the 'do' when the Duke of Edinburgh presented him with a sword. He was everybody's friend! If you ever walked through Newcastle with him, you got stopped every two minutes; everybody said Hello to him; everybody called him Jack. Maybe it was the way he talked or smiled and always had a word with people that made him as popular as he was. Obviously the memories of him playing football were very important to people, but there's got to be more than that for him to make that kind of mark on the area and the society.

I got a phone call from someone in Wallsend, asking if I would come up and open a new store. I said I couldn't come, and they asked if I knew anyone else who might do it. So I told them to get Jackie to do it. And it was publicised that Jackie Milburn was going to be there to open the store. And the people rang me the next day and said: 'Hey it was terrific! There were so many people here that the police had to stop the traffic.' And that was an example of how everyone loved him.

I probably got to know Jackie best when he was a journalist. When I went to Middlesbrough as manager in 1973, I used to get Jackie, Len Shackleton and Albert Stubbins coming through for a story for their respective papers pretty well every week. I used to get a phone call, and the secretary would say: 'I've got these three reporters down here, what should I do with them?' And I used to say: 'Don't leave fellas like that down there, bring them up to my office and give them a cup of tea.'

I'd not really done the job properly at 'Boro when I started to get offers of other jobs. I'd been there two years and we'd got into the First Division, but it wasn't time to leave. I always said I would stay four or five years at a football club and no longer. I had four good years at Middlesbrough, and I'm sure Jackie broached the subject once or twice about me taking the Newcastle manager's job then.

He did talk me into it eventually! Arthur Cox had just left, and when he left . . . I've always followed Newcastle United, to this day I'm a Newcastle fan. I was brought up black-and-white-eyed, and I don't think you ever change. Even when I was a player, the first results I looked for were those at Newcastle. When you're a Newcastle fan as a boy, you're a fan for life! But I don't think I would have even considered the job if Jackie hadn't approached me. I got on well with him; he came to see me a lot. I enjoyed it for the year I was there.

I still miss Jackie. I live up here and I'm still in football, so I get to Newcastle and Sunderland to see the games. I used to see Jackie at the matches. He would be leaning against the wall or around the corner, and we used to stop and have a natter about the game and the prospects. I miss him now especially when I go to St James's, because the first person you used to see when you walked through the doors would be Jackie stood there. It's very difficult to imagine Newcastle United without Jackie Milburn.

JACK CHARLTON
January, 1990

Introduction

I very nearly missed interviewing Jackie Milburn altogether. My appointment was for half past one, and by two o'clock I still hadn't found the right house. I was hammering on a door when a man living nearby, industriously painting his upstairs window, the base of his ladder wedged into a bed of bright summer flowers, shouted to enquire whom I was looking for.

'Jackie Milburn!' I said, almost reverently.

'You're in the wrong street, bonnie lad.' From his vantage point at the top of his ladder he pointed a finger in the direction of the adjacent terrace. 'He lives over there, second house from the end. In fact, if I'm not mistaken, I think that's him just leaving!'

Grunting a hurried 'Thanks' I scurried up some stranger's garden path, just in time to spot Milburn crossing the road. I shouted after him. 'Hello! Ja – er – Mr Milburn!' Surely not time for first names yet, I thought. He heard me and turned.

'You the fella who wants to talk about the play? I'd given up on you! I usually go for a nice long walk about this time. Come on, I'll take you into the house.'

He'd lost the harshness of the authentic Ashington accent, but the flatness of the vowels marked him instantly as being Northumbrian: and wasn't he proud of that! We sat opposite each other in a neat sitting room, walls speckled with photographs of past glories; one with Cardinal Basil Hume, both men being awarded the Freedom of the City of Newcastle; another shaking hands with Field Marshal Montgomery, Milburn with his arm in plaster. 'I'd broken my wrist days before, but it still didn't stop me playing. Against Bolton Wanderers, I think!' It took a lot to lay Jackie Milburn low!

'Would you like a drink? There's sherry there . . . or do you want a whisky? Just help yourself, Michael. I'm hopeless, me! I never touch the stuff.'

He sat on the edge of his chair. 'Aye, and you want to write a musical, eh! I don't know how you're going to manage that – you see, all I did was kick a bit of leather around a field. If you can make a musical out of that, whey . . . !' Milburn gave a little shake of his head and, to confirm his disbelief, an embarrassed wave of his right hand. His doubts aired, he then settled more comfortably back into his chair.

It had taken weeks to track the great man down, and it was mid-June before someone furnished me with his telephone number. We arranged to meet on a Thursday: 'Aye, Thursday's fine! That's wor lass's golf day, so she'll be out of the way.'

It transpired that he had been living in Ashington for the last five years. 'We were living in Benton but we got burgled, so I says to Laura, "Come on, kidda . . . we're going home!" ' Predictably, the house he had bought was only a couple of hundred yards away from the one in which he'd been born: 'That house was knocked down long enough since, though! Presto's got a car park there now. Aye, Ashington's all changed . . . for the better, mind. Oh, Aye!' I was to learn that, like a homing pigeon, Milburn returned to Ashington time and again throughout his life, whenever he was troubled or just downright tired. It was where he could relax completely with his friends and family all close by.

The question arose of where the play might begin – at which point in his life, that is. 'Whey, man, there's only the one place you can start; where it all began, with me walking up Wembley steps to get my first FA Cup winner's medal from the King in 1951.' It says much for the man's obsession with the game that he kept returning to football whenever asked to describe a particular highlight in his life. He didn't think that people would be interested in any facet other than that of the tried and trusted footballer.

Since he had retired from the football stage, Jackie had been very keenly sought after as an after-dinner speaker, and like all speakers he had a repertoire of regular stories to be trotted out at sporting functions and the like. It was at this point in the conversation that I began to feel that I was being given the after-coffee treatment! Somehow, I had to kick the ball into touch to get him talk about his childhood; who his young friends were; what he did at school; what was his first job; what were his hopes and fears. These were the things that interested me and, I thought, future audiences of a play or readers of a book. I gradually got Jackie to play on the same side as me, and then the stories really began to flow: 'I'll tell you this one. Mind, I was sworn to secrecy at the time.' The next three hours passed in a flash as Jackie weaved his way in and out of a life studded with glittering milestones.

Almost unnoticed, Laura, Jackie's wife, entered the room. She had returned from playing golf, and Jackie went through what seemed to be for him an embarrassed, awkward introduction. 'Have you not offered the lad a drink?' she asked. I tried to place the accent; it definitely wasn't local. 'Will you have a coffee?' I was infuriated by my inability to pinpoint Mrs Milburn's place of origin.

'Did you have a good game?' I asked, hoping to get it next time.

'Oh, not bad! Played up to my handicap, you know.' She was Scottish. I was sure; it was the upward lilt of the word 'handicap' that gave the game away.

'Have you finished with Mavis's Barbra Streisand video? Cos if you have, I'll take it back across to Jean's and get the eggs while I'm there,' she said. Mavis and Jean turned out to be Jackie's sisters, Jean living in the next street, while Mavis lived at Morpeth. Laura made ready to go.

'Got a card in, eh, kidda!' said Jackie. 'Champion! Haddaway put the kettle on!'

CHAPTER ONE

It was always football – I knew nowt else

Date: 28 April 1951. *Time:* 4.05 p.m. *Place:* Wembley Stadium, London. *Scenario:* A tall, well-built figure in a loose-fitting black and white striped shirt, a large black number 9 emblazoned on the back, stands poised, sharp as a pick. He checks his position: four yards into the opposing half of the field. He is onside when the ball is side-footed to him by a swarthy bull of a man, 'Pancho' to his mates.

Nevertheless he looks up, and left, to the official, desperately trying to keep up with him but hopelessly outpaced. The man, dressed in black tunic and shorts, is carrying a short stick tied to a rectangular piece of orange cotton. Ten attacks have already been aborted by the waving of a flag. This time it stays down, tucked into his side.

The stylish twenty-six-year-old has slipped the field. With every raking stride he takes, shirt billowing, the huge crowd senses that there can only be one winner. The rest are also-rans.

Only fifty yards now between the centre-forward and the goal. He closes his ears to the pandemonium cascading from the terraces. Somewhere up there is a frail King whose hand he shook only an hour ago. Two rows behind the Royal Box are the people who really matter to him: his mother, and wife Laura. Back home, his two baby daughters play unconcernedly while their minders crouch over a large bakelite wireless set, drinking in every word that pours from the moustachioed mouth of BBC commentator Raymond Glendenning.

A mere forty yards to go. Suddenly the ball changes to a stone and the rugged six-footer to a child. The green turf of Wembley becomes a backstreet gutter in a

1

north-east pit town, lashed by a cold North Sea. This is where it all began. This is where the footballing skill was first learned, kicking a battered old tennis ball up against crumbling coalhouse walls.

Thirty yards to go. Now he is a slim teenager, and the goalposts ahead of him are pit-props, capped by a wooden plank. Beyond lies daylight. He is racing outbye, and way behind are his marras without a hope in hell of catching him. It's the last shift of the week, and he's playing football that afternoon in the Ashington Miners' Welfare League. The one hundred thousand faces bearing down on him are rocks, threatening to fall about his ears and bury him in this black tomb.

There is only one escape, and that is through that shaft of light blazing from in between the white props, now only twenty yards in front of him. A burly figure emerges to bar his path. The vast crowd holds its breath. 'No! No! Get out of the way! You can't stop him now. Nobody can!'

'It's a GOAL!' And 300 miles away, joyous cries of delight from the half a dozen people dancing around the tiny sitting room startle two baby girls, Linda and Betty Milburn; they wonder what all the fuss is about. Back at Wembley Stadium their father Jackie, trotting back to the middle after scoring one of the most exciting goals in an FA Cup Final, was doing exactly the same.

We played the 1951 Cup Final against Blackpool, and I scored the first goal, and Morty, Stan Mortenson, playing for Blackpool, shouted when we ran back to the centre-circle: 'Great goal! Well done, son, I'm proud of you!' Cos he was a Geordie, you see. He played for Ashington during the war.

CHAPTER TWO

Cos I was brought up kicking a football

Aye! That's where I was born: 14 Sixth Row, Ashington. Presto's is there now. Overlooking the pit yard into the tankey shed, that's where I was born. The tankeys used to puff, puff, puff all day, and all night 'n' all, but you got used to it. I more or less lived there . . . that was me Grannie's house.

John Edward Thompson Milburn's life revolved around a smokey little pit town eighteen miles north of the Tyne. It was home. During his footballing career with Newcastle United and England, he had travelled to the far corners of the world – Brazil, South Africa, Canada, Scandinavia. He'd been cosseted in a first-class berth on the *Queen Mary*, and fed on the best that was going, but he was never happier than when crossing the Tyne Bridge, with the whiff of the pit heaps in his nostrils.

I just couldn't wait to get back to Northumberland; the greatest place in the world!

Milburn was born on 11 May 1924 in the upstairs flat of his Grannie Thompson's. A few yards away lay the cobbled colliery yard. The small houses were squeezed into a concertina terrace, overshadowed by the ever-moving winding gear strad-dling a pit riddled with thin, deep shafts. A thousand feet below the ground, strong sinews of coal spread out into the nearby pits, the names of which rang out like bells at Sunday worship: Shilbottle, Lynemouth, Linton, Pegswood, Woodhorn, Blackhill, Ellington, Whittle, Newbiggin, Broomhill, Longhirst Drift, and at the heart of them all Ashington, the biggest mining village in the world.

The first lease to mine coal in the Ashington district was issued in 1846, and a shaft was sunk to the High Main seam. Soon the Ashington Coal Company became the biggest employer in the North-East, employing over 5000 men and boys – as well as some girls in the early days. Five more shafts were sunk, and by 1860 six long rows of colliery-owned houses had been built: First Row to accommodate the gaffers, and the rest to house the work force. They were to be the first of many such rows of brick boxes with slate lids, all leading from the colliery yard, and known simply by their numbers.

In 1920 the Coal Company bosses, who had acquired a reputation for taking a great interest in the miners' well-being away from work, directed considerable funds towards the establishment of a Welfare Department embracing educational, sporting and leisure activities. It was this provision of sporting facilities which was to turn the pit village of Ashington into a 'football factory', out of which dozens of local lads were to stumble from the pit cage into some of the greatest football teams of the day. The blue scars of the mine were in their blood, but so was football. And if you asked where their hearts and ambitions lay, hungry eyes would turn in the direction of the Tyne and Newcastle United. For that was the only escape from the pits. It was a straight choice: the pits or football – but only if you were good enough.

I counted up one day, and I got as far as forty-seven Ashington lads who had made the grade in League football, and I mean First Division 'n' all, none of your lower League stuff.

The pitmen who went to Leeds, Manchester or London to further their footballing careers were without vanity or frills, and as uncompromising in their attitude and outlook as the marras they had left behind down the pits of Ashington. Above all, they were grateful. They had made it. They had got away.

Playing football was a doddle after working down the pit. When you've bounced your head against a misshapen arch girder, or your leg has been split wide open by a piece of jagged stone falling from the roof, what have you to fear from a misplaced kick by some unfriendly opponent? Given a choice between pit-props and goalposts, to the colliers of Ashington there was no contest.

It was football, football all the time with me. I knew nowt else. I got away, but I was lucky. In fact, I've been lucky all through me life.

Jackie, indeed, was lucky in being the first-born of Alec and Nance Milburn. His parents had moved into his Grannie Thompson's house as soon as they had been married. It suited Alec fine, as the house was right on the doorstep of the pit where he worked as a cutterman. Alec wasn't on short time and was able to provide quite well for his new family. Others weren't so fortunate, and had to make do with a working shift whenever it was offered. Weighing a hefty fourteen pounds at birth, young Jackie thrived, but for all that was very much on the small side when his school days began.

I remember the day I started school, and this is the gospel truth. Me mother took me to the Hirst North school. And she had knitted a special outfit. You know what it was like before the war – I'm talking about 1930 or 1929. Anyway, she had knitted a thing with a knitted top, and I cried my bloody eyes out because I hadn't a pair of pants like the other lads. You felt as if you were a jessy with your knitted stuff on.

Two years his junior, sister Jean recollects: 'Even at a very young age it soon became noticeable that he was pretty nifty on his feet, especially among the neighbours. One after another they would come around asking Jackie if he would run messages for them. He would get a penny here and halfpenny there, and it all mounted up.' Jackie Milburn was a professional even at six years of age!

Jackie couldn't wait to get out of school so that he could hurry home, kicking a piece of stone through the gutters of unmade streets as he ran. But he wasn't the only lad in Sixth Row who was football daft. Often there would be games in progress of twenty a side or more, scrambling after a little tennis ball. Some wore their fathers' old pit boots, and showers of sparks would fly up when one made contact with the narrow-gauge railtrack which bisected each of the long, clarty backstreets and was used to transport cast-iron bogies carrying the miners' free coal.

There was only me and my two sisters, and I was a bit spoiled, being the first-born. But it was more or less football all the way for me. I knew nothing else: that's all I wanted to do.

Christmas day 1932 was very special to Jackie: he was given a spanking brand-new pair of football boots. He'd owned a pair before then, but they were hand-me-downs from Willie Chambers who lived next door. The Chambers, with four sons at work down the pit, could afford new boots for their Willie.

We used to have great times as lads, specially on Cup Final Sa'day, cos that was the day you could listen to a live football match being broadcast on the BBC.

Me gran used to put her wireless set on the kitchen windowsill so that us lads could hear the commentary as we played our own match in the street. I remember Arsenal playing against somebody else, and the name Joe Hulme never seemed to be off the commentator's lips. He was Arsenal's right-winger, and he played for England.

I suppose, in a way, he must've been me first soccer idol, and I said to me pals: one day I'm gonna be a winger, just like him. I knew I was aiming high.

Football had been in the Milburn blood for three generations before 'Jet' screamed his way into the world. In 1886 his great-grandfather, a character nicknamed 'Warhorse,' had kept goal for Northumberland, Ashington and Morpeth.

It was always football, cos I was brought up kicking a ball. My whole family . . . my father . . . there was six brothers and three sisters on my father's side and every one of them

5

played football. Ladies and men played in organised football. So we knew nothing else, right from the start.

At that time I had cousins playing League football, and that was the lead-in for me because Jack, George, Jimmy and later on young Stan, four brothers, all played professional football; three at Leeds, and Stan went to Chesterfield.

Now their sister, Elizabeth, is Cissie Charlton, who had two sons, Bobby and Jack. Cissie was my full cousin; that makes Jack and Bobby second cousins.

George, Jack and Jimmy were my idols. When they came home in the summer months there was nothing I liked better (and I wanted to see more) than them kicking a ball about the back lane.

Kickabouts in the backstreets were to serve Jackie Milburn well, but he got his first taste of organised football at the age of eleven when he was picked to play for Hirst East Secondary Boys' School. He'd only just moved there from the junior school when he was chosen to play against Linton at outside right, his favourite position.

When I saw me name alongside the others pinned up on the tattered old noticeboard, I could have leaped and touched the ceiling.

Dickie Freeman, outside-left in the same side, recollects that he and Milburn were a year younger than the rest of the team, and that much smaller: 'But we must've proved we were good enough somehow, otherwise we wouldn't have been in the team, would we!' Tom Mackie, inside-forward remembers: 'We had a good team, but Jackie didn't stand out as being anything special. He was a canny runner, I'll say that for him, mind.' Jackie could hardly wait to get home to tell his mother. Alec Milburn was on night shift and wasn't due home until after midnight, but Jackie was determined to wait up for him so that he could share in the good news. In the early hours he was lying wide awake in his bed when he heard the back-door latch click and the heavy thud of pit boots on the lino floor. Jackie was ready to rush downstairs to tell his father when he suddenly thought better of it.

Mebbe after a hard shift aback of the cutting machine, I thought he would prefer his bed to me badgering him with news of me honour at being picked to play for the school, so I turned over and waited for him to come upstairs.

Downstairs he could hear Alec howking up woolly grey phlegm, and spitting coal dust into the back of the fire, black roundies still piled high into the red-hot glowing grate. After Jackie was sure everyone was asleep, he crept downstairs, pulled on his red and green school strip and sat in front of the fire all night, thinking of ways he could beat the opposing full-back in the morning – like Joe Hulme did for Arsenal.

6

CHAPTER THREE

People keep saying, 'Did you want to play for Newcastle?'

Childhood for Milburn was one long ninety-minute game of football, with added distractions like education merely tolerated – a sort of half-time interval between kickabouts. He wasn't an academic, but sported a wry sense of humour.

At school I was top in only one thing in me life, and that was a History exam. I sat next to a lad called Joe Morton, a great scholar, who wrote with his right hand, and I wrote with me left. And we were joint top with 73 marks each. Only time I'd ever been top. I could never understand why Joe copied off me!

The headmaster at Hirst East Boys' was Jack Denton, who had taught Jimmy Richardson, the Newcastle United player involved with a dubious goal in the 1932 Cup Final. Denton was instrumental in getting Jackie a place in the East Northumberland team, a prestigious side capable of holding its own against some of the best teams in the north of England.

I played for the school team, of course, and East Northumberland. I was playing for them when we played Manchester Schoolboys, and I scored a goal there at Maine Road; that was the first really big ground I ever played on. Whey, you know what it was like when you saw your name in the paper.

Milburn as a schoolboy had no burning ambitions to join Newcastle. In fact, through listening and playing to live broadcasts on the wireless, he confessed to a hankering after playing for Arsenal. Luckily he never followed that idea through, and I doubt if 'Wor Jackie: the Cockney Sparra', would have had the same impact in later years.

People keep saying, 'Did you want to play for Newcastle?' It just felt as if you wanted to be the best, wherever you were at the time. I wanted to be the best in the class, and I wanted to be the best in the school. You never thought about the higher-up things.

It was the same when you were playing for Newcastle; you wanted to be the best. And it was the same when I was playing for England; you wanted to be the best. People keep saying that when they were kids they wanted to play for Newcastle. I never gave it a thought.

Jackie put his tennis ball to a different kind of use in the summer. Out would come the dustbin lids to act as wickets and a little coal shovel for a bat. And for the long weeks of the summer holidays the game of cricket would take precedence, when a hit into the back alley was 'six and out'.

There was nothing Jackie liked better than pitting his skill and speed against all comers. At his last school sports day he entered every event – high jump, long jump and 100 yards – winning them all easily, in some cases setting records which stood for many years afterwards. The final event was the 440 yards, and he had a go at that as well.

Now by this time I was jiggered, but anyway I just managed to hang on and win. But as I crossed the line I fell to the ground, exhausted. I looked up, and there was me father glowering at us with a face as black as thunder.

'Get up!' he said. 'Get on your feet, lad! Call yoursel' a sportsman. No sportsman I ever knew finished with his head down in the clarts. If you're ever gonna be good at anything, lad, you've gotta finish with your head held high, like a man should.'

He was a hard man, me father. Very hard. But a good man – don't get me wrong. I never forgot the hiding he gave us that day. People have always said that I'm a shy, retiring sort of chap. Nowt o' the sort; I've had an inferiority complex ever since that day. I've never forgotten it.

Mind, he kept me feet on the ground, and in football that's got to be a good thing. He gave me some of the best advice I ever had as well. 'Demand the ball,' he always said. 'You are no good without it!' And of course, he was right. When you are out there on that pitch the ball is your best pal. You've got to keep demanding and demanding it.

One of the great myths that has grown up around Jackie Milburn, possessing all the attributes that made him everyone's idea of the perfect number nine, was that it was a position he hated and never wanted to fill. Much later, when he was first picked to play for England, he denied it. But this was the tale the pressmen loved to tell:

Funnily enough, I vowed I would never ever play centre-forward. I played once in that position

8

at school, and I was terrible! You know the way things always stick in your mind throughout your life.

I played one game against Linton School at Hirst Park, and I never kicked a ball. I was hopeless – absolutely hopeless at centre-forward, and I vowed then and there that I would never play in that position again, which I never did till Charlie Wayman left Newcastle.

For the last six months of his schooling Jackie transferred to the Bothal School, as Alec had brought his family back up to the top-end of Ashington. Near neighbour Ronnie Coulson struck up a firm friendship with Jackie: 'We were more than pleased to have Jackie at the Bothal School. He was only there a short time, but it was great having him in my house, cos I was house captain and he won practically everything on sports day. Knowing what a good footballer he was, we expected miracles of him. He made a big difference, but we still used to get walloped.'

Milburn, still only thirteen, was now getting used to the attention that was being directed his way from his contemporaries.

I'm not being big-headed, but I always took this sort of stuff in me stride. Because even at junior school I felt that people in the class sort of admired and looked up to me. Mebbe because of me running powers and footballing powers. Cos I used to score goals all over the place! It happened at lower school right way through to senior school.

Seemingly, it must be a marvellous thing for giving you self-confidence. I don't know, cos I'm a fella with no confidence at all. Cos that's all I could do, play football and run. Apart from that I was . . . phew!

You know why I think I got the breaks later on. It was because of the know-how around the goals. All my life I spent throwing balls on to the tilings, and hit them before they hit the bottom, into the netty corners. They were only about three feet wide, though. I spent all my life with a ball after school. I kicked the same stone to school for three years!'

During Jackie's last week at school, his teacher was asking each of the fourteen-year-old leavers what they wanted to be. Jackie held his head down when it came to his turn. 'Now then, Jackie, I don't suppose we need ask where your ambitions lie,' said the schoolmaster.

'Please, sir,' I said, 'I want to be a butcher.' I couldn't for the life of me think what to say, you see. Much to the merriment of the whole class.

Jackie Milburn, in fact, became a kitchen boy. One of his friends, Eddie Main, put him in touch with an agent whose job was to 'place' young boys and girls in service, usually down in the more prosperous South.

It was 1938, and times were difficult, especially in a pit community where there was a surplus of coal. The owners, complaining of a lack of orders, hadn't worked the colliery at full strength for many years. A large board, hanging prominently in the centre of Ashington on Station Bridge, informed the men when they needed to

9

report for their next shift. When Jackie and the other twenty lads in his class left
school, the notice read: 'NO NEW MEN REQUIRED'.

For me first job I went away to be a pantry boy near Dorking, in Surrey, when I was fourteen.
There was a lad in the same street called Lance Richardson; he went away on the same bus.
He was gonna be a jockey at Fred Darling's stable at Beckhampton. Gordon Richards was
there.

Me father had said, 'If it's the last thing you ever do, lad, you'll never go down the pit.'
Cos he worked down below, you see.

There was a woman in the Fifth Row who used to advertise for kitchen staff. She used to
do all the things for 'service' for all over the country. She was the agent in this area, and she
used to put adverts in the paper. We didn't know what the hell kitchen service was.

I had wanted to join the Navy. That's what I wanted to be. At least, that's what one or
two of the lads in the class wanted to be, so that's what I thought I wanted to be. But I was
only five foot and half an inch, and you had to be five one. I shot up nine inches in one year
after that.

Jackie was put on the overnight bus down to London where he was met by Captain
Evelyn, in whose country house he was to work. There followed a long drive
through country lanes in a chauffeur-driven limousine, passing field after field
stuffed with apple trees. He was amazed. It was the first time he'd ever seen apples
growing on trees.

I ran away the first morning! They put me to bed, and I got up and ran away. I got about
four or five miles, and they had to come and pick me up in the Rolls Royce, and they took me
back again.

When I went back that afternoon they told me I didn't have to work that day, just go around
the estate. And there were apple trees growing, and I must've picked about three or four stone
of apples and put them in the top drawer upstairs – because I had never seen anything like this,
you see.

I saw a football match going on outside the estate, and I started to cry. That's what I was
missing most, the football. I ran away the next morning and they didn't catch us this time. I
got the train to London – I had an Auntie Bella there and I knew her address. I got a taxi. I
was only fourteen, and I didn't have a clue. No money or nothing! So I got a taxi to Eton
Mews; 22 Eton Mews.

My auntie, my mother's sister, paid the taxi and she paid my fare home the next day. That
was after only four days. When I got back home I noticed someone had chalked on the gable-
end of the street: 'WELCOME HOME GORDON'. And then I twigged. It was for Lance
Richardson. He had lasted two days less than I did!

Jackie's next job was at the Ideal Stores, a general dealers on Ashington's First
Avenue. He filled bags of sugar and then weighed them, registering each weight
on the bag with a pencil. It was boring but it was a job, and he was earning money
on a regular basis for the first time in his life. He was also back home again where

he belonged; where he felt safe; and where the lads were playing football. The latter was the most important, and meant even more to him than the one shilling pocket money his mother returned out of his eight shillings a week wages.

But his father had always wanted him to get some kind of trade, and Jackie got his chance when the Second World War broke out in 1939. The government began yelling for coal, and the Ashington Coal Company responded by setting on more workers. It was then that Alec fixed it for his son to serve his time as an apprentice fitter, but that wouldn't happen until he was nearly sixteen.

My first job at the colliery was in the saddler's shop. I was there for about a year. They used to make the knee-pads and all the horses' bridles. I used to oil them and one thing and another, and make the belts.

Then I started me apprenticeship as a fitter, when I was about fifteen and a half. It was a five-year apprenticeship, but it was magic because you got six months at least in every part of the profession. You had six months on the cutters; six months on general; six months in the loco shed; six months in the garage. You covered every sphere of engineering, really.

I didn't mind going down the pit, but that's part of the reason why I left. We used to do stupid bloody things. I used to have nightmares when I came back here to live at Ashington. I used to wake up sweating in the middle of the night.

What brought it all about was . . . we used to work on big boilers. And I had to take the front off and crawl inside, cos they were full of pipes, and they used to get rusty, so you had to keep cleaning the scale off. Once or twice the lads used to put the big door with about twenty bolts back on so you couldn't get out. It was only daftness, and we all knew that eventually they would take it off again. But I used to have nightmares, thinking that if somebody left just one nut on . . . just one nut. Stupid! I never thought about it till I came back here again. It really did affect me for a while.

But anyway, we used to go down the pit as apprentices with fitters. First time I ever went down the pit I left me top coat on. This was me first time ever with a fitter. And we walked inbye about four miles, and I had me top coat on and me scarf, all the way. The sweat was pouring off me! I didn't know what it was all about, you see. I didn't have a clue! But he didn't have the sense to tell us to take me coat off . . . daft bugger!

Around this time, a group of miners began to bring the name of Ashington to the notice of intellectuals. Their forte was painting, and their work became so well known it attracted worldwide attention. They became known as the Ashington Art Group, and their paintings formed the basis of exhibitions throughout the country. It was something which had never been done before – a group of working-class men documenting their history on canvas. Ridley Warham, managing director of the Ashington Coal Company in 1938, said: 'Ashington has always been the home of surprises, and we have long since ceased to marvel at anything.'

At the outset of the war, Milburn began playing for local teams in the Midget League, a junior version of the Miners' Welfare League which contained teams from most of the local pits – Stobswood, Shankhouse, Newbiggin – plus many sides from the working men's clubs in Ashington.

The Coal Company had been formed initially by the Duke of Portland, and a lease had been passed on to Jonathan Priestman, a Quaker, who had banned the building of public houses in the town. The thirsty miners got around this blockade by opening private clubs at intervals of a few yards on the main thoroughfares of the town, some in ordinary dwelling houses, others in converted shops. They weren't there solely for the beer. A great camaraderie emerged, together with a fierce rivalry towards opposition establishments, which spilled over on to the football field.

I played for the Welfare Rangers and, later on, for the Rec Rovers. We used to get some terrible thrashings – 10–0, 13–0 – but I would rather have played in games like that, cos you were constantly in the game. What use is it playing in a cakewalk? I'll tell you, they were hard games with some hellish hard players in them, but hey . . . what a grounding.

By 1940 there were twenty-two clubs in Ashington to cater for a population which by then had risen dramatically to 30,000. Without exception they were men-only establishments. A regular attender at the Ashington and District West End Club was Jackie's father. Coal cutting was a thirsty affair, and Alec proved a good customer.

Jackie had become part of the folk lore of Ashington as early as 1936 when he became the first laddie to sell programmes for the newly opened greyhound stadium at Portland Park, which doubled as the ground of the home-town football team. Their nickname? What else but the 'Colliers!'

In the North-East, foot handicaps took place every Saturday throughout the summer months. Each village held an annual flower show where the miners could exhibit not only flowers but vegetables – in fact, practically everything that emerged from their rambling allotments. Any outsize leeks were kept for the more prestigious leek shows held in the September. There might be a three-piece suite to be won there, whereas the most they could hope for at the local show was a piece of coloured card proclaiming that they had won a particular section.

Jackie's first tangible prize for racing had come at twelve years of age when Cyril Brown, a professional footballer with Glentoran and later Sunderland, had organised a race around the backstreets and alleys in which practically every youngster in the area had participated. Jackie was to treasure the box of paints he won in that race for many years afterwards.

The colliery fitting shops, where he served his initial days as an engineering apprentice, were only a hop, skip and jump over a perimeter fence away from the recreation ground – the 'Rec' – a vast expanse of green which served two football pitches, one rugby ground, half a dozen tennis courts, a running track, and a fine gymnasium with modern showers and changing rooms, all courtesy of the Ashington Coal Company. Ronnie Coulson remembers how he, Jackie and scores of apprentices would clamber the fence at midday after eating their baits, which had been gulped down in five minutes flat leaving the lads with about twenty minutes of their break in which to have a game of football.

It was unbelievable. There we were, still in our overalls and pit boots, haring up and down after the ball. I learned to be a good jumper then, to get out of the way of them steel toecaps. But we must've enjoyed it, cos we hardly missed a day without getting some kind of game away.

At the end of his shift, usually about four o'clock, Jackie would go back to the Rec again, on his own this time. He kept to a strict routine. For the first hour there would be ball practice. He was well in with George Watson, the groundsman, who, against all rules, would leave a football for Jackie hidden under the gym floor beneath a pile of rubbish. Once united with his 'best pal', it was out on the pitch and bang, bang, bang! Hammering the ball goalwards from any angle and from any distance. There were no nets attached to the stanchions – they were a Saturday-match luxury – and Jackie inevitably had to run long distances to retrieve the ball. That didn't bother him at all.

After the football he concentrated on speed work. Prizes for winning the sprint at the local flower show varied according to the size of venue. A 'little 'un' at Wylam might have a first prize of a tenner, while a big event like the Whittingham Games would earn the winner maybe fifty pounds. However, prizes like these were well short of what could be made by betting on the side. Each event attracted about forty bookmakers who would line the makeshift running track shouting the odds, while waving thick wads of pound notes in the air. 'Come on, I'll lay you levels, you devils!' And the miner who was 'in the know' was everyone's friend. Wherever easy money is there to be made, duplicity is never far away. But runners who got together and 'squared' a race before the start would never dream of calling their collusion criminal in any way. It was simply part of the game. It was putting one over on the fat-cat bookie, and surely one could not be condemned for that!

The Powderhall Handicap, held annually in Edinburgh on New Year's Day, was the 'big one' as far as professional sprinters were concerned. It was the pro runners' Olympic Games. The competition was fierce but the money to be made was phenomenal, not just from the £200 in prize money but in the big long-odds bets to be struck before the runners in the first heat had even pulled on their spikes. It was a big, big day.

When he was twenty, Jackie was invited to be a 'workhorse' for a Scottish athlete who had been earmarked as a possible Powderhall winner. It was Jackie's job to act as a hare during secret trials held on a farm in north Northumberland. The Scot was on a 'keep' – a month's preparation. Les Common, Milburn's brother-in-law, recalls how the Scotsman tried to give Jackie two yards' start in a 120-yard race across a meadow. Ploughing through cow dung, Jackie 'pulverised this fella', to such an extent that the backers, never over-endowed with loyalty, immediately switched their allegiance to the Ashington Flyer!

Ronnie Coulson recalls accompanying Jackie up to Edinburgh the day before New Year's Day, when Powderhall was due to take place. They arrived at Newcastle Central Station an hour before the train was due, and decided to have lunch at a nearby café. Having ordered Jackie's favourite dish – rabbit – they found they did not have time to eat it. Jackie scooped up the rabbit, bones and all, into a newspaper, and the two colliery apprentices raced back to the railway station just in time to leap aboard their train. Once inside the packed carriage – it was full of servicemen and women – Jackie opened up his paper, extracted his rabbit and shared it with some hungry WRENS. Back at the café an astonished waitress clearing away an empty plate could only conjecture about the young miner who was so hungry he had devoured even the rabbit's bones!

On the track at Powderhall, Jackie won his heat so easily that there was consternation that he might be 'pulled' by the handicapper for the cross-tie, Jackie was advised not to win, but to save himself for the next year when a proper 'keep' could be arranged. It was decided to load Jackie's left running pump with a dozen pennies. Poor Jackie, running as lopsidedly as a whippet with three legs, was duly beaten into last place. Ronnie Coulson was even unluckier: he hadn't been told about Jackie 'carrying', and had backed his friend to win the race.

This was Jackie Milburn's only run at the legendary Edinburgh track. As a professional runner Milburn never did fulfil the potential that he had promised as a child, although he won a couple of 'ten-pounders' at his local Portland Park. In a way it was taken out of his hands by the calls made upon him by Newcastle, but he stressed that when it came to a straight choice between football and *anything*, then his commitment to football was always paramount.

CHAPTER FOUR

If we'd played as bad as Newcastle we'd 'a' been booed off

It was because of football that Jackie and a lot of his marras joined 1110 Squadron of the Air Training Corps in Ashington. Jackie admitted that the opportunity to move the entire Rec Rovers team from the Midget League to play for the ATC proved a far greater pull than the thought that the lads might one day get a crack at one of Gerry's aeroplanes. Through playing every Saturday, the young pitmen very rarely got the chance to see any of the major teams in action.

I never saw Newcastle play till I joined the Air Training Corps. I was eighteen. It was during the war and we were unbeaten for three years. All the lads that came up together joined the ATC, and I was picked for Northumberland. Raymond Poxton and I were picked in 1943 and we played Yorkshire ATC at Redheugh Park. Gateshead used to play there. And this morning we played this match, and there was a Newcastle director called Wilf Taylor came into the dressing room after the game and he invited us to go to St James's Park. All the lads. He just said: 'Show this card, and you'll get into the Paddock.'

So my mate Raymond Poxton and I went and watched. And we were standing in the Paddock watching this match, and I says, 'Raymond, we could play better than this, surely.' It was the last game of the season, and it was terrible! We were both eighteen, and we weren't trying to be big-headed or anything, but if we'd played as bad as that we'd 'a' been booed off.

With it being the last game of the season, we didn't think much more about it, because once the cricket season started you started to play with your pails in the back lane and your tennis balls and one thing and another. Then the new season came in, and there were adverts in the paper for writing to Newcastle for trials. So I said to Raymond, 'Hey, we could play better

15

than this lot.' I said, 'You write the letter,' because he was a better writer than me. He was a wonderful writer, Raymond Poxton. So he wrote the letter for the two of us to St James's Park.

We got a reply a few days later saying we had to report to St James's Park on the Saturday at a certain time. I think we had to report at one o'clock or half past one. We were there at eleven o'clock in the morning! Raymond and I were the only two there.

I'd had to borrow a pair of boots cos the ones I was using was falling to bits. At the time I had a good pal called Joe Smith who had just bought a new pair of boots, and he offered to lend them to us for the game.

Anyway, there we were sitting on the steps outside the ground with a pie and a bottle of pop apiece. Whey, we waited and waited until people gradually came in. Then they picked the teams: the probables and the possibles. That was the likes of Albert Stubbins, Harry Clifton – our heroes, who were terrific players during the war. They picked a couple of teams, and Raymond and I were left off, but we were put on at half time. Joe Richardson, the trainer, said, 'Hey, Jack, the fella that was playing in your position scored two in the first half, mind, so you'd better get out there and do something.'

In fact, I scored a couple and I had a canny game, though I was on a scrap side. There wasn't any big names to play with. You were playing yourself. Anyway, we were invited back the next week and I scored six goals in the second half.

Now this time it was different, cos we had a lad on the wing called Charlie Woollet who played in the first team, and the lad behind me was Bobby Jacques, who was captain of the school team when I'd played for Hirst East, and he was playing for Newcastle during the war. I was inside-left, and when you get an outside-left with experience and a left-half behind you with experience, whey. . . . On the other hand, Raymond Poxton was at left-half on the scrubbers' team. If he'd got the breaks, he was as good as most people. I was lucky. From that day on I was in the first team, and I never looked back.

Not long afterwards, Raymond was taken for a trial period to Derby County where he played for one of their minor teams. He later came back and signed for Ashington, playing as half-back with the reserve team before converting to centre-forward where he enjoyed great success in the Colliers first eleven. In 1949 a crunching tackle left him with a cartilage injury, and he never played again.

Raymond remembers that as Jackie was coming off the field after the first trial, he was approached by a number of directors, including Stan Seymour. The lives of Stan Seymour and Jackie Milburn are as inexorably entwined as nets tied to a goalpost stanchion. Like Milburn, Seymour was the product of a pit community, being born in 1893 in Kelloe, County Durham. He too followed an apprenticeship at the local pit, but as a joiner. And, similarly, he was given a trial at St James's when he was eighteen. Seymour, however, failed to impress, and was sent on his way with a half-sovereign in his hand and a word of advice in his ear: 'Come back when you've grown a few inches, son.' Seymour proved Newcastle wrong, excelled at Bradford City and Greenock Morton, and eventually came back to Tyneside – but it cost £2000 to get a player United could at one time have got for nowt.

In 1924, at the age of thirty-one, Seymour gained a Cup winner's medal with

United and helped them win the League Championship in 1926/27. During this period, very much the darling of Tyneside, he opened a sports outfitters shop in the centre of Newcastle, where one of his biggest customers was, of course, Newcastle United FC.

After playing for Newcastle for nine years, Seymour left in 1929 following an acrimonious wrangle with the club. By then thirty-six, he had thought that he could have gone on playing for at least one more season and so qualify for his second benefit on completion of ten years' service. Footballers then were entitled to a benefit of £750, less tax, for every five years' service. After ten years the club could arrange for a testimonial match. This rule was later to prove crucial to Jackie Milburn. Newcastle spurned Seymour's plea to be allowed to stay on for his tenth year, and gave him a free transfer. Seymour's bitter quote on leaving the club was: 'After that, and an offer of one pound a week for services rendered, I swore I'd never kick a ball again. It left a bad feeling between me and United for a long time.' Shortly afterwards, the name of 'Stan Seymour, Sports Outfitters' was deleted from the list of United's suppliers.

In 1938 Seymour was summoned to meet the directors at St James's Park. He thought that, as almost ten years had elapsed, Newcastle had decided to allow him to tender once more for supplies of equipment. United had, in fact, only just escaped relegation on goal average from the Second to the Third Division. Desperate situations call for desperate measures. On meeting Seymour, vice-chairman George Rutherford put a let's-make-up-and-be-friends-again arm around his shoulders and asked: 'Do you fancy being manager at Newcastle United?' Seymour declined the offer, but agreed to join the board as a director. And so it came about that Stan Seymour, one-time rebel, was allotted the five shares necessary to join the board, beginning a reign which was to last for over thirty years and make him the most powerful, successful and controversial director Newcastle United has ever known.

Jackie's first trial was a well-kept secret from his parents. But Alec found out and made him promise not to sign any contract. After the second trial match – in which Jackie scored six goals – Seymour asked him to sign on the spot. Most lads would have grabbed the pen from his hand, but between Stan Seymour and Alec Milburn it was Alec whom Jackie feared the most, and remembering his father's warning, Jackie refused.

Not used to rebuffs, especially from nineteen-year-old pitmen, Seymour persuaded Jackie to sign an amateur form. Clutching a copy of the form, Jackie left St James's Park, but not before promising Seymour that he would return in a few days with his father – if he agreed – to sign a professional contract. Seymour, now aware that news of Milburn's goal-scoring feat was spreading around the country, was fearful that other clubs would approach the young Ashingtonian. With this in mind he decided not to let another day slip by, and turned up on the Milburn doorstep early the next day, a Sunday.

Nance Milburn, flustered, full of excuses about the state of the house, made Seymour welcome with a pot of tea. Alec shook his hand, and very quickly Seymour was made to feel at home by the simple Geordie hospitality. The hours ticked by as he outlined to Alec the benefits Jackie would gain by joining Newcastle United. Although he could be signed only as a part-timer initially because of working in the pit, Jackie would be paid thirty shillings a week, plus two shillings and sixpence for his tea after the game, and the same amount to cover his fare on the bus.

Jackie, playing a very minor role in the proceedings, and content that his father was at least considering the offer, remembers hearing a curious noise coming from behind Seymour's back. It was the rustle of two crisp white fivers being rubbed together: the statutory signing-on fee. Whether it was this last crafty move by the wily Seymour which won the day or something else he said, Alec's resistance caved in and he promised Seymour, with another shake of the hand, that Jackie would sign for the Tyneside club the following day. An elated Seymour invited everyone out for a drink at the West End Club before catching the last bus back to Newcastle, happy in the knowledge that he had secured 'my finest ever signing' for ten quid and a couple of rounds of Newcastle Brown Ale.

So keen was Alec that he decided to take the Monday off work, an unprecedented occurrence. Not so lucky, Jackie worked his normal shift, rushed his tea down, and the pair of them caught the five o'clock number three bus from the 'stand', as the main terminus was known. They got off the bus at the Haymarket, nerve centre of the throbbing city, surrounded by theatres, cinemas, cafés, pubs, a university and a church. Streaming busily from the bus station lay Northumberland Street, the main shopping area, and beyond that the splendour of Grainger, Percy, Grey and John Dobson. The street names stood for elegance and style – all testimony to an era that cared about its cities. Aesthetic values, however, were far from the minds of father and son as they set out on the short walk that led them to Gallowgate, in their nostrils the sickly smell of the Newcastle brewery, as thick as toffee. But the scent of glory is a hard one to stifle.

Ushered into the boardroom, Alec, trilby hat in one hand, had a whisky glass thrust into the other; the preliminaries had begun. Another visitor to the ground that evening was David Halliday, ex Sunderland and Arsenal player, then manager of Leicester City. 'Let young Jackie sign with my pen,' he said, producing a gold-topped fountain pen. 'I think you've got a good un here, Stan.'

Jackie proved Halliday right when he reported for training the very next day. In a head-to-head over a hundred yards with Newcastle's fastest man, Albert Stubbins, Jackie coasted to an easy win. Trainer Norman Smith missed the confrontation, and hauled Milburn out of the bath for a rematch, 'I like your style,' commented Smith after Jackie proved the first run had been no fluke. 'We'll make a player out of you here, me lad. You see if we don't!'

Milburn's debut for United was away at Bradford City. Seymour invited Alec to accompany his son for the lad's first trip out of Tyneside, probably unaware that Alec had never crossed the Tyne Bridge either. They were booked into the impressive County Hotel, only yards away from Newcastle's Central Station where their train for Bradford was due to leave at 8 a.m.

There was little sleep for father and son as they played out their individual fantasies in restless dreams – Jackie's, perhaps, that he was sitting in front of the coal fire in his red and green school strip before playing his first ever game for the Hirst East Boys, and in his dream scoring goal after goal; and Alec reliving the Tottenham Hotspur offer he had spurned twenty years earlier, an offer that would have taken him away from the drudgery of the coal-cutting machine to bask in a glory he could now experience only vicariously through his son.

The following day came and went with neither dream being brought to fruition, Alec's because it was all in the distant 'what-might-have-been' days of the past, and Jackie's because of a huge Yorkshire crag of a man called Joe Harvey who scored both the goals that beat United 2–1. This was the very same Harvey who was to join Jackie as a team-mate two years later, and strike up a bond of friendship that was to comfort them both right through their working lives. However, it was back to fairy-tale time the very next Saturday when Milburn scored a goal with his first kick of the match on his home debut. United's opponents – Harvey's Bradford City!

Milburn went through his early days as a Newcastle United player in a daze. He had almost finished his apprenticeship at the colliery, using every spare minute of his working day perfecting one footballing skill after another, but still finding time to get through to St James's Park for official training three nights a week.

He was transferred to the nearby Woodhorn pit, and Jack Main, foreman joiner, had to reprimand the zealous youngster for thumping a tennis ball against the wall of the pit canteen, much to the annoyance of the foreshift men sitting inside trying to eat their breakfast in peace. Main, knowing that Jackie was also concentrating on speed work, arranged a race among the young apprentices. He paced out a hundred steps in the colliery yard, someone else shouted 'Go', and Jackie, the steel segs on his pit boots almost glowing as they skimmed the cobbles, crossed the chalk mark which signified the finishing line before most of his adversaries had gone half-way down the track.

It was during the 1945/46 season, with the League being split into North and South divisions, that Milburn, normally playing inside-left, was moved to the right wing to accommodate little Charlie Wayman, a County Durham lad who revelled in scoring goals. The first time they played in these positions was against Middlesbrough, and they won 8–2 with cheeky Charlie knocking in a hatful. Nearly every game brought a flurry of goals as United knocked in sixes, sevens and eights. There was an incredible 6–6 draw with Gateshead. They beat Bradford 11–0 – and didn't Joe Harvey get his nose rubbed in it later about that thrashing!

Stan Seymour obviously thought highly of Harvey, for he signed Joe in 1945 when he was still a company sergeant-major in the Army. He was introduced to the team who, apart from Harry Clifton, Joe Richardson and Dougie Wright, were nearly all raw kids of nineteen like Jackie Milburn. Harvey said later that he thought he was joining a Boys' Club team!

Joe turned out to be a diplomat as well as a good skipper. Playing Burnley at Turf Moor, soon after he'd been made captain, a free kick was awarded against United on the edge of the eighteen-yard area. The goalkeeper then was Tom

Swinburne – by all accounts as crazy as a loon – who arranged a 'wall' with young full-back Bobby Cowell, who had just come into the team from playing for the Home Guard, as the centre brick. The Burnley forward's free kick took a deflection off Cowell's outstretched leg and flew into the opposite side of the goal to where Swinburne was lying prone, thumping his goal-line in frustration. The goalie went berserk! Leaping to his feet, he shouted at Joe Harvey to send Cowell off the field. He screamed at Bobby: 'Whey, you silly bugger, you wouldn't even have been allowed in the dressing room before the war! Now bugger off home to your mammy!'

The disconsolate miner was actually trudging towards the touchline when Harvey caught up with him and with a fatherly hug led him back on to the pitch. 'Take no notice of him, son. Come on – get on with your game.' As Bobby trekked unhappily back to his position, Swinburne was still yelling, 'Get off! Go on – get off the bloody field!' This time it was the goalie's turn to get the Harvey bear-hug. 'Never mind, Tom, he's only young. He'll learn.' Swinburne, still smarting from conceding a goal, wrenched himself from Harvey's grasp and went back into the nets, muttering to himself, 'Bloody full-backs – I've shit 'em!'

Reminiscent of Bill Shankley's 'matter of life and death', football was a vitally important issue even them. And these fixtures were played when, supposedly, nothing was at stake. These were the games that saw Albert Stubbins scoring many of his 245 record-breaking goals in 199 matches. Wallsend-born Albert, the red-haired lad with the sure-fire shot, became the first post-war hero of the Tyne. Now he wore the number-nine mantle of the legendary Gallacher. His were the goals that were winning games and headlines, with an eager Milburn watching, learning, waiting in the wings, content and happy to be picking up a goal here and there and, above all, playing in a black and white strip.

I'll tell you who had a big influence on me, and that was Hughie Gallacher. When I was at school in the thirties, the big song then was: 'Do you ken Hughie Gallacher, the wee Scots lad, the best centre-forward Newcastle ever had?' I'll not argue with that.

He used to stand and wait for me outside St James's Park – just on the steps there – and tell us me little faults. Oh, it was tremendous! He killed himself, you know; put his head on a railway line. I could never understand how a man who had been idolised by thousands could feel so alone.

Ashington got through the war virtually unscathed. Of course there were air-raid warnings, with the Moaning Minnie wailing out from above the local police station, scattering schoolchildren from their desks into Anderson shelters. But German bomber pilots were never all that interested in the area as a target, although a couple did decide to unload a batch of land mines on the coast near Lynemouth.

The one big tragedy that befell the town happened in the middle of the night when a lone Wellington bomber, obviously short of the necessary fuel to get back to base, and with the pilot desperately trying to reach some open fields, hurtled just over the Milburn house into Fifth Row about a hundred yards away. Three houses were completely destroyed, killing all but one of the Cox family as well as the RAF crew of five.

When VE Day was announced, Geordie and his marras got back to what they had missed even more than a daily packet of Woodbines: the resumption of the Football League. Fans, still starved of meat and fruit, and with many of life's other luxuries remaining on ration, forgot their cares and came back in droves to support their local team. Competition to Saturday-afternoon football was almost non-existent. What else was there to do? Where else was there to go? The football authorities almost had a licence to print money. The vast sums of money that went into soccer in those early post-war days did not go towards improving the spartan conditions tolerated by spectators up until 1939, nor did it find its way into the pockets of the players. Milburn's first wage as a full-time professional was £10 in season, £8 in summer, with a £2 bonus for a win and £1 for a draw.

In 1945 Charlie Crowe, a twenty-one-year-old from Walker, made his first-team debut at St James's Park. It was against Stoke City before a crowd of 48,000 attracted no doubt by the appearance of wizard Stanley Matthews. Newcastle outplayed Stoke, and thanks to Crowe giving Matthews no room to manoeuvre, won 9–1, with Albert Stubbins getting five goals. The United team then, including Milburn, were all part-time pros and received the usual thirty bob, but amateur Crowe was given half a crown: one and six for tea and a shilling for travel expenses. Afterwards, when he'd had time to reflect, Charlie thought it 'a bit unfair'.

Even though slavery had been abolished for over a hundred years, soccer players found themselves tied to clubs, totally dependent upon them for their livelihood and accommodation, unable to negotiate a contract of employment, and subject to the whims of directors and officials who bought and sold them like chunks of meat in an abattoir. Few clubs were without guilt in this period of downright exploitation. One of Newcastle's greatest players, Hughie Gallacher, who some would argue was United's greatest centre-forward, was summoned to a hotel one day by the directors. Entering the lounge, the wee Scot recognised some Newcastle directors and approached their table. Very curtly he was pointed in the opposite direction to where a group of Chelsea directors was sitting. 'You are with them now, Hughie.' Another carcass had changed hands.

Seymour, now acting as honorary manager, set about assembling a team that could make Newcastle great again. Eventually United, submerged in the back waters of the Second Division and Third Division North for fourteen years, hauled themselves back up among the big boys in 1948. Always a side with a first-class pedigree, it took a team of mongrels to get them back into the First Division.

Seymour always said: 'Half a dozen Geordies, two or three Scots, and a couple of also-rans, and we've got a canny team.' He always said that . . . and he was never far away.

When Milburn arrived at St James's in 1943, there was already the nucleus of a good side. Experienced players like Albert Stubbins, Dougie Graham, Jimmy Gordon, Tot Smith, Harry Clifton, Ted Garbutt, Joe Richardson, Bennie Craig,

Dougie Wright and Tom Swinburne had been joined by local youngsters such as Charlie Wayman and Ernie Taylor. Shortly after that came other lads, many of them picked up coming straight out of the pit or through a shipyard gate. These were the likes of the three Bobbys – Cowell, Corbett and Stokoe – and Charlie Crowe: all destined to become regular United players for the cost of a £10 signing-on fee.

Bob Stokoe reflected many years later: 'There were so many of us in those days who only wanted to play for Newcastle United; we were black 'n' white daft! It meant so much to us and our supporters. And I think among the Cowells and the Crowes, Brennans and the Milburns and people like this, we were like a family. We cared for each other and cared for each other's performance.'

But Seymour recognised that the Geordie public, starved of the big time for so long, craved the star attractions. Fattened on the prime of Gallacher, anything less was unpalatable. Chequebook in hand, Seymour plundered the British Isles of the best footballing talent that was available. The list of players was impressive:

Joe Harvey in 1945 from Bradford City for £4500
Len Shackleton in 1946 from Bradford for £13,000
Frank Brennan in 1946 from Airdrie for £8500
Roy Bentley in 1946 from Bristol Rovers for £8500
Jack Fairbrother in 1947 from Preston for £7000
Frank Houghton in 1948 from Ballymena for £6000
George and Ted Robledo in 1949 from Barnsley for £26,500
Bobby Mitchell in 1949 from Third Lanark for £16,000
Alf McMichael and George Hannah in 1950 from Linfield for £20,000

United fans saw the addition of the glittering stars as a recipe for instant success, while cynics waited for the concoction to explode in Seymour's face like a Molotov cocktail. The rumblings began very quickly when prolific goal-scorer Albert Stubbins was transferred for £12,500 to Liverpool, where he became a firm favourite with the crowds at the Kop. Charlie Wayman moved to the middle of the attack, and George Stobbart was signed from the Boro as immediate cover.

Boardroom headaches were forgotten on 5 October 1946 when the Clown Prince of Soccer took centre stage at St James' Park. Len Shackleton had arrived! Newport County were the unfortunates to be mesmerised by the magic repertoire of the irrepressible Shack. United's team that day was: Garbutt, Cowell, Graham, Harvey, Brennan, Wright, Milburn, Bentley, Wayman, Shackleton, Pearson. Newcastle thrashed a bedraggled Newport 13–0, with Shack getting six goals, the last of which he knocked in cheekily with his backside! This amazing goals bonanza equalled the highest ever Football League score, and still remains Newcastle's biggest win and record score for the First and Second Divisions. Other scorers were Charlie Wayman (4), Jackie Milburn (2) and Roy Bentley (1). Incredibly, Shackleton had missed with a first-minute penalty.

For a long time during that 1946/47 season it looked as though Newcastle would get out of the Second Division at their first attempt. But January 1947 ushered in the year of the big freeze, and this coincided with United's rapid slide down a League table they had led at Christmas. The FA Cup had also been revived, and with thoughts of promotion melting away with the snow, Newcastle threw themselves into the new competition. In the third round they saw off Crystal Palace 6–2; a Wayman hat-trick beat Southampton in the next round; and Roy Bentley's winner against Leicester at Filbert Street put them into the quarter-finals. First Division Sheffield United were the next opponents, and a Bentley penalty and Milburn special booked Newcastle's place in the semi-final against Charlton Athletic. It was then that controversy, never far away from United's front door, sneaked in through the tradesmen's entrance.

Yorkshiremen Harvey and Shackleton had still not been housed to their satisfaction in Newcastle, despite numerous promises. Both aired their grievances to Seymour. Inexplicably, on the eve of the match top goal-scorer Charlie Wayman was dropped in favour of Stobbart. No explanation was given, but there were rumours of a dressing-room rift, hastily refuted afterwards. Drama was not confined to the Newcastle camp, however. On the Friday before the game, Charlton players, while visiting a local pie factory, were given contaminated sausage rolls to eat. The whole team were stricken with what was diagnosed as gripe, and were violently ill during the night.

As a grey-faced Don Welch and brooding Joe Harvey led out their respective teams at Elland Road the next day, neither was aware of the other's troubles. They obviously weighed far heavier on Newcastle than Charlton for, apart from their goalie, Sam Bartram, doubling up in pain while taking a goal kick, Charlton produced by far the more polished performance, and the London team won by an impressive 4–0.

The Newcastle dressing room erupted in fury after the game. Harvey and Shackleton swore they'd never play for United again and were adamant that they were both going home. As the game had been played at Leeds, neither had far to travel. United's players, who had been besieged by fans before the game wanting to know the reason for Wayman being left out, were also concerned at the decision they were convinced had compounded their side's troubles.

Within a couple of weeks a degree of harmony had settled on Newcastle, with Harvey and Shack being housed to their satisfaction in Gosforth. With the Cup no longer within their grasp, they settled back into playing out the remainder of a season which had promised so much but had ended in gloom and acrimony. They eventually finished a respectable fifth in the League, with the fans dejected and disappointed as the season came to a belated conclusion, extended by snow and ice into the middle of May. During the close season, Seymour, in the midst of his spending spree, announced that he was standing down as manager, and that George Martin of Luton Town would take over the club's affairs.

Soon after the 1947/48 season got under way, Charlie Wayman was transferred to Southampton, which left the whole of Tyneside wondering whom the directors would buy to fill the centre-forward berth. Although Martin was manager, the major decisions were coming from the board, and Seymour still had a big influence in the buying and selling of players.

Scottish international centre-half Frank Brennan says it was at his instigation that Jackie Milburn was moved from the right wing to centre-forward. 'I said to George Martin, "Look at the way Jackie plays. If you put a ball at his feet on the wing he'd run with it straight out of the Leazes End gate if the terraces weren't there. Why don't you play him in the middle, give him the ball, and let him run it slap bang between the opposition goalposts?" ' It was simple logic, but oh how it worked!

Now Charlie Wayman left Newcastle, you know for what reason – he couldn't find a peg in the dressing room to put his clothes on! It was true. We had two dressing rooms, and we had over seventy pros at the time. Seventy-odd pros who reported every day, and Charlie couldn't find a peg for his bloody clothes. So he asked for a transfer.

After Charlie left, George Martin must have thought that I could play centre-forward, and he put me in. I was playing wing or inside-forward at the time. At school I always played left full-back or right wing. Anyway, George says, 'I want you to go in there. You're going in, regardless, and giving it a try.'

I was frightened to death! I never slept a wink the night before. We were playing at Bury. Fortunately, after twenty minutes their goalkeeper was injured, and carried off. I scored a hat-trick. Just through this duff goalie being in there. From there on it just changed my life. Although, in all fairness, I never liked to play centre-forward at all.

Half-way through that season Newcastle were on course for promotion, yet good players were still allowed to walk away from St James's Park, some of their own volition, others slightly pushed.

Roy Bentley, living in a flat belonging to the sister of a director, complained that his bath was in a bad state, and requested a new one. It shows much for George Martin's status that it was he, the team manager, who came to inspect Bentley's suspect plumbing. He decided that Roy's plea was a frivolous one, and suggested a new coat of paint would do the trick. Bentley was indignant, and within two months was transferred to Chelsea. That was in January 1948, and one month later Len Shackleton exchanged his black and white cap and bells for the red and white of Sunderland as he took his clowning from Tyne to Wear. Shack's move was brought about by devious player power behind the scenes at St James's.

Shack was unbelievable! If he had had the guts or the will to want to do well, instead of joking and carrying on, he was untouchable as a footballer. He was my labourer at Hazlerigg workshops when I moved there after I left Ashington colliery. We both had to go there because of this reserved occupation lark. I used to have a motor bike, and we went back and forward to St James's three times a week for training. Shack was on the back, both with wor pit gear on.

He was absolutely the tops in ball control. He was doing these things all the time in training, making mugs of goalkeepers. I've seen Jack Fairbrother dive at his feet in training, and Shack would just let him come, then just ease the ball away. Whey, the ball was only inches away from Jack's fingers, and Jack was wild-eyed. He would've killed him if he'd got him.

Him and Tommy Pearson gave an exhibition one day at Newcastle against Cardiff, when they kept the ball between them with six or seven defenders around them, frightened to death to tackle. And this happened for ninety minutes, before we beat them 4–1.

It was sheer entertainment with Shack. He admitted later on that he had no interest, but he just wanted to feel that he'd entertained the public. Oh, he was unbelievable – but hopeless! Joe Harvey says to George Martin: 'We'll never win anything with Shackleton in the team. We've got to get rid of him.'

And it was true! I've nothing against Len, he was a smashing fella, but he had no interest other than entertaining the crowd. He would rather beat three men than lay on a winning goal. And we got rid of him! He signed for Sunderland.

Every year in the late forties and early fifties they were fighting against relegation. Although they knew what they were doing. Cos players used to get a hundred pounds a man for staying in the First Division, for the last six or seven games. Stuffed into their boots! It was worth it to the club. Whey, aye! Whereas we never got a penny.

That particular season Sunderland only just managed to avoid dropping into the Second Division for the first time in their history, finishing in twentieth place, only four points clear of relegated Blackburn and Grimsby. Loyal Wearside supporters still packed Roker Park, and home matches regularly attracted over 60,000 fans. Little wonder, then, that a drop in status was feared by the board: the lost revenue would have been enormous.

When the issue finally surfaced, it was a joint FA–League body who threw the first stone in the direction of Roker Park and called them cheats and criminals. But the footballing authorities were not entirely without blame themselves. It was they who decreed that players could not earn more than the maximum wage laid down – this had risen to only £10 a week by 1948 – and it was they who made it impossible for a player to negotiate his own contract.

Fined £100 for asking for more than the statutory £10 signing-on fee, Trevor Ford, Sunderland's Welsh international centre-forward, upset some of his fellow players, including Milburn, by daring to propose a sliding scale of payments – the system which, of course, prevails today. In his book, *I Lead the Attack*, he wrote:

I do not believe the star player is paid his worth. I feel ashamed that I had to try to secure my future and make my family comfortable by under-the-counter methods. Yet it was not my fault; it is the fault of the system and something should be done about it. I would not be prepared to let my son go through what I have been going through on that score. Clean up soccer, pay the top men top money, then football will regain its tarnished glory.

In spite of the comings and goings of star players, Newcastle managed to get into a challenging position for promotion mid-way through the 1947/48 season. Crowds flocked to watch the 'Toon' every Saturday. As many as thirty busloads left

25

Ashington, with Jackie Milburn content to wait his turn at the back of the queue, despite invitations to come to the front: 'Howway, Jackie, man, we're coming to watch you play!' Colossal gates were recorded during that season at St James's Park. An average of 56,351 people watched home matches, which was a world record until recently when overtaken by Manchester United. The entire North-East of England loved this team, and they showed it. Clothing was still rationed, but supporters amassed a pile of clothing coupons so that the players could be rigged out in smart grey suits in the winter, with navy blue blazers for summertime wear.

The Magpies had made a great start to the season by beating Plymouth 6–1, with Milburn keeping up a remarkable record of scoring in the first and last League games for four consecutive seasons. Eastertime was always crucial with so many games being played over that period, but United came out of it in second place behind Birmingham, closely followed by Sheffield Wednesday. As they were beaten again by Charlton, the FA Cup was no distraction. By mid-April Newcastle was almost there. They had beaten Fulham 1–0 at home, thanks to a George Stobbart penalty, to register their tenth consecutive home win, and were ready to take on the Sheffield side in the next match. A vast crowd of 66,483 filled the Gallowgate and Leazes terraces almost to bursting point.

For three months United had not conceded a home goal, yet within ten minutes Sheffield shocked them with a tenth-minute penalty goal. Stobbart levelled just before half time, and skipper Harvey nodded them into the lead soon after the resumption. The roar could be heard at Whitley Bay.

I've been all over the world and I've never seen anything like those supporters. They know the game backwards, and if you can play in front of them, and they take to you, you cannot possibly play for anybody better anywhere in the world.

They allow you bad games, because they understand. Whereas at other places you can have one or two stinkers – then they really get at you and hit you. Here they understand. Sunderland's just the opposite. You only get one chance with Sunderland, then you're down.

But the fans at Newcastle are the most knowledgeable in the world. They know the game inside out. And when players leave here, I cannot understand it. There was Beardsley and Waddle recently . . . how on earth can people give up the chance of playing for Newcastle United to go elsewhere, when they are the masters of football in the North-East: the people on the terraces.

I could never explain to people the feeling we got after we scored a goal at St James's Park. Running back to the half-way line, and the pounding we used to get. Every step you took running back . . . whoomph! It was absolutely unbelievable! You couldn't describe it. You had to really sense it, being there. Your head used to go whoomph . . . and that was every game that promotion year.

With only ten minutes left of that crucial game, Wednesday drew level. One point was no good to Newcastle – it was win or bust. Frank Houghton proved an unlikely hero. A half-back turned winger, Houghton scored two goals, breaking his arm in

26

the process of knocking in the second, after colliding with a goalpost. It was all stirring stuff, and the final whistle blew with young Frank still being borne by stretcher around the pitch perimeter. But Newcastle United were virtually there. Tyneside went wild when Newcastle officially clinched promotion, albeit in second place behind Birmingham. For fourteen years the Geordie fans had been starved of what they will always believe to be theirs by right: a place in Division One.

CHAPTER FIVE

1948
I got me first England cap; not only that – I got married

Jackie began to get noticed because of the goals he scored; it was his name that went on the score-sheet. But United's success was never just down to any one man. The Milburn name was synonymous with commitment, sportsmanship and modesty, but they were the virtues of the entire team. Later, he would admit that he fed off the likes of Ernie Taylor and Bobby Mitchell, and that it was skipper Joe Harvey's prompting which stirred him into putting that one last ounce of effort into his game. It was the image of the 'pit-laddie-makes-good' that enthralled the media, but it embarrassed Jackie to be singled out for praise.

1948 was the year of my life. That year without doubt, was better than everything else put together. It was the year that I will never ever forget, because we had only been in operation for two years after the war, and we won our way back into the First Division. There was a record 57,000 average gate for the season. Plus the fact that they had made me a centre-forward. That was the year I got me first England cap; not only that – I got married.

The way it happened was . . . in the November of 1947 George Martin took us to a place called Letchworth, just outside Luton, for special training. I walked into this hotel with Jack Fairbrother – Jack and I used to bunk together – and I saw this young lass working as a waitress. And I hadn't even spoken to her, and I said: 'Jack, I'm going to marry her.' And I did! This was in the November, and we were married in the February.

They said our dinner was at seven o'clock, so I went into the dining room at about half past six, by myself, knowing that she'd be there laying the tables. I just chatted and cracked her up.

She hadn't a clue about football, and she'd never heard of Newcastle United. In fact, she's only been to three matches in her life: three Cup Finals.

She was nineteen, I was twenty-three. I just talked to her and asked if she would go out. She said, 'Well, I'll see my mother first.' And after three or four days I took her to the pictures, and that was the start. I was engaged at the time, and I felt guilty coming back to Ashington. But there was just something about her . . . I just couldn't tell you. Just something sort of hit me. That was the best thing I ever did in my life! I've been very fortunate. She's that caring. And she's looked after me. Without her I would have done nothing, quite honestly. She is the number one. No doubt about it. We have wor arguments, same as everyone else. But she's done everything for me, that woman – everything.

Laura Blackwood was born in Glasgow. Never afraid to move around, she went down to Willesden Green in London at the age of sixteen to live with her parents. Her father had a hairdressing business, but Laura remembers that her first job was as a children's nanny. Her mother was working in a hotel near Luton, and suggested that Laura might like working at the same place. Laura agreed, and was eventually employed as a silver-service waitress. She had been there hardly a year before the Newcastle United squad invaded the hotel. Like Jackie, she couldn't put into words the immediate chemistry there was between the pair of them, but suffice it to say that she was content to put it down to 'love at first sight'.

In February 1948 Jackie and Laura were married in a registry office in London, and spent a three-day honeymoon by the sea at Folkestone. Back in Ashington, sister Jean remembers: 'My friends had been coming to the house for years, just hoping to get a glimpse of him. And they were saying to me: "Isn't he good-looking!" And I just looked at them, because to me . . . well, he was just my brother, so I'd never noticed.

Milburn, even from his young days, had always been attractive to women. He had natural good looks, was elegant in play and of a modest disposition. But for all the modesty, all the niceness of the man, there was an aggression welling up inside him, never far from the surface yet always hidden from view. This was the private face of Jackie Milburn; the setting of the square jaw when he knew he had to pull out that little bit extra to succeed. This was Milburn 'wanting to be the best' no matter where he was or what he was doing. United supporters sensed that something was 'on' whenever he got the ball, and he himself knew from the sound blasting his eardrums whether or not he would score a goal. There was an empathy between man and crowd that seemed to transcend the game of football.

Albert Stubbins puts it very well: 'When you're a centre-forward, you take on the role of a hunter, with the ball as your spear. It is like living in primaeval times, when it was solely down to you whether the people of the village starved or not. It was purely the ability, skill and aggression of the hunter that set him apart from the rest. You have to steel yourself for the inevitable flying feet and flailing fists that you know will come your way from those who are trying to defend their goal. The crowd, as villagers, can only stand at a distance chanting for their champion, first as he stalks his prey, then as he goes in for the kill, the ball lashing goalwards like a spear plunging into a bewildered quarry.'

Jackie was unaware that he was being singled out for analysis. His commitment to football was always total. But interpretations of style and play meant nothing to the lad who still had to go down the pit six days a week before emerging on a Saturday morning to don the famous black and white shirt.

I used to start at twelve o'clock on the Friday night to finish at seven the next morning, and then turn out at St James's in the afternoon. It was the same with most of the team. Some of them were in the pits or shipbuilding or the like, but some managers was better than others.

Now I worked at Woodhorn colliery for a while, and the pit was gonna come out on strike because the manager wouldn't let me off on a Sa'day. There was a Mick Bell, a lad with one arm, he was in charge of the Mechanics Union down there. He went in to see the manager, cos I was telling him what happened with me. I had to work on the Friday night starting at twelve o'clock to finish at seven or eight o'clock the next morning to get off to play. And, anyway, they were gonna organise a strike. He went in and told them straight: every bloody engineer, every fitter and electrician were coming out unless he gave me permission to get off. And they were gonna strike because of that!

Now the last time I was down the pit, I was down as a fully fledged fitter. Oh, aye, I finished me time. I was nearly twenty-five before I got out of the pits. Cos you weren't allowed out after the war; the pits was a reserved occupation.

I was down the pit this night. Something had happened to the coal cutter . . . something had broken. It was a Diamond cutter, and it was in the cut and the pawl had broke. There was nobody down the pit but me. So, what I had to do was go on to the face. I had to take the jib off which was in the cut, break the chain, take it off, take the pin out, leave the jib in the cut, and then I had to sylvester the cutter right to the barrier, cos I couldn't get the bloody lid off on account of the coal face not being high enough; it was only about eighteen inches. And I was playing the next day. This was on the Friday night, and we were playing West Bromwich on the Saturday afternoon.

Whey, you know what it's like when you're down there by yourself. The props are popping and creaking. The stone's falling and the roof's laying on. I says: to hell with this! It took us a long time, but I got the job done and I says: Hey, that's the bloody last – that's my finish!

I was sworn to secrecy at the time, but when I eventually did finish the pits, I went and saw this fella who had big salerooms at Gallowgate. He was Newcastle United daft. And I was telling him about this, and he says: 'I'll have to get you out of the pits then, Jack.' I asked how, and he says: 'Leave it to me' So he must've gone out and spoke to some doctors or other, and when he came back he says: 'Do you ever have any trouble with your ears?'

'Whey, now and again, like everybody else,' I says. 'I have a bit pick at them with a matchstick, and it runs a bit, but then everybody does that, don't they?'

He just sort of stood there and looked at us, funny like, and said: 'Oh, just leave it to me.' And he went away and saw this doctor, who told him: 'Just tell Jack to keep picking his ear, and I'll arrange for him to have a medical at the Royal Victoria Infirmary.'

Whey, it was nothing. Everybody did it. So they arranged that I should come out of the pit, cos I had this disease called external otitis. I don't know what the hell it is; seemingly, it's running of the ears or something like that. Whey, my ears never ran at all, but they got us out of the pits with that.

John Edward Thompson Milburn had worked his last shift below the ground. From then on he carried out his eight-hour shift on 'bank' – a miner's term for surface work of any kind. Like other players on the team, he could not be released permanently from the mines because conscription could still be enforced. The pits were still regarded as a reserved occupation.

If Newcastle fans had worried that their team would flounder in the First Division, these fears were quickly allayed as United surged up the League table from the first Saturday. In many ways the team found it easier than in the lower division where practically every game was a Cup tie as the opposition did their utmost to keep a lucrative fixture with Newcastle United on their calendar. The 20 per cent of the St James's Park gate, always in the region of 60,000, made the visit to Tyneside a big pay day for the poor relations of Chesterfield, Bury and Brentford. But now they were up with the big boys. Arsenal were League champions, while other teams like Wolverhampton Wanderers, Preston and Portsmouth were always chasing honours at the end of each season. Unfashionable sides by today's standards, such as Grimsby Town, Huddersfield and Burnley, made the First Division a hotchpotch of the talented and the mediocre.

People began to take notice of this Geordie team with the extravagant directors. Suddenly they were everybody's friend. Individual players began to be selected for honours; once United fielded nine internationals in their side. These were the days when, without the advantage of an under–23 side to bring young players along, the Football Association chose representative sides to play each other. Milburn was chosen to play for the Football League against the Irish League at Liverpool on 20 September 1948. Also in the team was Len Shackleton, by now playing for Sunderland. To say that Milburn made a great start would be to understate the facts. He scored a brilliant hat-trick, and was dangerous every time he got the ball. Jackie pays tribute to Shack for his own display that day, and says that, leaving his clowning aside for this match, Len gave a service to him that could not fail to produce the three goals he scored.

After such a start, the England selectors could do little else but choose Jackie for his first England cap a couple of months later.

I got me first cap in 1948 against Northern Ireland. What more could I wish for? I just picked the Evening Chronicle *up and read me name in the team. They didn't send you a letter or anything. What happened in them days . . . it was picked on a certain day, say Monday, at two o'clock. The first thing they did was to notify the press or the radio people. It was always in the newspaper or on the radio before the players got to know.*

I won thirteen caps, but I lost twenty or more through injury. Been selected and couldn't play. But it didn't mean nothing. It's lovely to have your first cap, but . . . there didn't seem to be any atmosphere somehow. I remember playing me first game at Wembley against Scotland, and when I walked out on to the pitch it was like a morgue.

My first game I played in Ireland. I had Stan Matthews outside-right, Billy Wright . . . all the big names were there. Of course, in the dressing room before the match everybody was coming up to you, wishing you well, clapping you on the back, saying: 'Come on, son, show 'em what you're like today!' Frank Swift . . . everybody, except one man; Stan Matthews. The very man that you wanted to come up and speak to you. You can say what you like, Stan Matthews was the greatest. Stan and Tommy Finney were in a different field to the rest of us.

But we gets on the field, and they played both national anthems. We stood there at attention. Then Stan came waddling across. 'Jack,' he says, 'I don't like to make a fuss of people back there in the dressing room, but listen, I'd like to wish you the best of luck on your first England cap. Now the first time you see me heading down the wing, get away to the far post, and just stop on the edge of the six-yard box. When I centre the ball, most of the time I put a lot of top on the ball to make it hang and fool the 'keeper, so that'll give you time to close in.'

First time he went down the wing, I did exactly as he had said. This bloody ball came over, and Jack Vernon, their big centre-half, and Smythe the goalie went up for it. And this ball was hanging, literally hanging, and they both missed it. It came to me, and – whey – the wife could have scored! And that was me first goal for England. Talk about actions speaking louder than words! It happened exactly as Stan had said. He was a man in a million.

England's team that day, 9 October, was: Swift (Man City), Scott (Arsenal); Howe (Derby), Wright (Wolves), Franklin (Stoke), Cockburn (Man Utd), Matthews (Blackpool), Mortensen (Blackpool), Milburn (Newcastle), Pearson (Man Utd) and Finney (Preston). England won 6–2, with other goals coming from a Mortensen hat-trick, while Matthews and Pearson got one apiece. As well as being Milburn's first cap, it was the first time Billy Wright had captained his country.

Jackie's lucky mascot, an ebony elephant given to him by Laura on their engagement and which he carried in all big games, was certainly working overtime for the twenty-four-year-old miner. The press were good to Jackie, and the following day's headlines all belonged to him. The *Sunday Sun* acclaimed: 'Milburn's Success as England's Leader'. But Jackie made headlines of a very different nature only two weeks later, when just about every newspaper in the country carried headings such as: 'Milburn Wants to Leave Newcastle' and 'Milburn Hopes to Move South'.

United were, once more, knee-deep in controversy. Milburn stated: 'I need to get away from the North-East because my wife's health is suffering.' But the timing of his transfer request, coming so soon after his first England cap, surely could not escape attention. Who knows what stories must have filled his ears as the team rested at their headquarters at the Slieve Donard Hotel at Newcastle, County Down, or on the ferry taking them back across the Irish Sea to Liverpool after the game. To a young lad who has been brought up in the shadows of half a dozen pit heaps, talk of London streets paved with gold might not have seemed so far-fetched at all. Naive he may have been, but Jackie Milburn always 'wanted to be the best', and if it meant leaving the place that meant more to him than anything in the world, then he was prepared to take that risk.

Many years later, Milburn put all the speculation of those few weeks at the back end of 1948 into perspective:

During my trip back to England on the night boat from Belfast [after his first cap] quite a number of soccer's 'wise boys' – those fellows who seem to know all the tricks of the soccer business – got talking with me about the big money to be made out of football. Quite bluntly, they whetted my appetite for a move when they suggested that an England player such as I had become could demand a good job outside of soccer if I was transferred to another club. And when I thought of my little home being bought on HP, and the struggle we were having, I decided I'd discuss the matter with my wife.

Always understanding, Laura left everything to me, but as she had not been in the best of health since moving to the North-East from the South, I decided to ask Newcastle for a move on her account. I must be frank and admit that the thought of possibly getting a good job with a new club appealed . . . on reflection, I realise what a foolish young chap I'd been to think there was easy money to be made out of football. . . . I know now that easy money isn't the kind that I would like to handle.

An early Christmas present for Jackie was a second cap for England, against Wales. Prior to his selection, a good deal was made in the newspapers of the merits of various contenders for the centre-forward position. Jesse Pye, rattling in goals for Wolverhampton, Jack Rowley, who led the Manchester United attack, and Milburn's old team-mate Roy Bentley, now performing well for Chelsea, were others in contention. England beat Wales 1–0 in a very dull game, but Jackie did enough to warrant his selection against Switzerland on 9 December at Wembley.

At the England team headquarters at the Grand Hotel, Brighton, he met up with the five new men who had been brought into the side. They were Ted Ditchburn of Spurs, in goal instead of Swift; Alf Ramsey, Southampton; Johnny Hancocks, Wolves; Jack Haines, West Bromwich; and Jack Rowley of Manchester United: all new caps, all brought into a side looking ahead to a possible World Cup trip to Rio in 1950.

After leaving Brighton in blazing sunshine, the team coach arrived at London moping miserably under a pall of grey fog, and the game had to be postponed until the next day. In a very one-sided game, played at Highbury, Milburn scored once – in fact all the debutants, apart from goalie Ditchburn and full-back Ramsey, scored as the Swiss were rolled over 6–0.

It was back to the bread and butter of League football for Jackie as Newcastle prepared to meet old rivals Sunderland in the first derby game for sixteen years. One player who made his debut for the Magpies in that game was the Scot Bobby Mitchell, of the mazy dribble, at outside-left. George Robledo, the robust Chilean nicknamed 'Pancho', was also included, at inside-right. Newcastle with both Milburn and Robledo in the team were in effect probably the first exponents of the 'twin-striker' tactics. It was Robledo who was to feed off Milburn's long shots at goal, poaching many of his goals from rebounds after a Milburn drive had been blocked or deflected.

The home game against Sunderland was played in a blizzard in a match that by today's standards would certainly have been abandoned. The United team that day was: Fairbrother, Cowell, Batty, Harvey, Brennan, Dodgin, Walker, Robledo, Milburn, Lowrie, Mitchell. Sunderland's line-up was: Mapson, Stelling, Hudgell, Watson, Walsh, Wright, Duns, Broadis, Turnbull, Shackleton, Reynolds. By a quirk of fate the referee for the game was Mr G. Sunderland. Nevertheless, Newcastle won the game 2–1, with goals from Milburn and Robledo.

United lost interest in that year's FA Cup at a very early stage, going out 2–0 at Bradford in a game they were expected to win. The glib riposte from every team that makes a quick exit from the Cup is: now we can concentrate on the League! Milburn was in fine form, scoring the three goals which beat Aston Villa 3–2. Old-timers were scratching their heads, wondering when they'd last seen such a performance from a Newcastle centre-forward.

I saw Hughie Gallacher play just the once, and everything I ever thought about the man wasn't as big as it should have been. He played in a charity game after the war at South Shields. The right-winger went down the field and crossed this ball, and Hughie was at the far post. As the ball came down he jammed it against the post with his head, and he rolled it around the post and it dropped into the back of the net. When you see a man do that, you think: God, what must he have been like in his prime? Because all my life I got it from me father: 'You'll never be as good as Hughie Gallacher. You'll never be able to tie his bloody bootlaces!'

Going into the final weeks of that season, Newcastle were intent on closing a three-point gap held by leaders Portsmouth. The vital game would be Newcastle *v* Pompey at St James's Park, three days before Milburn was due to face Scotland at Wembley. Over 60,000 fans again packed into the Gallowgate ground expecting to see the black and whites stake their claims as prospective League champions. But Pompey wrecked north-eastern hopes by winning 5–0, with winger Froggatt getting a hat-trick.

With Milburn on call for England, Newcastle slumped to a 4–2 home defeat by Derby County. The season which had promised so much ended with Newcastle slipping back to fourth place behind Portsmouth, Manchester United and Derby. Jackie Milburn was again United's top scorer with nineteen goals. At any other club this would have been looked upon as a good performance by First Division newcomers, but Newcastle, starved of honours, were impatient; they had waited too long already.

In the game against Scotland, Matthews was blotted out by Young and Woodburn of Rangers, and England lost 3–1. Milburn scored a consolation goal with a deflection from a Mortenson shot. Jackie said later: 'Our supporters politely applauded, like an audience having tea at an afternoon matinée.'

It was because of this lack of urgency among team and supporters that Milburn asked to be released from a proposed England tour of Norway, Finland, Sweden and France after the 1948/49 season ended. He had been chosen to travel with the squad, but Newcastle also had a tour planned, to Canada. Jackie approached Seymour and indicated that he would prefer to go with his pals rather than the

England team. Seymour obliged, contacting the FA on Jackie's behalf. Much was made of the situation in the press. It was said that a precedent was being set to accommodate Milburn, and that he was snubbing his country. Jackie put his side of the argument.

At that time there were many rumours regarding my withdrawal from the England side. The official FA explanation was that I was not considered for selection, which was an accurate one.

What I should explain is that I was having a rough time in the national side. True, we were frequently having changes, but I shall always insist that there were too many chaps who played for themselves instead of for the good of the team. It was every man for himself, the angle being if you did well as an individual you were 'in' for the next game.

Naturally, at centre-forward I relied quite a bit upon support from others. It did not come with the smoothness I knew when playing for Newcastle United. I worried about the unhappy experiences I had in the England team and told Mr Seymour of my fears, so when he asked me whether I would prefer to travel to Canada with Newcastle rather than accompany England, I became selfish myself for once and plumped for Canada. It was then that Mr Seymour asked the FA if they would not consider me for this tour; they agreed and off I went to Canada.

The directors of Newcastle United were always keen on taking the team on tours during the close season. The board saw them as good opportunities for team-building, while both Charlie Crowe and Bobby Cowell say they looked upon the trips to faraway places as being 'a bit of a holiday'.

In June 1949 the Newcastle United party embarked on the *Queen Mary*, bound for New York. Pit lads like Milburn, Cowell, Taylor and Walker could be excused for thinking that this was some kind of belated April Fool's Day prank that someone was playing, as they surveyed their first-class cabins while the majestic *Queen* slid out of Southampton waters. For the next three days they were able to relax and wallow in the comforts that the stately ship had to offer. Meals were served on a grandiose scale. A prodigious eater, Frank Brennan found the buffet lunches exactly to his liking as he scoffed delicacies from each of the silver platters piled on to the huge table.

Evening entertainment was provided by Geraldo and his Orchestra, with a young Ronnie Scott playing saxophone solos in the ensemble. The colliers danced alongside millionaires, and never put a foot out of place. This was what made the hard slog of an English football season worth while. Overawed they may have been, but the Geordie lads were determined to enjoy the high life while it was on offer; life on the dole was only a couple of bad matches or a broken leg away. The Statue of Liberty beckoned. 'Howway the lads!', and the squad disembarked at New York and headed for the train that would take them on the trip of a lifetime, taking in the magnificent Rockies and romantic Niagara Falls.

Ten matches were played in the next six weeks, Newcastle winning all of them, some by huge margins, as they played exhibition soccer in front of the appreciative Canadians. One team, obviously having had advance warning of Jackie Milburn's devastating bursts of speed, brought in the fastest American Indian in the country, Charlie Greyeyes, in an attempt to stifle the Ashington Jet. This magnificent athlete, with his black hair tied back in a pigtail, could run like the wind, but he had never kicked a ball in his life, and United won the game 16–2, with Milburn scoring five.

The crowd that day, most of them wearing traditional costumes with colourful headgear, stood in inscrutable silence for most of the game. With the match over, someone tried to organise the Indians into a group photograph, using a pidgin English it was thought they might understand. After several abortive attempts to get the Braves to smile, one of them pulled the plumage from his head, threw it to the ground, muttering through his teeth with true John Wayne grit, 'Come on fellas, let's-get-the-hell-outta-here.' The crowd dispersed as the sheepish camera-man put away his Brownie and stalked off, no doubt in search of firewater from the team wigwam!

'Wherever ye gan yor sure to find a Geordie.' So goes a very well-worn north-eastern song, and the Canadian province of Vancouver proved it to be true. It was while United were staying there that Jackie Milburn was asked if he would lay a wreath on the grave of a fellow Ashingtonian, Hugh Cairns, one of the town's rare Victoria Cross holders. Hugh had emigrated to Canada with his family shortly before the First World War. In France in 1918, showing complete disregard for his own safety, he had captured over fifty Germans in three separate incidents. He died from his wounds shortly afterwards. Obliging as ever, Jackie took some of the team with him, and they made the short pilgrimage with the Cairns family to the cemetery where the wreath was duly laid.

Then it was back to the football as United reeled off one win after another to finish the tour with ten wins out of ten, scoring seventy-nine goals, including a personal contribution of thirty-one from 'Wah Jackie', as the Canadians affection-ately labelled him.

The voyage back home on the *Empress of France* was not without incident either. On the first night out, obviously impressed with United's victories, the captain ordered a special commemorative menu to be made up in their honour. The menu listed the team members and results of all the matches played, and added a very ingenious list of dishes named after the Geordie lads who had upheld the good name of English football abroad.

Late that night, and by now in mid Atlantic, a violent storm struck the vessel, which was tossed about to such a degree that Bobby Cowell remembers lying on his bunk feeling very poorly and thinking that his days were numbered. His fears were confirmed as a very plaintive 'Should aald acquaintance be forgot/And never brought to mind' began to drift around the cabin. Fearing the worst, he looked over the side of his heaving bunk to see a small music box floating across the floor every time the ship lurched in the swell. Cabin-mate Tommy Walker, who had

Newcastle United Football Club

CANADIAN TOUR-1949

●

—OFFICIALS –

Dr. R. Rutherford (Director)
Mr. Stan Seymour ,,
Mr. W. B. Taylor ,,
Alderman W. McKeag ..

———

G. S. Martin (Manager)   Norman Smith (Trainer)

●

—PLAYERS—

J. Harvey (Capt.)	R. Mitchell	B. Craig
R. R. Batty	R. Cowell	F. Brennan
T. J. Walker	E. Taylor	F. C. Houghton
N. Dodgin	R. Fraser	D. Graham
J. E. T. Milburn	J. Fairbrother	T. Thompson
	G. O. Robledo	

●

PLAYED TEN—WON TEN —GOALS : For 79 - Against 15

Montreal	...	...	...	...	4 — 1
Toronto	...	...	...	...	8 — 2
Saskatoon	...	...	...	...	13 — 2
Edmonon	...	...	...	...	16 — 2
Vancouver	...	...	...	...	5 — 2
Seattle	...	...	...	...	11 — 1
Vancouver	...	...	...	...	8 — 1
Winnipeg	...	...	...	...	7 — 4
Toronto (Swedish International Team)	...	4 - 0
New York	,,				3 — 0

MENU

—o—

MELON COCKTAIL FAIRBROTHER

CANAPE AU TAYLOR

FRASER OLIVES   SALTED NUTS HOUGHTON

CONSOMME HARVEY   CREAM ROBLEDO

FILLET OF SOLE GRAHAM

BROILED HALIBUT BATTY '

EMINCE OF BEEF CRAIG   BRAISED HAM, SAUCE COWELL

ROAST CHICKEN MITCHELL

VEGETABLES

GREEN PEAS BRENNAN   NEW POTATOES NORMAN SMITH

COLD SELECTION

ROAST LAMB THOMPSON   GALANTINE OF TURKEY WALKER

SALAD GEORGE MARTIN

SWEETS

MAGPIE PUDDING

PEACH MILBURN   GATEAU ST. JAMES

SAVOURY

CROUTE DODGIN

DESSERT   COFFEE

EMPRESS OF FRANCE   WEDNESDAY, JUNE 29, 1949

37

bought it as a present for his wife, looked wanly over at Bobby before spewing up Peach Milburn all over the offending article, silencing it once and for all.

The 1949/50 season had scarcely broken sweat when Newcastle, always with an eye for a bargain over in the Emerald Isle, bought two Linfield players for the price of one when they purchased George Hannah and Alf McMichael. Hannah, a stylish inside-forward, was English by birth, while McMichael, a ginger-haired Irishman, proved to be one of United's best full-backs and went on to gain more caps as a Newcastle player than anyone before or since.

Both made their home debuts against Manchester City in front of a crowd of 58,142 in January 1950, helping United to a convincing 4–2 victory. Hannah scored one of the goals but twisted an ankle late on in the game. As he was being assisted from the pitch by trainer Norman Smith, cheers rang out from all parts of the ground, indicating to the young lad that the Geordie crowd had been impressed by what they'd seen. Two of the Newcastle team's mainstays, Harvey and Brennan, had returned for this game after spending the early part of the season on the physio's table.

It was while Harvey was prone one day that Ernie Taylor decided to get his own back for an earlier roasting the skipper had given him. Together with Charlie Crowe he was passing the treatment-room window, through which the pair were able to see Harvey lying on a table, face down and naked apart from a towel thrown nonchalantly over one shoulder. Rubbing oil along Joe's craggy back was club physio, Alec Mutch. Taylor spotted a bottle of ether on a shelf. Ether was used as a painkiller to get injured players back on their feet again during a match when the magic sponge had lost its mystical touch. But trainers were very careful when applying the liquid anywhere near a man's private parts, because it could cause a nasty burn.

All five-feet-four of Ernie shook in anticipation as he primed Charlie to lure Mutch out of the room. But prior to that he ran cold water into a bath situated next door. Crowe fulfilled his part of the dirty deed, and Taylor crept up behind Harvey, poured three drops of the ether just above the crack in the Yorkshireman's hairy backside, and retired to a safe distance. In two seconds Joe let out an almighty roar, leaped like a hairy hippo off the table and, clutching his painful parts, plunged into the bath of cold water in the next room. But cold water, far from being a soothing agent, merely exacerbated the pain from poor Joe's stinging extremities. Archimedes would have been proud of the way the Newcastle captain launched himself from the bath, shouting not 'Eureka' but 'If I find the – – s. . . .'

Newcastle were down to fifteenth place in the table mid-way through that season. Wholesale team shuffles were the norm, and for a home game against Stoke City five changes were made, with Charlie Crowe and Tommy Thompson getting their first game of the season in the first team. The poor form of the side was reflected in the gate that day: down to less than 38,000. One feature of the game was the battle of England team-mates Milburn, for Newcastle, and Franklin, centre-half for Stoke. Pundits reckoned that Milburn won the day, scoring the goal that put Newcastle on the way to a 4–2 win. But Neil Franklin didn't rate Jackie all that highly. Coming off the field he was asked: 'Well, Neil, what do you think of Newcastle's centre-forward?' Franklin replied sharply: 'He's not a Tommy Lawton.'

It was the comparison between Milburn and other prospective number nines that was the main talking point in what was a desultory season for the Magpies. Would Milburn get among the caps again, and perhaps be chosen to travel if England won their way into the 1950 World Cup Finals to be held in Rio, South America? The top two teams in the home championships automatically qualified for the Finals, but Scotland vowed they wouldn't go unless as outright winners.

England's first game was to be against Wales on 15 October. Five players were still in contention for the leader's shirt: Pye, Rowley, Bentley, Lawton and Milburn. Nat Lofthouse had been getting among the goals at Bolton, but wasn't considered 'ready' for the England team. None of his rivals had the Milburn flair in running at players at speed. He could do things in a tight space, in a split second, where lesser players needed time and room. Milburn was top goal-scorer to date in the League with ten goals, and although Lawton had nine, they had all been scored in the Third Division South for Notts County.

A week before the England team was due to be announced, Jackie gave the selectors a further reminder that he was the man in form when he prompted United to their first away win of the season, 2–1 at Burnley. When Jackie picked up a paper the following week, it read: 'Milburn and Shackleton Picked for England'. Some papers expressed surprise at Milburn's inclusion in the side after being released from England's Continental tour to go to America with Newcastle, and being passed over for the first game of the season against Eire, which England lost. The defence from that Eire game was retained *en bloc*, but only Tom Finney from the forward line kept his place, moving from outside-left to the more familiar right wing. The England team that day was: Williams (Wolves), Mozley (Derby), Aston (Man Utd), Wright (Wolves), Franklin (Stoke), Dickinson (Portsmouth), Finney (Preston), Mortenson (Blackpool), Milburn (Newcastle), Shackleton (Sunderland), Hancocks (Wolves).

Jackie joined up with his old pal Shack at the Seabank Hotel, Porthcawl in Glamorganshire; the game was to be at Cardiff. It was a case of the most expensive player in England – Shackleton had moved for £20,050 – playing alongside the Ashington pitman who had cost Stan Seymour only a tenner! They should in fact have been playing in opposition that Saturday instead of as team-mates. A Sunderland *v* Newcastle derby game took place, but without the two stars the expected bumper gate never materialised.

Len Shackleton had a great game as England trounced the Welsh 4–1 in front of their own crowd. But if Shack was great, Milburn was tremendous, scoring three goals – two of them fine headers – and making the other goal for Mortenson. That the players had an eye on the World Cup was made apparent by the ferociousness of tackles which left five of the England team with injuries before the match ended.

That England *v* Wales game was one of the highlights in a Jackie Milburn career that saw numerous peaks. It was not just the way he had taken his hat-trick – with luck it could have been five – but his positional play was excellent. Unselfish running off the ball opened up the game for colleagues, and he well and truly laid one myth to rest: 'Jackie Milburn cannot head the ball.' That Milburn was here to stay as an England international was now never in doubt, and pundits who had queried his selection came out and admitted how wrong they were.

Charles Sampson: 'England has solved her centre-forward problem. Jackie Milburn scored three goals, and if his display is anything to go on he's in the England team to stay.'

Joe Hulme: 'Milburn has come to stay.'

Ivan Sharpe: 'The story of England's World Cup winning send-off against Wales at Cardiff is the story of Milburn's success at centre-forward.'

Roy Peskett: 'Step forward Jackie Milburn to be congratulated on as brilliant a centre-forward display as I have seen for years.'

Ray Glendenning: 'Milburn has come to stay as England centre-forward. I have put forward the claims of Tommy Lawton . . . but Milburn was chosen and justified his choice.' (Glendenning was Lawton's father-in-law.)

England's manager from the time official internationals were resumed after the war had been a former Manchester United reserve-team player, Walter Winterbottom. But he was only a part-timer with a part-time team. He was able to spend practically no time at all with players, and was hamstrung by an unwieldy selection process. But he had inherited a team that looked invincible abroad. Due to a long-standing rift between the British Football Associations and FIFA, none of the home countries had entered the three World Cups before the war. But competition at world level was exactly what was needed to shift the English game from its stereotyped approach.

That Jackie had given his usual 101 per cent against the Welsh was evident in the X-rays taken after the game, which showed a broken bone in his wrist. The right hand and forearm were put in plaster, and a surgeon at Newcastle's Royal Victoria Infirmary put on a new liquid-glass support which would enable him to play. Milburn said:

I am over the moon with the news that I may be able to play on Saturday. I feel perfectly fit in myself, and am sure the wrist will cause me no trouble. It is a relief to know that I will not be a spectator for several weeks, as was at first suggested.

But it was two weeks before Jackie pulled on a black and white shirt again, in an away game against Bolton Wanderers. The club doctor, Bob Rutherford, had warned him not to play but, keen as ever and knowing that England were due to play the following week, Jackie had his way. Still, George Martin wasn't taking any chances with a man who could put 20,000 on to a gate just by tying his laces in the centre-circle, and Milburn was banished to the right wing for his own safety.

Jackie was pleased to be back in action again as the team lined up before the game to be presented to Field Marshal Montgomery. Newcastle chairman John Lee did the introductions, going down the United line-up one by one. Charlie Crowe was puzzled when Monty came face to face with Frank Houghton. He considered there to be an extraordinary length of time while the two men stood looking at each other without speaking. At half time, Charlie and the rest of the lads had a good laugh as Frank came in, face like thunder, threw himself down on the bench and moaned, 'What the hell chance do I have here when even the soddin' chairman doesn't know me name?'

Bolton certainly knew who Milburn was, and after an unexciting display on the wing in the first half he moved to centre-forward, and the 32,000 spectators suddenly woke up. He showed the England selectors present that, even with a plaster upsetting his balance, he was still the man to watch. One other reason why Jackie *had* to play in that game was wearing a number-nine strip for Bolton. Nathaniel Lofthouse was the heir apparent. He was rugged, held his forward line together well, and was excellent in the air. Joe Harvey was again out of the side, and Lofthouse gave his deputy, Tot Smith, a real runaround. Centre-forward honours were shared, with both Milburn and Lofthouse getting late goals in a 2–2 draw. But it was generally considered that Milburn had done enough to warrant selection for the next England game.

In spite of Jackie's good showing, plaster cast 'n' all, he was not considered for the game against Northern Ireland at Maine Road, Manchester. Local man Jack Rowley stepped in and helped himself to five of the goals which saw England beat a bemused Irish side 9–0. Again the question arose as to who was the best centre-forward in England. No wonder Jackie had been convinced that he must play, even with an arm in plaster. It would take just one lucky break for someone to rob him of that trip to Rio, and that was what he had his heart set on: the chance to be the best in the world.

England's next game was to be against the Italians on 30 November at White Hart Lane. When the side was announced, Jackie's fears proved to be well founded when he was chosen only as first reserve. His cast was removed three days before he joined the England party in London. As a consolation for being left out of the full England team, he was given a run-out at centre-forward for the Football League against the Irish League at Windsor Park.

Jackie had good company as he crossed the Irish Sea to play on his favourite Belfast ground. Joe Harvey, fully recovered from the injury which had laid him low for most of the season, was in the League team at right-half, and Jackie's young cousin Stan, then playing for Chesterfield, was at left full-back. Jackie almost beat the Irish on his own, with a hat-trick in a 3–1 victory. The call went up once more: 'Milburn most go to Rio!'

One startling piece of news to hit the football world at the time was that Eddie Quigley, a twenty-five-year-old inside-forward with Sheffield Wednesday, had been transferred for a world-record fee of £27,000 to Preston North End, relegated into the Second Division the previous season. Quigley was considered to be no more than an average player. He had never been capped, and hands were thrown up in horror at the thought of this chequebook soccer that PNE were playing. Two weeks earlier they had bought Willie Forbes from Wolves for £18,000. This was seen in some quarters as the beginning of soaraway transfers. Guesses were made as to what some international players might be worth. Random opinions were: Billy Wright £60,000; Jackie Milburn £80,000. And some said both were a bargain even at those prices!

Undismayed at missing out against Italy, Jackie set about showing the selectors that he was still the number one at number nine by scoring eighteen goals which helped to lift Newcastle from a mediocre placing in the League up to fifth spot by the end. Against West Bromwich Albion, in the mire of a winter-ravaged St James's Park, he floated over the mud, scoring twice and making two others for Walker and Robledo. United trounced their opponents 5–1, with hapless Irish centre-half Jack Vernon wishing he'd never heard the name of Milburn.

Newcastle's progress in the FA Cup, after a great 7–2 win in the third round against Oldham with Jackie scoring yet another hat-trick, was brought to an abrupt end before a record 65,000 gate at Stamford Bridge. Chelsea, the butt of many music-hall jokes, had the last laugh, spoiling Newcastle's fun by winning 3–0.

It became apparent during this period that Jackie had grown in confidence. He was proving to be an opportunist, full of skill and acceleration – the best striker of the ball in football. He had perfected a long, loping, sliding tackle which, although it had been used by defenders as a last-ditch method of defence, had never been used as a part of a forward's repertoire. Jackie's leg seemed to glide under his opponent, crook the ball between calf and thigh, and he was up and away before the other man had even realised he was being tackled. Asked about this special technique, Jackie said:

I've no idea how it really started. My father tells me I was doing it when I was five or six. Now it's just natural, and I find myself doing it probably not more than once or twice a match, purely on the spur of the moment.

Milburn was passed over again by the England selectors for the remaining games of the home internationals. However, he was selected for a short tour of Portugal and Belgium. The tour was billed as a pre-Rio taster, and Jackie saw it as his last chance to get on that South American plane. The team were issued with a new light-weight boot, and they enjoyed their first kickaround with their fancy footwear in a deserted Wembley Stadium. Winterbottom's reason for using Wembley was that it was the one pitch in England which by this time – mid-May – had any grass left on its surface.

Jackie always wore a size six football boot, even though his feet were a size eight!

He would wear the boots without socks, soaking them in cold water for hours at a time so that they became moulded to his feet. Prior to using this revolutionary footwear, Jackie had used a boot with a heavy sole in order to put some 'beef' into his shot. Most of the team liked the new boots, but the canny Geordie packed his familiar old ones in his suitcase before the team left from Northolt Airport, bound for Lisbon.

The Portuguese government had spent £350,000 on building a vast National Stadium near Estoril, levelling a whole valley in the process. For the playing surface they had imported lush turf from the Cumbrian coast. The Hotel do Parque had been set aside for both teams, and the players found themselves in the strange position of sitting down to dine with their opponents the night before the game – the England players uncomfortable in ties, blue blazers and grey flannels, and the Portuguese looking very casual in sky-blue track suits.

Like so many Continental sides, Portugal had installed an Englishman as coach and manager. Ted Smith, formally a centre-half with Millwall, had also coached leading Portuguese team Benfica. Smith had taken the trouble to learn the local language, customs and backgrounds of his players, and had built up a fine understanding with his team. England's last game against Portugal, in 1947, had resulted in a 10–0 victory, but the English knew that this game would not be so easy. Ted smiled as he recalled that game, when the Portuguese had introduced a schoolboy's size four ball into the game once England had gone a goal ahead.

On the first morning's training England drove off in a motor coach (taking with them a size four ball 'just in case'), while the Portuguese players were ferried by friends in massive limousines.

For the game Milburn occupied his favourite position at outside-right, but would have loved to be in the middle, knowing full well he was bound to be compared with Tom Finney or Stan Matthews on the right wing. England won the game 5–3, with Finney at outside-left getting four, two from the penalty spot, and Mortenson getting the other. Although Jackie didn't get among the goals, he felt that he had played well, especially in the second half as England grew in confidence.

Next stop was Brussels. Greeting the England squad at the airport was Bill Gormlie, former Blackburn Rovers goalkeeper and now in charge of the Belgian national side. Anderlecht was another team to benefit from Gormlie's coaching. A win for England was expected, but if the Portugal game was anything to go on, 'The Masters', as England had long been known, were in line for a caning once they came up against a team with sufficient belief in themselves.

The game was played at the Heysel Stadium. It was to be England's last game before a squad was chosen for Rio. Jackie was again given the number-seven jersey. As the game progressed he was playing well, getting good service from Boro's Wilf Mannion, when, on a typical Milburn dash down the touchline, his right foot went over, catapulting him to the ground. It was thought the ankle was broken, and he was carried away by ambulance men.

'Goodbye, Rio!' was the thought running through Jackie's head as he lay in the dugout watching his old friend and colleague Jimmy Mullen run on to take his place. This was the first substitute that England had ever played in an international match. The ironic thing about the incident was that, within minutes, Jackie was able to shrug off the pain and begin sprinting without showing any signs of trouble. Soon after Jackie's exit Belgium went ahead, but England retaliated with goals from Mannion, Mullen, Mortenson and Bentley to win the game comfortably. His season over, a despondent Jackie went home to Ashington thinking that the only competition he'd get that summer would be with his local cricket eleven.

CHAPTER SIX

1950
World Cup, the whole bunch of us played cricket

Within a week of getting back home Jackie saw, scribbled on a newspaper billboard, 'England Team for Rio'. Racing across to the news vendor, Jackie saw the following:

England's World Cup Party

Goalkeepers
Williams (Wolves), Ditchburn (Tottenham).

Full-Backs
Ramsey (Tottenham), Aston (Man Utd), Scott (Arsenal), Eckersley (Blackburn).

Half-Backs
Wright (Wolves), Hughes (Liverpool), Dickinson (Portsmouth), Nicholson (Tottenham), Taylor (Fulham), Watson (Sunderland), Cockburn (Man Utd).

Forwards
Milburn (Newcastle), Matthews (Blackpool), Mortenson (Blackpool), Bentley (Chelsea), Mannion (Middlesbrough), Finney (Preston), Bailey (Tottenham), Mullen (Wolverhampton).

Local papers the next day were proclaiming: 'North-East Trio for Rio'. So Jackie was on the road to Rio! First stop: Dulwich Hamlet. It was there that the England squad trained for a few days while officials were taking care of the administrative side of the tour. Visas were filled in; players were measured for tropical suits; and dreaded yellow-fever injections were given. Then on 9 June 1950 it was off to London Airport to pose for the media, then on to a Panair flight with Brazil Constellation Airways. The plane took off right on time at 12.45. What Jackie later described as 'the greatest of all England's soccer adventures' had commenced.

Little was made of the fact that not one but *two* Newcastle United players were destined to take part in those 1950 World Cup Finals in Rio. Jackie's close friend George Robledo was off to help his native Chile, who were to be England's first opponents.

The aircraft carrying the England players made two scheduled stops, first at Paris and then at Dakar, on its way to Recife in Brazil. Before being allowed to leave the plane, Jackie and the rest of the team had to undergo a humiliating spraying with insecticide to eliminate any mosquitoes which may have stowed away while the plane was in Africa. Immigration officials proved troublesome too, as Tom Finney found that he had mislaid one small section of his entry-documents. Once his explanation had been accepted and the team ushered outside the airport, it was the turn of the South American press to bar a very weary set of Englishmen from a shave and shower. Their questions ranged from 'What do you think are Brazil's chances of winning the Cup?' to 'Where was your father born?' Milburn later described the scene:

The Luxor Hotel where we stayed was a miniature skyscraper about twenty yards from the beach of Copacabana. From the balcony of the room which I shared with Stan Mortenson, I stood and digested the scene, thinking aloud, 'A big difference from Ashington!'

Winterbottom had laid down a strict routine for the players which consisted of early-morning training; rest in hotel between 12.30 and 3 p.m. to avoid the harsh sun; and another session of training in the evening. Not everything went as the England manager had planned, however.

My mind always goes back to when we went out to Brazil in 1950. We went out training on the first morning, and Walter Winterbottom came and started talking to the press. He left us three bags of balls. Normally, when a bag of balls is left with a football team you're lucky if you can get one. Everybody wants one, two, three of his own if he can possibly get them.

We played cricket! The whole bunch of us played cricket! What I'm trying to say is, once the season has finished, it doesn't matter how willing you are; there's nothing left. I've said all along that England will never ever have a chance of winning anything in the close season unless it's playing on their own soil. Like in 1966 when we won the World Cup! Cos believe you me, when you've had nine months of a hard English season, you've had enough. This was proved in the European Championships [1988] by the likes of John Barnes and Peter Beardsley. They couldn't kick the ball. Couldn't run. Couldn't do nothing.

Now it was different with Jack Charlton's young lads, because Eire had nothing to lose. Nor had they the skills of the other teams. It was sheer effort that carried them through. You've got to have the skill to win. But once you've had a long English season, you've had it. You cannot do it. And we'll NEVER win anything out of season.

Jackie Milburn's thoughts were echoed by Bobby Charlton as England prepared for 'World Cup Italia 90': 'Our main problem isn't one of technique. We struggle because we don't send our players into World Cup and European Championship action fresh and rarin' to go. If we are going to make any changes let's alter the structure . . . English players have too many matches close to top competitions.'

Aye, Walter Winterbottom was in charge of the team then. Nicest fella I've ever met in football. Very knowledgeable man on tactics and coaching. He was the best. But man-management – he fell down on that. He was too nice a fella. It's not a question of being ruthless. Some players need bollocking and others need an arm around their shoulder. He could just put his arm around somebody's shoulder. He couldn't bollock them.

The first match coincided with the feast of Saints Peter and Paul. Rio donned its festive sombrero to provide a spectacle that Milburn and his English friends had only read about in travel books. The coach taking them to watch the opening game between Brazil and Mexico was splattered by fireworks as it sped along the freeway. It was stopped by a horde of laughing Brazilians, and one negro pushed his smiling face against the coach window, dazzling the players with a mass of gold teeth. Joker Bill Eckersley shouted, 'Hey, he's got more money in his mouth than I have in the bank!' They were soon caught up in the massive throng descending on the newly built giant Maracaña Stadium, and had to walk the last few hundred yards. The national stadium had not been completed on time, and the players had to scramble over lengths of pipe, barbed wire and piles of rubble, all the while breathing in the smell of damp concrete.

Hosts Brazil were to play Mexico in the opening game. But the whole concept of a truly 'World' Cup was completely new and alien to the England players getting their first taste of soccer South American style. As Milburn says, how could they be expected to cope with the carefree Latins when they had left their best efforts on the mud flats of White Hart Lane and the sandy sweeps of the Baseball Ground? Brazil gave the watching 'Masters' an object lesson that afternoon as they beat Mexico 4–0. But the English team shut away what they had seen and prepared for the appointment they had the next day with Chile and George Robledo.

Jackie didn't get to play against his mate, as England chose the team which had finished the game against Belgium after he'd been injured. It seemed as though England's fears were unfounded as they coasted to a comfortable 2–0 victory, the goal-scorers being Mannion and Mortenson.

England's next game was to be against a mishmash of nationalities, mostly

European, masquerading under the name of the United States of America. And the next day they set off for their next base, above the mountains of Belo Horizonte. This was the way Reuter supplied information on the build-up to that fateful game, under the heading: 'England's Team Tune Up for Cup-Tie with USA.'

The England team are training for their second World Soccer Cup game against the United States at Belo Horizonte on Thursday, at the British mining camp 1000 feet in the hills above this city.

They are the guests of the British-owned gold and silver mine of St John del Rei – the largest mine of its kind in Brazil, and one of the largest in the world.

The team arrived from Rio in time to reach the camp – 16 miles from Belo round the steep mountain roads with 67 acute curves – for lunch, which contained bacon and eggs. After a short rest the team played a little cricket, had a brief swim, a game of snooker, and generally amused themselves.

Today they will have training in the morning and after lunch go down the 8000 feet mine, though it is unlikely they will go the whole distance.

There might be a change or two in the team from that which beat Chile 2–0 on Sunday. There seems a possibility that Jack Milburn (Newcastle United) will be given a show at centre-forward in place of Roy Bentley (Chelsea), but Mr A. Drewry, who is in charge, will not announce the team until the day of the match.

Fortunately, I missed the first two matches, cos you used to have these inoculations, and my arm swelled up like – oh, unbelievable! And it was in one of those games that America beat them 1–0.

Whether Jackie meant to say '*un*fortunately' will never be known. In a way, he was probably better off with a swollen arm than with the bruised pride suffered by those eleven Englishmen who played the 'no-hopers' of the USA. Not one critic in the press box, situated directly in front of team reserves Milburn, Matthews and Bailey, had given the Americans a chance. But the one goal they scored will haunt English footballers each time they pull on a white strip to face an underdog in a World Championship. Who coined the phrase 'the Cup is a great leveller'?

Defeat had seemed out of the question as England, through Mannion and Mortenson, put on a show before the appreciative Latins. But for all their class, England began the second half in arrears due to what Milburn described later as a 'freak goal'. As the game progressed nearer and nearer to the referee's final whistle, any kind of goal – freak, fluke, 'hand of God' – would have been acceptable to the frustrated Englishmen and their worried supporters. The American goalie performed miracles, stopping shots that he sometimes knew nothing about. Every English player was dashing upfield to have a pot at goal, including dapper Alf

Ramsey. But nothing would go right, and as Tom Finney recalls: 'It was just one of those days when you wish the ground would open and swallow you up.'

As the humiliated England squad landed at Santos Dupont airport from Belo Horizonte, there were no crowds to greet them; none of the world's pressmen was present as they had been to wave them off. The defeat was a bitter blow – but not, as yet, a mortal one. England still had one more game to play in their group. Each section was played on a League basis, and they needed to beat Spain in the next game in order to go to a play-off, again against Spain who had won their two previous matches.

At eleven o'clock the next morning, after discussion with Arthur Drewry, Walter Winterbottom announced the following team: Williams (Wolves), Ramsey (Spurs), Eckersley (Blackburn), Wright (Wolves), Hughes (Liverpool), Dickinson (Portsmouth), Matthews (Blackpool), Mortenson (Blackpool), Milburn (Newcastle), Baily (Spurs), Finney (Preston). It proved to be a panic selection. For Eckersley and Baily this outing was to be their first full international; Matthews had not played for England for over a year; Finney was playing in a position he loathed; and only days before, during a practice game, Milburn had fallen heavily and brought on a painful spell of fibrositis. The morale of the team was low. Little wonder that they had no appetite for this vital match.

The Brazilian spectators gave the anxious England team a true South American welcome as they were led on to the Maracaña pitch by a determined-looking Billy Wright. The Latins needed England to continue in the competition if they were to recoup their massive outlay in staging the event. The English were still a big box-office draw, and the chances of them making an early exit had been unthinkable only days earlier.

Referee Galeati of Italy seemed unaware of this as he disallowed, on the grounds of offside, what was later proved to be a perfectly valid Milburn goal. Sadly, photos verifying the authenticity of the goal appearing in the papers next day could not be used in evidence. Again it was just the one goal that beat England, but the Spaniards were guilty of turning the game into a farce as they resorted to handling the ball whenever danger threatened. If the game had not been so important it would have been highly amusing as the Spanish players threw themselves about like slip catchers on a cricket field, holding on to every ball that came their way.

Five minutes from the end, when it became obvious that a totally frustrated England team would be taking the early plane home, thousands of spectators began waving their handkerchiefs in a mocking farewell. And so England bade a final adios to the 1950 World Cup. Brazil went on to reach the Final by putting seven goals past the Spanish goalkeeper who had kept a clean sheet against England. Surprisingly the Brazilians failed to win the Final, losing 2–1 against Uruguay. It says much for England's unwillingness to learn that instead of staying to watch the rest of the tournament they left the day after being eliminated.

One more slice of drama came England's way on the journey home when their plane developed engine trouble and the pilot had to put down at a small airport in the north of Brazil. It was here that the team sat down and talked about what had gone wrong with their play. A few years later Jackie wrote:

In our discussion it was generally appreciated above all else that the teams we'd watched put a tremendous amount of thought not only into their play, but also their preparations. . . . Shooting used to be the strong point of our football, but in Brazil – even as a forward I must admit this – it was our weakness! True, we always fought hard, and our footballers could never be accused of being chicken-hearted. But in keen competition of this calibre a big heart isn't enough. The World Cup series of 1950 emphasized this fact.

CHAPTER SEVEN

You never had the feeling you were going to lose

Before the 1950/51 season began, Jackie performed one of his regular celebrity spots by refereeing a game of old 'uns v young 'uns at Pegswood, a tiny pit village near Ashington. One familiar name on the old 'uns team sheet was Alec Milburn, Jackie's father. It was the first time Jackie had seen him play, but he had heard glowing reports from other people of the tremendous power of Alec's kicking.

People had always been telling me how good a left foot he had. And I just thought: Oh, aye! But there was this charity game, and I was referee – George Robledo was running the line. Me father – he was a full-back – took this goal kick as the goalie had been injured, and he kicked that ball over the opposition team's crossbar, at the far side of the field, without it touching the bottom!

And he only took a size four shoe! You wouldn't credit it, would you! But folks had been telling me he'd been doing this regular. He could've gone to Tottenham! They wanted him to go down to London, but him and my mother had just got married – so he didn't bother.

The charity match, in aid of the Ashington Welfare Athletic and Pegswood Welfare football teams, raised £25. Jackie donated two handkerchiefs he'd brought back from Rio, autographed by the England team, for a raffle, which was won by a very grateful Mr B. Clarke of Pegswood. Pegswood won the match 7–3 thanks to the fine wing play from Jackie Dryden, ex-Newcastle, then Ashington FC's trainer.

Newcastle's first League game of the season was against Stoke, and if anyone thought that he might still be suffering from the aftermath of the Rio debacle,

Jackie very quickly reassured them that he was back to his best form. Showing great speed in his Rio light-weight boots, he whizzed around the Stoke defence, now without Neil Franklin who had absconded to Bogotá, to score after a typical raking run through the middle. Later he put the game beyond Stoke's reach with a penalty.

Newcastle had begun the season in fine fettle, and this victory began a record-breaking run of ten games without defeat. Milburn scored the two goals which beat Burnley 2–1; Newcastle swamped Huddersfield 6–0; in a top-of-the-table tussle Arsenal, under skipper Joe Mercer, were beaten 2–1; and so it went on. The Magpies were sitting pretty, and there didn't seem to be another team around in the First Division to knock them off their perch. The team was blending well. Fairbrother was now established in goal and proved an invaluable last line of defence.

Jack Fairbrother was the finest goalkeeper I ever saw in my life. Typical of him was when he used to ask me to go back two or three afternoons a week with him to train. And, mind, Jack when he came to Newcastle was twenty-eight or something and he was thirty-one when he left, I think.

Him and I used to go to St James's Park, and he had two long ropes on the goalposts. He used to have me running in from various angles, and I used to come running up, and he would shout 'STOP!' I would be tearing in, and as soon as he shouted I put my foot on the ball and kept running out of the road, so the ball was left at an angle where he was in comparison with the posts. I used to run straight on, and Jack never moved. The ball was left there, and we'd get the rope from one post to the ball, and the other post to the ball, and if Jack wasn't in the centre of that rope we used to have to do it over and over again until he got it to perfection. And this took hours. He was an 'angle' goalkeeper.

Ronnie Simpson was brilliant, but he was a goal-line goalie. Relied on reflexes. But Jack was just the opposite. As a forward on the field, whenever the opposition press your goal, you sometimes get a sinking feeling because you know they're going to score. You never had that feeling with Fairbrother. As soon as he started coming away from the line we knew that his angle was right. We weren't always right, but you never had the feeling that you were going to lose.

When Newcastle did eventually lose a game that season, there was great drama behind the scenes. United's unbeaten run had attracted great publicity. Many players were being put forward as potential internationals. Milburn, Taylor and Harvey for England, Brennan and Mitchell for Scotland, and McMichael for Ireland were all suggestions by the sports writers of the national papers.

Milburn was considered a certainty for another cap against Ireland in the first game of the home internationals on 7 October. But, inexplicably, the selectors went for Jack Lee, Derby County's leader, and gave Jackie a seat on the reserve bench. Knowledgeable journalists blamed Jackie's poor showing in the last of the World Cup games for his sensational omission. The game against Spain had not been vintage Jackie, and he had seemed to lack the confidence to have a crack at goal

52

Sixth Row, Ashington, in 1946, with father Alec, and sister Jean, while mother Nance holds the pet dog, Vic

Our reluctant five-year-old hero poses with his sister Jean

Above: ATC camp at Belford near Morpeth, in 1941. Jackie is second from right, back row

Right: 'Half-time at the Rec', 1936, from a painting by Oliver Kilbourn

Above: Ashington Mining School Youth Group of 1943. JET is second right, back row

Left: Ashington lads descend the Bothal Dickie shaft, 1938

Below: Jack Charlton, bare-headed, back row centre, with trainee miners in 1950

'It doesn't hurt a bit, sir!' Meeting Monty at Burnden Park,
Bolton, 1949

Right: Honorary Pilot Officer Milburn, 1110 Squadron ATC, on
parade

Milburn's first Newcastle team, in 1943. Harry Clifton and
Albert Stubbins head the line-up, Charlie Wayman and Jackie
complete the eleven

Jackie stands next to towering goalkeeper Frank Swift for his first England team photo in October 1948

Left: Typical Milburn challenge on Swiss full-back, 1948

Below: Jack and Shack in England tracksuits, before the game against Wales at Ninian Park. Milburn scored a hat-trick in a 4–1 win

Jackie meets King George VI prior to the
1951 Cup Final . . .

. . . which Newcastle won, beating Blackpool
2–0. Joe Harvey is hoisted aloft by Milburn
(who scored both goals) and Brennan

Laura Milburn on her way to her first football match: the Cup Final against Blackpool. Behind
Ernie Taylor is young reserve, Bob Stokoe

Spurs' Ditchburn and Ramsey foil Milburn goal attempt at St James's Park in 1949

Tom Finney looks on as Milburn threatens Portugal's goal, in the 1951 Festival of Britain game at Goodison Park

In an unfamiliar England red shirt, Jackie scores the winner against Argentina, 1951

Newcastle's twin strikers, Robledo and Milburn, often trained in the gym at Ashington Rec

Brennan, Milburn, Cowell and Crowe, bare all

Newcastle United's 1952 squad included Ashington's other international, Jimmy Jackson, seated, front right

It's Wor Cup, and Jackie says a personal thank-you to his wee friend Ernie Taylor

Ashington's Central Hall is packed to honour its favourite son, 1951

when offered the opportunity. Whatever the selectors' reasoning, Lee was to be given the chance to prove himself, with Jackie playing the role of understudy.

The Newcastle board, metaphorical feet flying, waded into the controversy. If Milburn was just going to kick his heels at Belfast, then United wanted him for an important League game at Villa Park. Seymour applied to the FA for Jackie's release. This was the second time that Newcastle had dared to ask for a player to be released from international duties – Milburn in both cases. Would they be allowed to get away with it again? This was the question being asked in many club boardrooms, where it had long been thought that the Football Association had no divine right to call upon a club's players. They were all looking for a precedent; perhaps Newcastle United could provide one.

One possible solution put forward by Newcastle officials was that Milburn could travel to Belfast with the England squad, but if it became apparent that he wouldn't get a game then Newcastle would pay to have him flown back to Birmingham airport in time to take the field against Aston Villa. When Newcastle United think, they think big. 'Milburn to be the First Flying Footballer' was the headline in the papers after manager George Martin gave the following press release: 'Milburn has been chosen as a reserve, and we do not relish the idea of his sitting on the sideline in Belfast while we play our important game against Aston Villa. But if the FA would agree to his becoming a flying reserve I do not think that we should raise any objection.'

The terse reply, received the next day, was: 'The Football Association have refused Newcastle United's appeal that Milburn, their centre-forward, be released from England reserve duty against Ireland next Saturday.'

Other clubs were sympathetic towards Newcastle's plight – it could well have been any of them – and they agreed to support them at the next FA meeting. Until then, Rule 41 which stated that a player selected for international and other matches *must* play, had never been challenged. There was a growing conviction among League clubs that international fixtures should be played mid-week, as the top teams invariably supplied two or even three of their star players to help their country and it was virtually impossible to find suitable substitutes to deputise for them.

Newcastle were well able to vouch for this as their forward line, bereft of their dynamo, failed to spark at all and United went down 3–0 at Villa Park as Jackie Milburn watched his England colleagues win a poor match against Ireland 4–1. John Graydon's headline in the *Sporting Chronicle* on the Monday read: England Won, but Missed Milburn's Speed and Thrust'. But it was small consolation for a Newcastle team that had now lost its place at the top of the First Division.

Jackie had a chance to thumb his nose at the England selectors as United took on Derby County and his England replacement Jack Lee at St James's. Obviously well primed by his pal, Frank Brennan didn't give Lee a sniff of the ball for the full ninety minutes. And 54,753 United supporters went home wondering just what their man had to do to get back in the England team after opening the scoring that put Newcastle on the way to a 3–1 win.

George Robledo was proving to be an excellent buy from Barnsley, and was profiting a great deal from being Milburn's back-up man. Frank Brennan was later to say:

George was doing great, knocking in hat-tricks all over the place. But most of them were put down to Milburn. Jackie would have a crack . . . aye, from twenty or thirty yards, and they would come off the woodwork or a defender's body, and there would be George to put them away. He was always poaching around the goal-mouth.

We were talking about a particular incident in our penalty area after one game, and George pipes up with 'I didn't know that happened!' And Joe Harvey barks at him: 'George, how the hell would you know what happens in our goal-mouth – you never come into our half of the bloody field!'

Joe Harvey's attitude and actions on the field were entirely pragmatic. If the only way to stop an opponent was to bring him down, then down he came. If the only way to motivate a player was to curse him, then he had the language for the occasion. Jackie and the rest of the side had a lot to thank him for as they set about taking the world of football apart in that 1950/51 season.

I'll tell you why I admired Joe Harvey. He wasn't a good player, and he used to get more bollockings off the crowd than cheers. But even so, I couldn't understand how a man could get that kind of stick off the crowd and still guide a team the way he did. In other words, he forgot what the crowd was saying. He still kept at us: 'You bloody well do this . . .' and such, even though he was having a stinker! It takes a good man to do that. I couldn't understand how a man could do it. Because if the crowd began to get at me, I used to go into me shell.

At school, with being sports champion, a lot of people looked up to you in the class, and it made you feel good. I'd never had that before – never had any bollockings. And when it did happen, you didn't know how to react. I would rather have gone into me shell and hid somewhere, or pretended I was injured. And yet he shrugged the whole lot off, and said 'Bugger them!' to guide the team. It takes guts. He was an extraordinary character, was Joe.

People have often asked me if I'd like to be playing now with all the big money that's floating around. Now, I know the money would have been nice, but if it meant missing playing with the lads that we had at St James's just after the war – the Brennans, Cowells, Harveys, Crowes and Mitchells – whey man, there's no way I would ever have missed that. It was a laugh a minute with the lads. The likes of Jack Fairbrother . . . they were so dedicated. There's no money would ever have been able to buy that team.

The next international game that season was against Wales at Roker Park, Sunderland. One good thing that the FA were doing at the time was spreading the international games among the provincial arenas. But with the games being played in all parts of the country, it was difficult to tell if a man was chosen on merit or purely because he was a local lad, put in to swell the attendance.

The North-East had three representatives playing at Roker: Mannion of Middlesbrough, Welshman Trevor Ford, Sunderland's new signing, and Jackie Milburn. It was always Milburn who could be relied upon to bring the fans rushing through the turnstiles, although the appearance of Sunderland's Willie Watson, brought in as a last-minute replacement for the injured Billy Wright, meant that the Roker team had two representatives. In an exciting game England kept up their unbeaten record and won 4–2, with a Milburn goal clinching the match barely a minute from the end. Critics were well pleased with England's performance, apart from Arsenal's Leslie Compton, brother of Denis, who had been hopelessly outgunned by the robust Ford. Once again Jackie Milburn was tipped to hold his place for the next England game against the touring side of Yugoslavia.

But the formation of an England team was proving as difficult to forecast as an earlier Grand National when an unconsidered Irish horse, Caughoo, had won at odds of 100–1. Milburn was dropped once again, evidence to some that he had been included at Roker only because of the proximity of the venue to Newcastle. An outraged John Thomson of the *Sunday Pictorial* wrote:

England football selectors have a curious way of showing their gratitude to the team which fought so magnificently against Wales. They have promptly changed it!. . . . Most surprising is the omission of Milburn of Newcastle United, who needs only a little more confidence to be one of the greatest centre-forwards ever to lead an England line. This is a fine way to increase a lad's confidence!

Anyone who was at Sunderland and thought Milburn a failure must have been blindfolded!

For a while it looked as though Jackie had lost confidence, and it was George Robledo who knocked in two consecutive hat-tricks as United continued to be among the First Division front runners. Milburn, now the father of six-month-old blonde-haired beauty Linda, asked if he could move back to Ashington from the club house he was renting in Gosforth. He told a reporter:

No one knows better than me that I have been playing below my form in recent weeks. Living in Ashington will mean a lot of travelling, but it will be nice to know that I am going home to my own people when training and matches are over.

The wife and I have felt very lonely in Newcastle, and I have worried about her being on her own when the club has been away from the city. Newcastle can be a very lonely place.

While it was always understood that the names of Milburn and Newcastle went together like strawberries and cream, the sweetness in Jackie's life was invariably sucked from out of the sooty air which enveloped the colliery rows of Ashington. Jackie Milburn meant a great deal to the people of the North-East, but it was specifically to the folk of Ashington that he was 'Wor Jackie'. He belonged to the town, to the pit, and to the pitmen. His was the first name on everyone's lips on a Monday morning at work, whether United won, lost or drew – the result was not important. 'How did wor Jackie gan on, on Sa'day?' was the question that hummed around the coal workings of the Bothal, Duke and Carl pits.

This was to be the first of many homecomings for Wor Jackie. Fortunately the trick worked, and Jackie was back in business – the newspaper business. He was paid by a Newcastle-based newspaper on a freelance basis.

The only way I could make ends meet in those days was writing a column in the North Mail and Chronicle. *I used to write a weekly article. That was me pocket money! Cos when you've got a family and your wage is twelve pounds a week . . . .*

I used to spend – whey, I'll tell you, to write 300 words used to take me all day. You see, the lads used to have a day – every Wednesday – to be playing golf, either at Ponteland or Morpeth. They were all on the course for half past nine. They used to come in, play nine holes, get their dinner, and they were away for eighteen in the afternoon. I used to get there early, and here's me sitting in the corner of the clubhouse all day, trying to get this word-perfect. I would be tearing it up and writing it again.

But it stood me in good stead, cos it wound up that I was twenty-three years at the News of the World. *I used to write about personalities in the game, anything. All football, of course. I've thrown all the cuttings away – I think there might be a boxful left in the loft.*

Milburn showed commitment in whatever he did, wherever he was. He was never still for a minute. Laura was told by a new neighbour that she was lucky to have a husband who wasn't a 'nine-to-five' man. But the truth was that living with a professional footballer brought with it pressures and problems never imagined by ordinary housewives. Laura tells of having to live with a man whose sole intent from Monday to Friday was to build up an inner energy which would be ready for release at exactly 3 p.m. on the Saturday afternoon. Adrenalin had to be carefully stored, aggression nurtured to such a fine degree that it would spill over only with the ball at his feet, surrounded by burly defenders trying to steal it from him. It was never easy for Laura sharing a house with a growing family and fifty thousand fans.

A rejuvenated Jackie joined up again with United after being laid low by fibrositis. He found that team affairs had been taken over by Stan Seymour, with George Martin leaving Newcastle to take up a similar position with Aston Villa. Martin, although being in charge of Newcastle's promotion-winning side of 1948, had never enjoyed full control over either team selection or tactics. According to left-half Crowe, a typical Martin team-talk went like this:

To Jack Fairbrother:	'Jack . . . the 18-yard area . . . make it your own. You're the boss!'
To Cowell and Corbett:	'Now . . . the two Bobs . . . these two wingers . . . put a rope around their necks!'
To Joe Harvey:	'Joe . . . keep 'em going!'
To Frank Brennan:	'Frank . . . put 'em in your pocket!'

To Charlie Crowe:	'Charlie . . . give them the usual!' (*Bashing one fist against the other*)
To Walker and Milburn:	'Tom . . . Jackie . . . show 'em your arses!'
To Ernie Taylor:	(*Ruffling Ernie's hair*) 'Aha! . . . The little man!' (*Nodding his head as if to emphasise some point*)
To George Robledo:	'George . . . the far post!'
To Bobby Mitchell:	'Mitch . . . that extra man . . . don't overdo it!'
	'Right then, lads – out you go!'

Newcastle kept on piling up the points and were well in contention with Arsenal, the League leaders, when they went to White Hart Lane to take on newly promoted Tottenham. Spurs put a stop to United's gallop, flashing seven goals past a bewildered Fairbrother who was getting the angles wrong for once, in front of a colossal 70,000 crowd, to go top of the League.

The FA Cup got under way, with Newcastle easily disposing of Second Division Bury 4–1. Fourth-round opponents Bolton Wanderers proved far more difficult, even at St James's Park. Bobby Mitchell got United's head in front after only four minutes, to send a 67,596 crowd wild, but a defence without big Frank Brennan was always going to find Nat Lofthouse a handful. Brennan's deputy, McNeil, was panicked into giving away a needless free kick just outside the Newcastle penalty area. From the resulting melee Moir headed an equaliser. Mattie McNeil began scything Lofthouse to the ground at every opportunity. During a lull in the game Nat asked Charlie Crowe: 'Who the hell is this fella? Does he think he's playing rugby, or what? He'd better watch himself or I'll have him.'

Just before half-time Lofthouse and McNeil clashed again in a grinding tackle that left the Newcastle player flat out on the ground. As Norman Smith was giving him treatment, the big centre-half was yelling across at Lofthouse what he'd do to him when he got back on his feet. Nat strode across, and with a voice full of menace said: 'Lad, you're not going to get up again: you're out of the match.' The Bolton player was right, for McNeil from then on was a virtual passenger on the wing.

Lofthouse, now with acres of space, laid on another goal for Moir, and United found themselves behind in a game which they had completely dominated from the first whistle. The game was held up for five minutes while the police cleared the field of jubilant Lancashire fans. But if the Bolton supporters thought the game was won, they had reckoned without Jackie Milburn! Standing almost unconcernedly with his face to his own goal, he received the ball, swivelled on his heel, and shot the ball past Hanson before the goalie even sensed there was any danger. This was the drama of a man who could turn defeat into victory in an instant. Minutes later, as an immobile Bolton defence stood appealing for offside, Milburn walked the ball through into the net to put the Newcastle marble into the bag for the next round.

In the fifth round Newcastle proved far too good for Stoke City at the Victoria Ground, winning easily 4–2 with Robledo scoring twice. Brennan returned for this game to stiffen United's defence. Near neighbours Sunderland were also through, but in a thrilling replay went out to Wolverhampton Wanderers, defeated 3–1. Newcastle's next Cup tie also went to a replay, as they were held to a goalless draw at home by Third Division Bristol Rovers. The game at Eastville proved less difficult, and goals from Taylor, Crowe and Milburn were enough to scupper the Pirates 3–1.

Eager ears listened for the semi-final draw at lunch-time the following Monday. Newcastle's opponents would be Birmingham, Blackpool or Wolves. Of the three, United would probably have preferred Birmingham or Blackpool. They were drawn against Billy Wright's Wolves.

Joe Harvey, surely tempting fate, wrote the following article for the *Newcastle Journal and North Mail*, printed on the morning of the match. It was headed: 'Next Stop Wembley!'

Wembley – here comes Newcastle United! That heartfelt wish just about covers the range of my hope and determination this morning. As I have been disappointed in one semi-final since the war, this game means a great deal to me.

Why does the Cup bite so deep? It's not the brass, though I'm six-foot of Yorkshire in that sort of collecting. We all know the League is the real test. In the next couple of months United will pull out their last reserves for the Championship run-in. But the Cup? Well, it's an adventure.

And when you get there? How should I know? I've only seen Wembley stands rising in the distance when travelling, and gazed longingly at the ground itself at the cinema.

And now we are nearly tossing a coin for the lucky dressing-room. I cannot get my thoughts past that . . . WEMBLEY, HERE WE COME!

Newcastle played Wolves at Sheffield's Hillsborough ground, and the other two teams met at Maine Road, Manchester. For the first time since 1912, both semi-finals ended as draws – and goalless draws at that. Two would-be England centre-forwards were on view at Hillsborough: Newcastle's Milburn and Roy Swinbourne of Wolves. Both had the ball in the net in the first five minutes but their efforts were disallowed, Milburn's for 'offside' and Swinbourne's for 'hand-ball'.

The Newcastle *v* Wolves replay was arranged for Huddersfield, and the other game was scheduled for Goodison Park, home of Everton. Wolves' team for that game on 14 March 1951 was: Williams, Short, Pritchard, Russell, Shorthouse, Wright, Hancocks, Walker, Swinbourne, Dunn and Mullen. The Newcastle side was: Fairbrother, Cowell, Corbett, Harvey, Brennan, Crowe, Walker, Taylor, Milburn, Robledo and Mitchell.

For a long time that day it was doubtful whether the match would get under way. Incessant rain had flooded the pitch and terraces, and huge pipes were brought in to pump out the water. Minutes before the kick-off the referee declared the pitch fit, but there was no time to clear away the metal pipes, so they were stacked behind the goals.

Wolves shocked the thousands of United's travelling fans by scoring an early goal through inside-right Walker. Now under extreme pressure, Newcastle gave away a corner on the left which was quickly taken by Wolves' England winger, Hancocks. Big Frank Brennan rose above the Wolves attack to head clear, but in doing so stumbled and fell off the field, banging his head against a metal pipe. Stan Seymour swore he heard the crack up in the directors' box.

Norman Smith raced on to the pitch to where Harvey was bending over the motionless Brennan, whose face had by now turned ashen grey. Joe turned round and said, 'My God! He's got to be dead.' Smith produced the magic sponge and smelling salts, and administered both to the Big Fella in large doses. Eventually Brennan rose shakily to his feet, eyes rolling around in his head. Harvey pleaded with the trainer to pull him around. A little colour seeped back into Frank's craggy face, and Smith held up two fingers: 'Frank, how many fingers have I got up?' The Scot mumbled and swayed, but said nothing.

Brennan got a little more coherent, and the referee, eager to get the game away after such a long stoppage, waved Newcastle's trainer from the field. As he was running off, Smith turned to Brennan and shouted: 'For heaven's sake, Frank, let your head clear before you attempt to head the ball again.' Brennan nodded, but in Wolves' very next attack he met a vicious drive square on the forehead, and the ball flew thirty yards upfield. The Newcastle players held their breath, expecting Frank to topple once again, but he just grinned as they looked on in astonishment.

The game was another personal triumph for Jackie Milburn. Newcastle refused to be flustered by that early Wolves goal, and Jackie had a simple tap-in after a piece of Taylor magic had opened up the Wolves defence. Minutes later it was Milburn's turn to do the donkey work and leave the rest to the sweet left foot of Bobby Mitchell.

Joe Harvey's perilous prediction had come true. Wembley, here we come!

CHAPTER EIGHT

1951
Cup Final, Shack insisted we were playing for buttons

That win put Newcastle into the Cup Final for the eighth time. They had been the bookies' favourites for a long time to lift the trophy, and were very well placed to do the 'double'. Immediately after the final whistle had blown after the replay victory, Seymour raced into the Newcastle dressing room, threw his arms around each player in turn and announced: 'Thank you, everybody! It was a wonderful performance, and I'll tell you all straight away, there's going to be no worrying about who plays in the Cup Final. Whatever happens, you fellows who've brought us this far will play at Wembley.'

Unbelievable! There were still nine matches to be played in the League, and United had to win only about half of them to win the Championship. Yet the Newcastle manager had handed the players what amounted to a free hand in the way they would approach the remaining games. Milburn wrote:

It was during this pre-Final waiting period that I realised what a tremendous strain was being placed upon the men due to play at Wembley. Although none of us ever thought of holding back from a tackle for fear of being hurt, or taking a chance which may have brought us an injury, I'm confident that, quite unconsciously, every man who is going to play in a great match doesn't put everything he possesses into ordinary League games before the great day.

For the next six weeks the Newcastle team tottered from one defeat to the next, disappointing their worried followers and causing the bookies to install opponents

Blackpool, who had seen off Birmingham, as new favourites to win the Cup. The match was now being hailed as the 'Matthews Final', with every neutral football fan in the country hoping that Stan, now approaching forty years of age, would get the one honour that had eluded him for so long.

Four weeks before the Wembley game, the teams met in a dress rehearsal at Bloomfield Road. Blackpool, mid-placed in the League, rested Matthews and Perry; Newcastle played without Ernie Taylor and Joe Harvey. Blackpool inside-forward Alan Brown, who was to break a leg in a later game and so miss Wembley, was prominent with long, strength-sapping runs through the mud and water that clogged up the middle of the pitch. It was from one of these runs that the first Blackpool goal was scored through Mortenson: a great header stemming from a prodigious leap.

Milburn gave goalie Farm an ominous taste of what was to come at Wembley by firing in the equaliser with a twenty-five-yard oblique shot. Only seconds later Mudie put Blackpool ahead, again from a Wardle centre. Bob Stokoe, getting a rare game in Harvey's absence, kicked into an open space for Robledo to run on and level the scores once again. The match ended that way – 2–2 – and a report in the *Sunday Pictorial* ended with: 'If these two teams can produce at Wembley the same quality of football as on this occasion under such adverse conditions, it augurs well for a great Final.'

A week before the Final was due to be played, the United team and directors headed for the beneficial Spa waters of Buxton. The team had used the Derbyshire town before for special training, and it had got to be a lucky hideout for them, with United always winning big matches after staying there.

Jackie now had two children, Linda and Betty, who were getting used to Daddy being away sometimes for weeks at a time. The Milburn family were still living in Ashington, now in Ellington Terrace quite near Jackie's sister Jean, with his parents only a matter of yards away. It seemed that Jackie's life not only gravitated towards the pit town but, more precisely than that, to one particular part – the 'top-end'. It was where he had been born, brought up at his gran's, had kicked a tennis ball up against the netty door, worked in the fitting sheds, and loped around the running track at the Rec. All those places put together could fit quite comfortably into a medium-size soccer ground.

Team talks from trainer Smith and manager Seymour tended to be short and to the point. No blackboards here with pin-men moved around like robots; this was the era of 'gut' football. Players felt instinctively what was the right thing to do. The advent of the all-knowing soccer coach had not yet made inroads into what was a rousing game, exciting to watch, and a thrilling spectacle which still pulled in massive crowds in all kinds of weather.

Coaching was looked upon as something of a joke by the long-serving pros. Walter Winterbottom had been giving an England side some slide-rule advice, and ended with: 'When it's on, I want Wright to transfer the ball to Finney, then Finney to Mannion. Mullen and Milburn will then go on dummy runs, and the ball will be switched back to Finney who will get to the bye-line and cross for

61

Shackleton who will put it into the net.' Biding his time, Shack paused before quipping: 'Ah yes, Walter, but what side of the net should I put it in?'

Charlie Crowe, who later became a qualified coach, remembers the coaching jargon that Winterbottom himself coined. One such piece of gobbledygook went: 'On getting the ball use your *peripheral vision*.' Charlie says what he meant was: 'Watch your back'!

The 1951 Wembley Cup Final will go down as the match that very nearly wasn't played. There was not one, but three crises, any one of which could have ended up with only one team on Wembley's red carpet to shake the hand of King George VI. Crisis number one loomed up in the shape of wise-cracking, briar pipe-smoking Len Shackleton.

That's why I came to admire Shack more than anybody. He insisted that we were playing for buttons. He insisted on this, way back to the war years. Aye! In fact, he came over just before the '51 Final – he was playing for Sunderland at the time – and spoke to the lads. 'Hey, you want to refuse to go on the bloody pitch,' he says, 'because they're making nearly forty thousand pounds on the gate.'

It was three and a tanner for a ticket then, and about a couple of quid for a seat, or something. And he went through the whole routine of what they were clicking, the FA, and how much they were making, and what we were getting.

Len Shackleton was a man before his time, not only with his inimitable style of play, but also his foresight into what was happening in the game at that time. A great deal of money was being made, with attendances holding up very well, although not as high as in the immediate post-war years. That the money wasn't going to the players was obvious, when the maximum wage at that time was only £12 in season and £10 in summer. Shack, together with players' champion Ernie Clay, was later to be instrumental in the FA taking a closer look at the whole idea of the maximum wage. The Newcastle lads decided not to take Shackleton's advice, however, the consensus being that if they refused to play, the board would soon draft in another eleven lads more than eager to pull on a black and white strip in a Cup Final.

Crisis number two was of a petticoat variety. Just before the squad left for Buxton, Ida Harvey, Joe's wife, noticed that the ticket she had been allocated for Wembley was a standing one on the terraces. On checking with other spouses it was found that, indeed, all the players' wives would have to stand. Ida, when roused, could be just as formidable an adversary as her husband, and she demanded that Joe, as skipper, should sort things out. No seat – no Wembley. Joe took another couple of players along for support when he approached Stan Seymour with the ultimatum. Seymour, sensing that with ladies involved this was one fight he couldn't win, said that the ticket allocation was an error, and the wives were given seats two rows behind the Royal Box. Yet another catastrophe had been averted. Not so easy was crisis number three!

While at Buxton the United team had been given the run of the place and its facilities – snooker, golf, tennis, swimming, etc. – and everyone took full advantage of the very relaxed atmosphere. Even night-time drinking – in moderation – was allowed, but only up until the Wednesday night; after that a strict curfew was imposed, which players might defy at the risk of being sent home. Eleven o'clock was made the deadline.

Two players thought they could beat the system, and stayed out in Buxton until midnight. On entering the reception area, the pair spotted four directors sitting in such a position that the errant duo could not fail to be spotted. Player One decided he would try to enter the hotel through a window, while Player Two, less adventurously, chose to sneak past the directors, still deep in conversation, by the more orthodox front door. Both were apprehended. Seymour demanded an explanation, and as the two unfortunates obviously didn't have one, they were told to wait in an adjoining room until it was decided what action would be taken. A few minutes later the miscreants were summoned before their betters and told they were to be punished, as had been threatened, by being sent home and their places in the team given to two of the travelling reserves.

The two men were shattered. Totally shaken. Not for one moment had they suspected that the Boss would carry out his threat, but Seymour, backed up by his fellow directors, was adamant that a rule had been broken, and that those guilty of breaking rules must pay the penalty.

An uneasy Newcastle United went to their beds that night, not wanting to believe what had happened in the last couple of hours. Not just the players, who saw everything they had worked for that season crumbling before their eyes, but also the management, because of the reception they knew they would get from a hostile press and an even more savage set of supporters should the two players – both crowd-pleasers – be dropped.

'If you have a problem, sleep on it' is a worthy old adage which worked wonders for United. Seymour awoke, accepted apologies from the two latecomers, and the good ship Magpie was back on an even keel.

The Newcastle squad left Buxton on the Friday morning to travel to Weybridge where they were to stay overnight at the Oatlands Park Hotel. The players' wives made their own way down to the capital the same day, having been booked into the Great Northern. Also in the Newcastle party were two Geordie entertainers who were to keep the players in high spirits the night before the game and also the morning of the match. At last the players were relaxing and getting the 'feel', of the big occasion. They had climbed a mountain to get this far, but from now on it was all downhill.

After arriving at their hotel, unpacking, then having a light lunch, the players went with Seymour straight to Wembley Stadium, which was only a few miles away. The psychological advantage of a team walking on the Wembley turf a full day before they are due to take part in a big occasion like a Cup Final is tremendous. The players spent a full hour getting the feel of the dressing rooms, treading every bit of the lush turf, taking time to stand and stare without the attention of 100,000 pairs of prying eyes feeding off their every move, searching for cracks in their armour. And then it was the journey back – relaxing, laughing, joking, but with their mind's eye still keenly focused on the twin towers shadowing that massive expanse of green.

Jackie Milburn's room-mate at Weybridge was his pal 'Pancho'. There were laughs all round when it was found out that they had been allocated the bridal suite. It had been a two-year marriage of convenience for the Newcastle strikers with the contrasting styles, yet complementing each other perfectly. Milburn, in spite of that mid-season hiccup, was still slightly ahead on the goals-scored sheet.

After dinner that evening the team got together for what was to be the last pep talk before the big game the following afternoon. Seymour knew better than to talk tactics, but he singled out one man of the opposition who would need special attention. That man was Stanley Matthews. The Blackpool winger was notorious for drawing players away from the game, pulling them out of position and so making more space for Mudie and Mortenson. The Seymour plan was simple: Matthews was not to be followed, but was to be taken by the nearest man.

Milburn and Robledo retired to their room still suffering from the friendly jibes of joker Fairbrother and company. Both players were avid readers, and settled into their beds to while away an hour before getting to sleep – at least, that was the plan. Very soon they were playing out the next day's Final in earnest conversation. Jackie was saved by the bell – the telephone bell. Later, he described what happened that night.

We'd both read a couple of pages of our respective books, then, much as we disliked it, found ourselves discussing what might happen in the match on the morrow. Fortunately for me, my wife, ever a considerate soul, knew this would happen, so at about half-past ten she telephoned from her hotel, and for nearly an hour we talked about the children, the new curtains she needed for the living-room, our forthcoming holiday, and the new dress she had bought for the banquet. Laura – bless her – talked about everything except the Cup Final, and for an hour at least I was made to realize that there are other things in life in addition to football.

There was still little sleep for George and Jackie as they were awakened at about seven o'clock by a group of Geordie supporters singing 'Blaydon Races'. Jackie forgave them as he waved from his bedroom window.

The Saturday morning was spent pottering around the hotel grounds, playing snooker, table tennis, a friendly game of three-card-brag – anything to keep over-active minds from dwelling too long on the afternoon's affairs. The two travelling Geordie minstrels, comedian Harry Goodfellow and his pianist Benny Needham, played and sang a medley of north-eastern favourites, including 'She's a big lass and a bonnie lass/And she likes her beer/And they call her Cushie Butterfield/And I wish she was here.'

Back in Ashington almost the entire population wished they were there, too. It was their boy who was playing at Wembley, and dozens of coaches were already spilling out their human cargo, colouring the streets of London black and white with Magpie flags, rosettes, hats and scarves. The majority of Ashingtonians had to make do with their wireless sets, some already tuned in three hours in advance, but a few of the town's more prosperous citizens had got together and hired their own plane. Their twin-engined Dakota left Woolsington Airport at eight o'clock that morning, disembarking an exuberant party into London two hours later.

After lunch it was time for George Robledo to leave for the game. George was a poor coach traveller, and Seymour, taking no chances, had arranged that Bobby Cowell and trainer Norman Smith should accompany the Chilean on the short train journey that would take them direct to the stadium. As Jackie waved them off he shouted, 'I hope we see you later!' and when the full significance of that remark hit George, his face shadowed with a look of concern. 'You know, Jackie, I hadn't thought of that,' he said.

The coach containing the rest of the team arrived at the ground ninety minutes before kick-off; ample time to go through the superstitious rituals which footballers build up during a Cup run. Jack Fairbrother sensuously pulling on his policeman's gloves of the purest white; Bobby Cowell wearing a particular tie; Frank Brennan with the battered boots, large enough to take little Ernie Taylor's size fours as the wee man climbed into them still wearing his own; Jackie Milburn with his ebony elephant: and captain Joe Harvey entrusted with a very special 1901 penny already carried by two Newcastle United players in previous Cup Final victories, and now entrusted to Joe to carry to a hat-trick of wins. Dare he even think of failure?

Getting ready in the 'south' dressing room, Jackie was so worked up that he went into the toilets for a crafty drag, only to find he could hardly get in there for players of a like mind. The sounds of 'Abide with Me,' his favourite hymn, took Jackie, together with George Robledo – who had made it after all – down the tunnel to sneak a look at the singing crowd. They were there for only seconds before being beckoned back into the dressing room. A pity, for they missed the next song, conducted by Wembley regular Arthur Caiger: 'Blaydon Races'. Strictly impartial, the band of the Coldstream Guards next struck up with 'She's a Lassie from Lancashire', satisfying both sets of happy supporters.

Now it was approaching ten minutes to three, and there began the long walk up the narrow tunnel, side by side and shoulder to shoulder with the opposition, afraid to glance across lest anxious eyes betray the fear which was turning sturdy legs to putty. Leading the parade of the gladiators was Mr John Whitty, a compact little man, bowler-hatted – marshal for the afternoon. A member of the FA, his job was to issue instructions to everyone so that they knew what was expected of them once out on the field.

On the pitch a game was already in progress: catch the duck! Blackpool hotelier Sid Bevers, dressed in a tangerine and white suit, had run on to the field carrying a large box which he placed on the centre spot next to the Coldstream Guards band. Out of the box sprang Donald, a spotlessly white duck who had been present at every Blackpool tie and was looked upon by the Blackpool supporters as unofficial mascot. Donald strutted and waddled for several minutes before the Wembley security police converged on him. The duck, however, was enjoying the laughter and applause from the amused crowd, and managed to evade everyone until his owner, Sid, successfully captured the indignant bird with a rugby tackle.

And now the teams were emerging from the tunnel, Newcastle led by Stan Seymour, holder of a Cup winner's medal, and Blackpool by Joe Smith, who had won two. The ripple of noise from those standing near the entrance turned into a torrent as the players came into full view of the 100,000 people who had paid a record of £39,336 to witness what had been hailed as the match of the century.

Introductions now, as a pale King George VI was guided towards the teams. He shook Joe Harvey's hand, asking, 'Have you played here before?' 'No,' replied Joe, 'but our chief has.' Further down at the end of the Newcastle line, Stan Seymour confirmed, 'Yes, indeed. I had the honour of receiving a Cup winner's medal from Your Majesty in 1924.' Formalities over, the two teams ran to their respective ends, looking up into the vast crowd trying to pinpoint friends and relatives bobbing around in that vast sea of faces.

The Newcastle team for the Final was: Fairbrother, Cowell, Corbett, Harvey, Brennan, Crowe, Walker, Taylor, Milburn, Robledo, Mitchell. The Blackpool side was: Farm, Shimwell, Garrett, Johnston, Hayward, Kelly, Matthews, Mudie, Mortenson, W. J. Slater, Perry. Blackpool had been forced to play an amateur, Bill Slater – who had not played in a First Division game for six months – because of an injury to their regular inside-left, Alan Brown. Newcastle fielded the side who had been promised their places after the semi-final, in spite of injury scares with Brennan and Harvey.

Immediately before the kick-off there was still a brisk market of tickets at Wembley Park Underground station. One young Newcastle United supporter openly touted a three-shilling ticket for £4, eventually having to be satisfied with £3 10s.

Referee Bill Ling got the game away at precisely 3 p.m. Initial play was scrappy as both teams displayed obvious tension. Milburn had the ball in the Blackpool net after ten minutes, chesting it down before sliding it past Farm. Ling thought that Jackie had handled the ball, and disallowed the goal. Jackie, on the point of protesting, remembered Seymour's last warning before going on to the pitch: 'On no account are you to question the referee's decisions.' He turned away, masking his frustration beneath lowered eyes.

Now it was Blackpool's turn to be disappointed. Matthews, target for all of the Seasiders' passes, evaded three tackles from Newcastle defenders before pinpointing the unmarked Slater. The unhappy amateur, with far more time than he realised, hooked his hurried first-time shot inches the wrong side of the post. Three relieved Geordies looked sheepishly at each other, having forgotten their original plan: leave Matthews to the nearest man, and don't get drawn out of position. The dejected Slater was probably unaware that he was only the third amateur to play in a Cup Final or, even more ominous, that both his predecessors had finished up on losing sides. Meanwhile, the two Blackpool full-backs were also playing to orders. The policy of Eddie Shimwell and Tommy Garrett playing so far up the field and so dangerously square was not deliberately to set an offside trap, but to keep close to wingers Walker and Mitchell. The main reason for this was that Mitchell had had such a good game against Shimwell in the Cup rehearsal at Bloomfield Road only weeks earlier. The ploy worked in that they succeeded in keeping the wingmen quiet, but it left centre-half Hayward completely uncovered in the event of a swift counter-attack from the speedy Milburn. Purposely or not, the Blackpool defence caught United's forwards offside nine times in the first half. Most of the decisions were hairline ones, giving the impression that it needed the defenders to be only a fraction too far forward to let Newcastle in with a chance of springing the trap.

Jack Fairbrother made complete nonsense of an attempted catch from a Perry corner, and was left marooned as Mortenson got a free header. The ball had 'Goal' embossed into the leather until ex-pit joiner Bobby Cowell miraculously emerged, as if from out of the Wembley turf itself, to head it off the goal-line. It was proving to be a dour, hard match, and from a Robledo tackle Blackpool captain Harry Johnston fell, writhing in agony for several minutes before resuming with a definite hobble. At last Milburn showed his heels to the Blackpool defence after good work from Brennan and Taylor. Once in the clear he let fly from twenty yards, only to see Farm parry the ball with one hand, upwards and over the crossbar.

The half-time whistle went with Blackpool still looking like being the team to have a bet on. Fairbrother had taken thirteen goal kicks to five from Farm, and Blackpool had won three corner kicks to two from Newcastle. Half-time talk in the Newcastle dressing room was to the effect that it was 'so far, so good', with the proviso that more long balls, hit to the wings, might unsettle the opposing defence.

Newcastle chairman John Lee, sitting between Queen Elizabeth and the Duke of Gloucester during the first half, said later: 'I found Her Majesty enjoyed the football very much. At two or three stages she passed comments concerning offside and other decisions which showed me that she has seen quite a deal of football, and has followed it with enthusiastic interest.'

The game restarted at approximately 4 p.m. The sun was now in Fairbrother's eyes, and he donned a cloth cap. Five minutes and twelve seconds later, Newcastle took the lead. Robledo came out of a tackle with the ball, looked up, saw his number nine in acres of space, slotted the ball through to him, and stood back and enjoyed the lethal finish. Jackie Milburn had done it! Through his exceptional speed and accuracy of shot, he had proved himself a star in the greatest footballing production in the world: the FA Cup Final.

But the drama was far from being played out. Barely four minutes later, the Ashington man was centre stage once more to grab what many people have expressed to be one of the finest goals scored in a Cup Final. It sprang from a Blackpool error by, of all people, Matthews. Following the Newcastle opener, the desperate men in tangerine played every ball to the right wing in the hope that the maestro could save the game for them. Stan, hustled as always by Crowe, hurried an inside pass which went astray, and was then swept upfield to the Newcastle right-hand side. Ernie Taylor described what happened next.

When I got the ball from Tommy Walker, I was wondering whether to try a shot or not, but out of the corner of my eye I saw a black and white shirt streaking along. I knew that only Milburn could move like that, so I decided on a back-heel. My back was to goal when I heard the thud of a shot, and as I spun round I saw the wonderful sight of the ball in the back of the net, and Milburn sitting on the ground grinning!

The game had been won and lost in the space of five minutes. A crestfallen Blackpool side looked stunned as Mortenson got the game away again. But every-one knew that the spectacle was over, and that the Cup, thanks to two pieces of Milburn magic, was bound for Geordieland for the fourth time in their history; the luck of the 1901 penny lived on.

The remaining few minutes of the match were played out with the pathetic sight of Stanley Matthews, all hopes of a winner's medal gone for another year, trying to score a goal himself, so bereft of goal-scoring attempts were his colleagues. But a jubilant Newcastle defence kept a firm hold on the game until referee Ling confirmed what everybody else had known for some time: it was Newcastle's Cup.

Even on Wearside, Sunderland fans, fed up with watching their team playing out a dull 1–1 draw with West Brom, tuned in to a radio commentary of the Final and cheered like mad when Milburn scored his second goal.

Joe Harvey led a breathless United team up the steps to receive the winners' medals, as a forlorn Blackpool eleven trooped off the pitch almost unnoticed. Both the King and Queen in presenting the Cup and medals thanked the Newcastle team for the entertainment they had provided. The Queen emphasised that she had thought the football very enjoyable. As a grinning Jack Fairbrother passed her, Princess Margaret remarked, 'A lovely day for you!'

After the medal ceremony it was back down to the pitch once more to acknowl-edge the 12,000 loyal fans who had played their own special part in the victory, spurring on their favourites with familiar chants and songs. Joe Harvey, holding the Cup above his head, was lifted on to the broad shoulders of Frank Brennan and Jackie Milburn, with the rest of the laughing team grouped closely, making a fine tableau for the nation's press.

Back in the relative haven of the dressing room, the champagne corks popped and Jackie had his first taste of bubbly out of a Cup now bedecked with Black and white favours. 'By, that's champion!' said Jackie, licking his lips.

Now it was the turn of the reporters to get their own particular stories from each of the players. 'What about that second goal, Jack?' Jackie smiled. 'It could have gone anywhere,' he replied modestly.

Statistically Blackpool would seem to have had more of the play, with Newcastle having to take twenty-six goal kicks to Blackpool's eleven, while Newcastle gave away fifteen free kicks against only two from the Blackpool side.

A losing Cup Finalists' dressing room is never a happy one, but Blackpool had already tasted defeat only two years earlier, which made it an even more desolate place. Manager Joe Smith was reported as saying that he thought the first goal had been offside. Asked about the second, he replied, 'I couldn't see it for a pillar.'

Captain Harry Johnston, 1951 Footballer of the Year, said of Milburn's second goal: 'Surely this was the finest ever Wembley shot.' Stanley Matthews paid tribute to Milburn's two goals in an article some years later.

It was definitely Milburn's match! His terrific speed made the first. He raced through a gap as wide as the Sahara desert to take a George Robledo pass, calmly drew George Farm, and slipped the ball into the net.

The second was right out of this world! It was the greatest goal I have ever seen, and certainly the finest ever scored at Wembley. A goal that every player dreams about.

That goal is now history, but how many other players would have chanced such a shot, especially in a Wembley Final? Very few would have had the courage. Certainly only a player with the Milburn brand of confidence in his own shooting power.

Jackie Milburn showing confidence! Matthews was right. The shooting power, together with the terrific speed, gave Jackie no problems at all; he knew he was the master. If only life for Jackie Milburn could be a series of fifty-yard sprints, ending with countless shots at goal . . .

. . . Cos me, I'm a fella with no confidence at all!

A coach whisked the Newcastle players back to the Great Northern Hotel to enable them to change into their best bib and tucker, for that evening they were off to a celebration dinner at the plush Savoy in London's trendy West End. Prior to that, however, they met up with their wives who offered kisses in return for a first look at the precious gold medal in the small blue box. There followed a small reception when the players and their wives were joined by the directors to toast the team's victory in champagne. On the way to the Savoy, the Newcastle coach passed through streets bulging with jubilant Geordies intent on letting the world know who had won the Cup. Fans crammed Piccadilly, Leicester Square and Trafalgar Square where they sang 'Blaydon Races' and the praises of Wor Jackie. Not even a sudden downpour could dampen their joyous enthusiasm, and the festivities went on late into the night.

Over two hundred people were gathered under the brightly lit chandeliers of the Savoy, and it is doubtful whether Jackie Milburn knew a quarter of them. Faces he might have been expected to recognise were of members of Newcastle's great 1910 Cup-winning side: Peter McWilliam, Jimmy Howie and Jackie Rutherford. They were joined later by the legendary Bill McCracken, who hadn't even bothered to go to Wembley; he'd gone on a scouting mission for the club. 'I'd rather watch the on-coming youngsters,' he said. Of Jackie Milburn, Jackie Rutherford was quoted as saying: 'Here is one whom we would have been proud to have in the sides of my day.'

The previous three times that Newcastle had won the Cup had been in 1910, when they beat Barnsley 2–0; in 1924 when they again won 2–0, this time against Aston Villa; and in 1932 when Arsenal were beaten 2–1. In their four losing Finals, United had been beaten 2–0 by Aston Villa in 1905; 1–0 by Everton in 1906; 3–1 by Wolves in 1908; and 1–0 by Bradford City in 1911.

Even before the soup courses at the Savoy had been served, the first Newcastle supporters were arriving back on Tyneside. Thirty-two excited fans who stepped from the same Dakota plane which had taken them down to London in the morning were united in saying that it had been a day to remember. As the first, Mr Robert Cooper of Ashington, stepped from the plane at Woolsington, he was mobbed by visitors to the airport eager to get a first-hand view of the Final. 'The lads did us proud,' he said, 'but it was still Jackie's Final.'

In Ashington the working men's clubs were overflowing, and pints of beer were being raised in a toast to the local lad who had made the Cup victory possible. There was a sense of pride about the place once again; Jackie Milburn had put Ashington on the map. And Jackie's two-goal Final did a good turn for the Ashington YMCA. That night they were able to sell all the tickets for the forth-coming Ashington v Dunfermline Athletic match on 19 May in which Jackie and George Robledo had agreed to take part to boost YMCA funds.

Back at Trafalgar Square, as darkness set in, some sympathetic north-eastern souls thought that Nelson looked a little cold and began to collect material to light a bonfire. Five London bobbies soon put a damper on that idea. Over in Piccadilly, reinforcement police had to be called in to keep the crowds moving, as large traffic jams were being caused by masses of Geordies who would suddenly stop and give a rendition of 'Blaydon Races'.

Away from the genial mayhem, polite speeches were being made at the Savoy. Joe Harvey again praised his team; Arthur Drewry, vice-president of the Football Association, paid tribute to Stan Seymour and trainer Norman Smith, while at the same time hinting that the England selectors had taken note of 'some fine Newcastle United performances' – a clear indication that Milburn was once again in line for an England cap. The Duke of Northumberland, Viscount Allendale and the mayor of Newcastle, Alderman Chapman, assured the players that all the North-East would be very proud of their achievement.

Newcastle United had a League game at Wolverhampton on the following Wednesday, and decided to stay on at London overnight then move camp to the Royal Albion Hotel at Brighton until mid-week. So it was not until Thursday, 3 May that the FA Cup arrived on Tyneside, to be welcomed by close on a quarter of a million raucous Geordie supporters. The train carrying the Newcastle team in a specially hired carriage was coupled to an engine bedecked in black and white, bearing the slogan: 'IT'S OURS AGAIN.' The usually drab Central Station was dressed to the number nines as the train swept into the main platform. The fireman and driver left their posts momentarily to thrust Newcastle's colours aloft as the train came to a halt beside an enormous banner which proclaimed: 'WELCOME HYEM, CANNY LADS'.

First to jump from the train was Joe Harvey, the Cup held for all to savour.

70

Policemen linked arms to keep back the good-natured crowd which threatened to swamp the platform in a deluge of black and white flags and scarves. Nearly 600 Tyneside bobbies were on duty that fine May evening. Most of them lined the 'victory route' which took the open-roofed bus up Neville Street, past a bewildered Lord Grey, through to Blackett Street and on to Gallowgate. An estimated 200,000 Tynesiders shouted and sang themselves hoarse on the pavement, while others, leaning from second- and third-floor office and shop windows, showered the coach with a New York style tickertape welcome. Frank Brennan remembered: 'We were all amazed, you know. All these milling masses – we had never seen Newcastle like this.'

More was to come! Another 30,000 people were packed into St James's for a Central League game as the news was announced on the loudspeakers at 6.40 p.m.: 'The Cup is back in the North-East.' Forty minutes later the coach, with a huge mass of bodies snaking along behind it, arrived to a new welcoming cheer. The team appeared in the grandstand headed by Joe Harvey, still clutching the precious trophy.

The Cup had cost £50 when bought in 1910, after being made by a Bradford firm. It was, in fact, the third FA Cup to be used in the competition, which has been in existence since 1871. The first, which played such a thrilling part in the history of English football, was stolen on the night of 11 September 1895 from the shop window of a Birmingham football manufacturer. Aston Villa, the holders, were fined £25 by the Football Association for lending it out.

When the cheers for Harvey had subsided, a chant of 'We want Jackie' surged around the ground, gradually increasing in volume until the ever-modest Ashington collier's son sidled up to the microphone, right arm tucked self-consciously into his grey jacket. It was a further three minutes before the crowd would let him speak. He finally silenced them with 'Come on, let's get on with it. I'm gettin' nervous stannin' here.' The fans needed no encouragement to laugh at this typical Milburn-ism. He continued: 'This has been the proudest moment of our lives.' And he turned to Mitchell, Harvey & Co. for support. 'Hasn't it lads?'

I think we must've kidded you on these last few weeks. But we knew in wor hearts that we could win on Sa'day. Anyhow, we darena' come back withoot it! We won because we have the finest bunch of lads in the world, the finest skipper, and the best supporters. Thanks a lot!

For being a self-confessed shy man, Milburn had the knack of saying, as well as doing, the right thing at the right time, and his awkward little speech was exactly what the crowd wanted to hear. But then, they knew they could always rely on Wor Jackie not to let the side down.

After that it was a case of 'after the Lord Mayor's Show' as the team paraded around the pitch behind the Newcastle Corporation Brass Band (no prizes for guessing what tune they played), then back into the club quarters where, during a celebration party, Joe Harvey cut an enormous cake, iced and set out like

Wembley Stadium. On the icing were the figures, dressed in club colours, of both Newcastle and Blackpool players.

Councillors in Jackie's home town were also busy planning a civic reception in Ashington's Central Hall. This took place the following week, and Jackie brought along his two friends George Robledo and Jack Fairbrother. After being entertained by Mr Normanton Baron on the organ, a presentation of a briefcase was made to the man who had written the name of Ashington into the annals of football history.

In spite of winning only one of their last eight games, Newcastle finished the season in fourth place, Jackie being top scorer again with seventeen goals. Arthur Dewrey's broad hint that Jackie might get into the England team turned into fact when he was chosen to lead the attack on 10 May against Argentina. For a long time it looked as though England might lose on their home soil for the first time. As the teams left the Wembley pitch at half time it was the Argentinians who led by a goal to nil.

England, in their unaccustomed red shirts, had hammered a one-way route to the Argentine goal for forty-five minutes, but their forwards had squandered more than a dozen chances, or seen them saved by Rugilo, a mixture of goalkeeper, athlete, high diver and comedian who saved shots he had no right to stop. Jackie Milburn was guilty of missing the chance of the half when, after a solo run had taken him almost to the goal-line, he fluffed his shot completely. Still dominating play after the interval, it wasn't until the last ten minutes that England scored. The first goal came from Mortenson, and Jackie got his foot to a header from Hassall to push the ball over the line for England's winner.

As in Rio the previous summer, England's weakness was proved to be in their lack of a marksman. It wasn't a good game for Milburn who, only a fortnight earlier, had almost won a Cup Final on his own. His conviction that he just didn't fit into an international side that played like eleven individuals was confirmed when he was picked only as a reserve for the game against Portugal ten days later.

Newcastle officials planned a short seven-day tour of Europe for the team during the summer of 1951. It was a happy-go-lucky trip which none of the players took all that seriously. Charlie Crowe remembers that one of the games was against Anderlecht, the Belgian League champions, at the Heysel Stadium. It was billed as an exhibition match, but rumours were flying that the Belgians were on to a huge bonus if they beat the English FA Cup holders. The Newcastle lads were on to the usual £2 for a win.

Ernie Taylor, proving just as wily off the field as on, persuaded Joe Harvey to ask the Anderlecht captain, Mermans, to 'square' the game. The plan was that if they played an exciting game with an equal number of goals being scored by each team, then the Belgians' bonus could be shared by everyone. Mermans, who later became chairman of the Belgian FA, was of the opinion that his side could beat the Geordies without resorting to collusion, and refused to enter into any bargain with the opposition. His decision proved ill-advised and cost him a lot of money as United thrashed Anderlecht 5–1.

Jackie Milburn spent most of that summer relaxing at home in Ashington, taking time out to return to his old Hirst East School to present prizes at their annual sports day, held in the Hirst Welfare. Appropriately, the school's Milburn House carried off the boys' challenge shield by gaining most points.

Together with many of his footballing team-mates, Jackie showed off his prowess at cricket when a Newcastle eleven took on an Ashington side in a testimonial match for the Ashington pro Jack Watson.

It was during the close season that most of Newcastle's successful Cup-winning side were approached by manufacturers, both local and national, to endorse their products or even to take up part-time positions with their firms. Jackie, now seen by advertisers as a successor to Denis Compton as everyone's image of the handsome, swashbuckling sportsman, was soon advertising 'Quaker Oats is my food for action – it gives me Cup-winning fitness.' The Royal Society for the Prevention of Accidents used Jackie's voice on a 78 rpm record to urge car drivers to be more safety-conscious: 'This is Jackie Milburn talking. Now you know me, I'm always liable to take a chance or two when I'm on the field playing for Newcastle United. But you car drivers out there should *never* take a chance on the road. . . .'

Jackie, now twenty-seven years of age, had already begun to look to the future, and was forever on the lookout for some business venture which he could step into when it was time to throw his boots away. He wasn't alone: most of the Newcastle team started to look and plan ahead. Frank Brennan joined Bainbridges, one of the largest stores in Newcastle, in the sports department; Charlie Crowe became involved in the building trade; and William Crook, a boot manufacturer of Gateshead, wanted Jackie Milburn to take a part-time position as representative with his firm, advertising a 'revolutionary' football boot.

Jackie had already signed a contract, and adverts had appeared in the press showing him holding a Jackie Milburn 'Own Design' Sports Shoe, when the Newcastle Board proved unwilling allies in the players' quest for financial security. The following article appeared in the *Daily Mail* under the heading 'Club Bans Milburn from Job'.

Jackie Milburn, the centre-forward whose two goals gave Newcastle their Cup victory at Wembley in April, was told by the club directors yesterday that he must not accept a part-time job.

Milburn had already signed a contract as a part-time representative for Mr William Crook, a boot manufacturer. Mr Crook said: 'Jack has signed a contract with me which comes into force on August 1st, and I have already reorganised my areas so that he looks after Northumberland and Durham. There is no reason why Milburn should not earn £1000 a year with me and eventually become a director of the firm.'

Mr Ted Hall, the Newcastle secretary, announced after his board's meeting with

Milburn that the player had left on friendly terms but had *not* resigned from the club.

'The board informed Milburn that their decision that no player should accept part-time employment was still in force,' said a statement from the club.

Last week Newcastle United directors met Joe Harvey, who captained their team to victory at Wembley, and told him they could *not* consider releasing him to take over the managership of Carlisle United.

All the Newcastle players bowed to the wishes of their employers.

CHAPTER NINE

No money would ever have been able to buy that team

With all the players adhering to their master's wishes, they had a brand-new season to look forward to, with the first game an English/Scottish Cup winner's match in Scotland against the might of Glasgow Celtic. True to form, the Newcastle board managed to alienate some players right from the kick-off. For the game against Celtic – a highly prestigious and lucrative one for the team – three players from the Cup-winning team were left out; Taylor, Corbett, and Crowe. Seymour said at the time that it was to give a first-team blooding to others. The trio were very upset, and voiced their displeasure. Seymour refused to change the team.

Ernie Taylor, around whom most of United's attacks were built, banged in a transfer request almost immediately. The Newcastle board saw Taylor's action as a fit of petulance, and, not prepared to bend to individual pressures, agreed to listen to offers. Joe Harvey, when he heard that there was a strong possibility that his wee friend would be leaving, pleaded with Seymour: 'Stan, for God's sake don't give the little fella a transfer. Transfer me – anybody! But keep Ernie; he makes everybody play.' Blackpool manager Joe Smith, obviously impressed with the little man's performance against his beaten team, snapped up the talented midfield schemer, and Ernie went to the Seasiders in the October for £25,000. The whole Newcastle team suffered by his departure.

The next of the disgruntled trio to go was Bobby Corbett. Corbett, who began his career as a left-winger with Throckley, was a carefree lad, playing the game as if he really enjoyed it. Early in the 1951/52 season when United were away to Bolton Wanderers, Corbett misplaced a pass and Joe Harvey jumped on him straight away with his typical barrack-room manner, calling him a 'stupid bastard'. Bobby, very uncharacteristically, squared up to Joe, and for a few seconds feelings ran very high at Burnden Park. But it was just like God-bless-you to Joe, and both players were soon shaking hands and getting on with the game, the incident forgotten. Not so with Seymour, and a month later Corbett was off over the Transporter Bridge to play for Middlesbrough.

Charlie Crowe, still sore at missing the opening game, and having been replaced in the first team by George Robledo's brother Ted, also asked to be placed on the transfer list. Seymour rejected Charlie's request, and refused to discuss the matter with the player. 'I called to see Stan Seymour, sometimes two or three times a week,' says Charlie. 'Seymour used to shake his head and say, "Resign yourself to the fact, you are *not* leaving Newcastle. No! No!". There were times when he wouldn't look at me. He was convinced I had been "nobbled" by another team, that another team had talked to me. I was in the reserves at the time, captaining the team alongside Jack Fairbrother, who had been dropped for Ronnie Simpson.'

Simpson had joined United a couple of months before the Cup Final against Blackpool. A Newcastle journalist told Fairbrother then that he wouldn't be in the first team for the coming season. Jack, always one to take things to heart, packed his bags and was on the platform at Newcastle Central waiting for a train when Joe Harvey arrived to persuade the goalkeeper: '. . . don't be so silly, forget it, and come back with me'. Fairbrother returned and played his part in winning the Cup, but when the new season got under way, sure enough, Ronnie Simpson was wearing the first-eleven goalkeeper's jersey. Jack later moved on to be player/manager of Peterborough, then playing in the Midland League. Crowe, still niggling away, played most of the new season in the reserves.

And so it was that Newcastle United, who had finished on such a high note at the end of the previous season with a set of players that Jackie Milburn said were priceless, started rebuilding their side. The inside-forward position vacated by Taylor was filled by Billy Foulkes, who joined United from Chester for a record fee for a player from the Third Division.

United got off to a good start, although Jackie missed a number of the early games through a pulled leg muscle. With Newcastle now playing only one striker up front, George Robledo's name was the one filling the score-sheet. In Newcastle's first four home games they amassed twenty goals, with only three against.

Stan Seymour got a shock when his England centre-forward, Milburn, walked into the office one day, and asked if he could play for the reserve team. Jackie said, 'I know you cannot change the present forward line. Fair enough – I'll play for the reserves.' Replied Seymour, 'Thanks, Jackie. It's the fair way out for everybody. You'll go in against Bolton Wanderers' reserves tomorrow.'

Jackie's appearance in the Central League team the following day boosted the gate by an extra 10,000. But he was soon back in the first team, and he and Robledo renewed a partnership in a United forward line that was to score ninety-eight goals by the end of the season. Four times Newcastle knocked in six goals, and twice they recorded sevens! By the time that the FA Cup ties came around,

Newcastle were already being shouted as favourites to win both the Cup and League.

In the third round Newcastle were drawn at home to Aston Villa. United's old manager George Martin, now in charge at Villa, anticipating a result, arrived at St James's Park two days before the game with a briefcase full of replay tickets to be sold on the Sunday after the game if it ended as a draw. He was probably hoping that Newcastle's luck would run out, as no team had won the Cup in consecutive seasons since 1890. The Villa side now contained three ex-Newcastle forwards: Thompson, Dixon and Gibson. Alf McMichael and Ted Robledo, who had both played only one game in the run-up to the 1951 Cup win, were now regulars in the Newcastle side. Jackie Milburn, who was beaten by George Robledo in the race to be the first Newcastle player to score a hundred League goals, got as far as ninety-nine a week before the Cup-tie when he scored against Preston.

Among the favourites to win the Cup again, Newcastle nearly came down at the first hurdle. Before a stunned Geordie crowd of 56, 860, Aston Villa led 2–0 before fifteen minutes had elapsed. Billy Foulkes, in Taylor's old position, reduced the lead after twenty minutes' play. Then Villa were blitzed by two quick goals from Bobby Mitchell. Right on time, George Robledo pinched another to leave the Midland side wondering just what had hit them. United fans breathed again as their team began their Wembley march.

Newcastle were next drawn away to Tottenham Hotspur, the League champions. Spurs manager Arthur Rowe said of the tie: 'There's only one thing wrong with Spurs *versus* Newcastle – it should have been at Wembley!' Newcastle had nothing to fear from the London club, for they had thrashed them 7–2 at the beginning of the season.

Playing at Turf Moor on 20 January, Jackie slammed in his hundredth goal, but still ended up on the losing side as Burnley beat the black and whites 2–1. A feature of the game was an incredible seventy-five-yard run by Burnley centre-half Cummings, culminating in what Milburn later described as 'The best goal I've ever seen'.

Jackie felt obliged to speak to inquisitive journalists about his own future.

I can take all the knocks that are coming on the field of play, but I object to these stories that have persistently linked me with other clubs. I have never been happier than I am now with Newcastle United. I have two lassies and a new house, and if I leave Newcastle it will happen because *they* have kicked me out.

At the time he gave that comment, Milburn's name had been linked with Spurs, United's next Cup opponents and, ironically, the team his father, Alec, had turned down just before Jackie had been born.

· On 21 January the Victoria Club, known all over the world as the racing man's Stock Exchange, held a call-over on the FA Cup. This year was the first time they had done this in the ninety-two years of its existence. The odds were as follows:

11–2	Arsenal
15–2	Portsmouth
10–1	Tottenham Hotspur
10–1	Liverpool
11–1	Blackpool
14–1	Newcastle United
14–1	Wolverhampton Wanderers
16–1	Chelsea
16–1	West Bromwich Albion
16–1	Middlesbrough
25–1	Stoke City
33–1	Birmingham City
100–1	Others

Newcastle announced the same side for the tenth consecutive week to take on a Charlton team who had lost their last three games. United, although doing well near the top of the League, were still looking for the same stability which had brought them success the previous year. Jimmy Seed, Charlton's popular manager, arrived on Tyneside joking, 'I don't suppose Jackie Milburn is off with a cold or something?' He was referring to the late goals which Jackie had got against his team the previous season when United had won 3–2. Unfortunately for the Charlton side, Jackie was on top form, scoring twice, Newcastle won 6–0, and but for veteran Sam Bartram's inspired goalkeeping could easily have smashed that 13–0 record, so many chances did they create.

United were now travelling in style, and set off to Brighton for a week's special training, in their own railway carriage. Soon after arriving at the southern resort, the mayor of Brighton arranged for a sherry party to welcome the group. Interviewed in Brighton by a *Newcastle Journal* reporter, Stan Seymour, director/manager, said: 'We've come here to escape from ticket pests. They've worried the lives out of all of us. The football public up there are Cup-tie mad, and it has been proving an ordeal for players and officials. A second reason for the trip was to give the players a break. They had a stiff Christmas programme and now face both Cup and League matches, which puts an extra strain on them.'

The players trained at a greyhound stadium owned by one of the Brighton directors, but found that there were no facilities for showers, so mini-cabs were summoned to ferry the players to a nearby gymnasium. In their hotel they were fed on the best, including liberal helpings of oysters.

Back in fish-and-chip country, the night before the game against Spurs a special train left Newbiggin by the Sea at 11.18 p.m., picking up at Ashington and Bedlington before taking the normal route to London's King's Cross via Newcastle Central. The local supporters would not get back home until 8 a.m. on the Sunday morning, but if Jackie Milburn was playing, they were determined to be there.

It wasn't just Milburn who was making local news that weekend. John Sinclair, an eighteen-year-old Ashington pit apprentice, became the British Youth Billiard

Champion at Burroughes Hall in London. And in a fifth-round English Schools Shield Game, Milburn's old boys' team, East Northumberland, were due to play Hull Boys. In the East Northumberland team that day were many Ashington lads, including Bobby Whitehead at right-back who later played for Newcastle United, and thirteen-year-old inside-forward Bobby Charlton.

The game at White Hart Lane – given the all-clear only hours before kick-off by referee W. H. E. Evans – was played in atrocious conditions with players having to plough through a sea of clarts up the middle and skate over bone-hard surfaces near the touchlines. Spurs tried to play it too close and suffered accordingly. Newcastle, swinging the ball around the park, went into the lead with goals scored by George Robledo and Mitchell. In the final minutes the Chilean, prone on the ground and surrounded by three white shirts, managed to hook his second, and United's last, goal as they cracked their London hoodoo to win 3–0.

Jumping out of the bath after the game, a jubilant Mitchell obliged with the following ditty, written to the tune of 'A Gordon for Me'.

> *Six oysters a day, then play Spurs away,*
> *The tasty wee oysters worked wonders today,*
> *The Magpies were braw, supporters an' a',*
> *But the wee Brighton oysters take pride of it a'.*

Some quick-reaction views after the one-sided game were:

Arthur Rowe: 'It was not our day, and it is no disgrace to lose anywhere to such a display as Newcastle's.'

Alf Ramsey: 'The better team won, and good luck to United's back-to-Wembley bid.'

Joe Harvey: 'A big hand to management for our grand holiday, and to the trainers who tuned up the whole team to such form.'

Jackie Milburn: 'All the lads say they are going for League points just as hard as for a Cup bonus.'

Jackie was referring to United's slide down the League the previous season, caused by a sudden rush of Cup blood to the head. But Cup fever ran even higher a couple of days later as Newcastle were drawn away for yet another tie, this time at Swansea. United had played only one post-war game at the Vetch Field, and that had been during the 1946/47 season when a 2–1 win for the Magpies had helped to push the Welsh side into the Third Division.

Swansea, whose small ground held only 28,000, allocated 6610 tickets to the Geordie club, who could have found takers for that paltry amount in the bar of any one of Ashington's clubs. Ticket demand at Swansea was so great that the General Post Office there ran out of half-crown postal orders. They sold 7000 of that denomination in two days, as eager Welsh fans sent in postal requests for tickets.

In spite of the claims of Harvey and Milburn about fighting for League points, Newcastle were very disappointing in their next outing, going down 3–0 at Molyneux where Wolves had their England goalkeeper Bert Williams back in the side for the first time in three months. Swansea were showing no such reluctance to have a go, and beat Birmingham 4–0 to record their sixth consecutive win.

Sunday Times sports correspondent Arthur Appleton was also a BBC Radio producer at the time. 'The BBC asked me to record the sound of a Newcastle goal being acclaimed by the crowd,' he said. 'I followed them from match to match and they never scored a goal; they were keeping themselves for Wembley. I told this to Jackie many years later, and he said, "Whey man, Arthur, you should've told us – we would've scored one for you." '

In Porthcawl, where the Newcastle team were staying, an injury scare arose over Bobby Mitchell who had sprained his back, but he managed to go with the rest of the team to the cinema on the Thursday night and duly took his place in the line-up for the match. On the morning of the game Newcastle were installed as 4 to 1 second favourites to lift the Cup, behind Arsenal whose odds had shortened to 7 to 2.

Swansea, fielding a Geordie centre-forward, Ronnie Turnbull, played a very physical game against Newcastle, causing them many problems. Mitchell scored the only goal of the match in the forty-first minute, but only a desperate last-minute save from Simpson prevented the Welshmen from getting a well-earned equaliser.

Virtually every house in the North-East was tuned in to the Light Programme the following Monday to hear whom the lads had drawn in the sixth round. But the wooden marbles could not have been more unkind – Portsmouth away – and a great groan went up over the Tyne which could be heard almost as far south as Scotch Corner. The fans immediately got out their maps and rulers to see how far they would have to travel this time. Already they had spent long hours and good money in support of their team, and with a 674-mile round trip to the Hampshire coast in the offing, their travels took on a Marco Polo look:

> Round Four: Tottenham Hotspur – 542 miles
> Round Five: Swansea – 624 miles
> Round Six: Portsmouth – 674 miles

At St James's Park there was now talk of a new Milburn. Seventeen-year-old Alec Tait, a ginger-haired lad who, like Bobby Charlton, attended Bedlington Grammar School, was picked to play for England Youths against Wales. The speedy youngster, already a Northumberland tennis champion, showed the Welsh defence what Geordie centre-forwards were made of when he celebrated with four goals. Tait was a product of the Newcastle Youth team – the 'Ns'. Alec drifted in and out of the reserve side, but it was Vic Keeble, a £15,000 signing from Colchester, who was being groomed as Milburn's immediate successor.

The Portsmouth–Newcastle game drew out every superlative from all those privileged to see it. It was the 'Cup tie of the decade', said the man from the *Sunday People*.

I shall remember this as the greatest final Wembley never saw. Thrills? It had them all – and to spare! Clever football? Tons of it! Mistakes? Yes, a few; excusable too. And towering above everything it had a Milburn hat-trick, all worked into a grandstand finish.

The scores were level at 2–2. Milburn, already twice a scorer with half-chances, breaks away and veers to the left. Froggatt and Gunter run alongside him like dogs on a leash. Then with the sudden venomous flash of an adder's tongue, Milburn's left foot strikes. Almost before goalkeeper Butler can move an arm the ball is in Portsmouth's net – fired there from a range of 25 yards.

Now Newcastle lead 3–2. Portsmouth throw everything into a do-or-die finish. Even fullback Gunter moves upfield. Then, in the dying seconds, Newcastle defender McMichael clears his lines with a run upfield. Again that man Milburn comes into it. This time he flicks the ball deftly to burly George Robledo – and Newcastle's fourth goal is in the book.

As the last whistle goes the crowd break in, Milburn disappears in a scrum of jubilant Geordies, and every Newcastle man is mobbed in turn. We are all a step nearer Cup history.

Newcastle I salute you . . . if anyone deserves a two-year lease on the Cup in these modern times, you do.

If Newcastle's success was essentially a team effort, Milburn's contribution was among the highest. He was hailed the next day.

Sunday Sun:	'He went for the chances, the half-chances, and no-chances-at-all with the abandon which we have always said would make him the undoubted centre-forward of the age.'
Sunday Times:	'Froggatt brought out all the arts of this tireless and determined centre-forward.'
Empire News:	'Don't even think of any other centre-forward . . . he carried the Newcastle attack on his shoulders.'
News of the World:	'If any player knocked Portsmouth out of the Cup it was Milburn – with electricity in his heels and dynamite in his feet.'
Reynolds News:	'The United leader was back at his dynamic best . . . only Milburn's left foot hits goals like that.'

Sunday Pictorial:	'Each goal revealed the powerful, accurate shooting, the instinctive sense of balance which makes the great player.'
Sunday Express:	'Without exaggerating I should say that Milburn turned in one of the best centre-forward displays of all time.'

With this one game, Jackie Milburn achieved everything that he had promised himself on the football field.

. . . it didn't matter where you were . . . you just wanted to be the best.

CHAPTER TEN

1952
Cup Final, I didn't feel the same satisfaction

Present at Fratton Park that day were England FA selector A. H. Oakley and team manager Walter Winterbottom. It seemed only a matter of course for the United leader to gain another cap on 29 March when England met Scotland. Indeed, with Scotland selectors George Graham and Jim Frew also in the crowd, some pundits forecast that it would be an all-Newcastle duel at Hampden Park between Brennan and Milburn. But the most imminent question for United's fans was: Whom do we play in the semi-final?

As a result of the draw, Newcastle were to play Blackburn Rovers at Hillsborough, with Arsenal playing Chelsea at White Hart Lane. After the Gunners had only just scraped through against Luton, and as Newcastle now seemed to have the easier passage through to the Final by being drawn against Second Division Blackburn, the Geordie team now became the bookies' favourites. The odds were: 6–4 Newcastle; 2–1 Arsenal; 5–1 Chelsea; 15–2 Blackburn.

Tickets for Newcastle's semi-final went on sale on Friday 21 March. British Railways put their allocation of 4000 on sale at 6 p.m., but by then 6000 people were in a queue which stretched from Central Station to Marlborough Crescent Bus Station. Altogether, BR turned down block bookings for 15,000 unlucky fans. Thirteen train-loads eventually made the trip to Sheffield.

While United were at Buxton prior to their match against Blackburn, one of Jackie Milburn's rivals for the England leader's position, Tommy Lawton, moved clubs for the fourth time in his career. Lawton, who signed for Burnley for just £10, was only seventeen when he moved to Everton for £6500. From there he went

83

to Chelsea for £11,500 before moving to Notts County for £20,000. His latest move had been to Second Division Brentford for £12,000. In all, a massive £50,000 had changed hands as the stylish centre-forward moved clubs. His legitimate share of this: £50.

On 24 March, five days before the semi-final, Jackie was half asleep as he was summoned to the telephone of his Buxton hotel at 5.15 a.m. It was Sister Sarah McMahon speaking from the Ashington Nurses' Home. 'It's a boy!' she said, and five minutes later Jackie had woken the entire Newcastle party to share in his good news. Jackie junior was born at 5.10 a.m., weighing eight and three-quarter pounds. Now the proud dad just had to get to Wembley not once more but twice, in order to win medals for all three children. When asked later about one for his wife Laura, Jackie joked, 'What for? She's got me, hasn't she!'

When the England selectors met two days later they decided there was no room for Milburn, and chose the same side which had pulverised the Irish League 9–0 in a representative game. Nat Lofthouse got the centre-forward slot, but it was suggested that Milburn had been passed over because of his Cup commitments.

On 29 March, semi-final day, Newcastle were being called the 'Cup team of the century'. From 1905 they had appeared in eight Finals and had twice been beaten semi-finalists. Seven of the team who had gained Cup winners' medals were still there from the previous April. Newcomers were the boyish-looking Scot Simpson; Ireland's new captain, McMichael; the younger Robledo brother, Ted; and Billy Foulkes, who since joining United had been capped for Wales, netting his former club an extra £500, being part of the condition of his transfer.

Once again Newcastle were held to a draw at Hillsborough in a semi-final match. Blackburn, far from being overawed by the Magpies' mighty record, earned the right to be treated as equals in their first gale-swept meeting. Jackie might have scored early in the match, but his header was well off target. Later, carried right through by sheer pace, and with only the Blackburn goalkeeper to beat, he sportingly stepped aside as Elvy dived at his feet. A draw was probably more than a lethargic Newcastle United deserved. The game, and most of United's 20,000 travelling fans, moved on to Elland Road, Leeds, the following Wednesday.

This time Newcastle began with far more urgency than they had displayed at Hillsborough, but squandered at least three good chances in the first half. Soon after the restart, Milburn got clear on the right wing and crossed to George Robledo, who headed United into the lead. With only ten minutes left, a young Ronnie Clayton supplied an accurate ball to Eddie Quigley, who equalised for the Rovers. Then, with less than five minutes to go, a Robledo effort was handled inside the penalty area. All black and white eyes turned in the direction of Jackie Milburn; he was the team's regular penalty taker. In an experiment conducted by Walter Winterbottom only the year before at St James's, it had been proved conclusively that a penalty kick struck full force by Milburn would beat a goalkeeper every time, even if hit close to the 'keeper's body.

Jackie lowered his eyes and walked away from the ball, which Joe Harvey had placed on the spot for him. Harvey chased after him. 'What the bloody hell is wrong, man?' he asked. Jackie rubbed his knee, indicating that he was carrying an injury. He was reluctant to take such an important kick, which would either take the team to Wembley for a second time, or perhaps knock the stuffing out of the whole side if it was missed. Harvey swung around and looked about him; the Newcastle team turned away to escape his searching eyes. Losing patience, the man with the magic left foot, Bobby Mitchell, without being asked, stepped forward and hit the ball as hard as he could. It could have been only a couple of feet from goalkeeper Elvy's right ear, but the speed and power of the shot left him rooted to his goal-line. Newcastle were a goal up, and back at Wembley! Some after-match comments were:

Jackie Bestall (Rovers' manager):	'Well done Newcastle! Now go and win the Cup for the North.'
Stan Seymour:	'The toughest semi-final imaginable! A great battle to win.'
Joe Harvey:	'I've never been in a harder struggle.'
L. Kelly (Rovers' centre-half):	'May I pay tribute to Jackie Milburn, the best centre-forward I've ever seen or played against, and a great sportsman.'

With Arsenal also through – their semi-final had been postponed initially because of a waterlogged pitch – the Gunner's manager, Tom Whittaker, had this to say: 'It should be a crackerjack Final. Both teams have been to Wembley since the war so the players know the ground and should have no Wembley nerves.'

In a board meeting at St James's Park, Stan Seymour was appointed vice-chairman, a position held up until then by A. G. Stableforth, who had recently died. Charlie Crowe was still a regular attender at Seymour's office, asking for a transfer. Ted Robledo was the man who had taken his number-six shirt, and it was obvious from the way the Chilean was playing that he would take some shifting. Fed up with Charlie's persistence, Seymour made him a proposition.

Look, Charlie, forget all this talk about wanting to be away, and I might make it worth your while. What would you say if I offered you a hundred Cup Final tickets (up till then Crowe, not in the Cup Final squad, had been allotted only thirty-two) and put your name down as a definite for the forthcoming tour of South Africa?

Charlie, a canny lad who knew a bargain when he saw it, immediately agreed. Shortly afterwards the party to go on tour was announced. It was the Cup Final team plus Ron Batty, George Hannah, Bob Stokoe – and Charlie Crowe. Newcastle had arranged a mammoth ten-week close-season tour of South Africa, and letters winged in to local papers from Geordie expatriates enquiring if the Tynesiders would be visiting their particular area.

On 9 April Newcastle, Sunderland and Middlesbrough were among nine First Division clubs who were fined fifty guineas for contravention of a rule regarding 'spending money' to players. It all resulted from a questionnaire circulated to all clubs in the Football League asking whether spending money was paid to players. Some clubs replied with a No, others with a Yes. All those who replied in the affirmative, including Liverpool, were fined accordingly. Newcastle had been in the habit of giving their players £2 a day 'pocket money' while away from home for more than a couple of days. FA regulations stated that £1 was the maximum, so the United board fell into line with this ruling, giving their players the statutory £1 – and a packet of Player's cigarettes.

The following day Seymour made a telephone call to Swansea's manager, McCandless, offering £35,000 for Ivor Allchurch, who had been very impressive against United in their Cup tie. On hearing this, Welsh international Allchurch said, 'I hear that Newcastle are interested in my future. My only comment is that Newcastle is a little too far north.'

Newcastle continued to lose points in the League, prompting letters of complaint to the local press, including this comment from 'Frustrated Season Ticket-holder': 'Both last season and this, United had a remarkable chance of doing the 'double'. But what has happened? We all saw this last year: no win between semi and final. And this season: 6 points out of 18 since the Cup run started. We sit and suffer while Arsenal go out for every point.' Arsenal had then gone seventeen games without defeat, and were only two points behind League leaders Manchester United.

The following week Newcastle went down to London for a Cup rehearsal game at Highbury. Obviously not wanting to show their strong suit, United fielded: Simpson, Cowell, Batty, Harvey, Stokoe, G. Robledo, Walker, Davies, Keeble, Hannah, Prior. Arsenal brought back thirty-nine-year-old Leslie Compton at centre-half in place of Ray Daniel, who had fractured his arm in a previous game. Seymour said, 'If Daniel is fit and chosen to play at Wembley, we could not possibly consent to him wearing a plaster in the Final.'

From their League encounter at Highbury, Newcastle brought back a point and a boxful of Cup Final tickets which some members of the Arsenal team had been unable to sell.

Writing in the *Newcastle Journal* a couple of weeks before the big Wembley game, Stan Seymour was in philosophical mood.

In football today there are far too many men holding a seat and directors who do little or nothing to aid the game. There is a little army of people in the game for no more than a good time or to satisfy a personal vanity.

I blame the system that operates whereby a few men holding blocks of shares can control Club elections by use of the proxy vote. Every Club belongs to the people. Why should the few holding large share blocks rule the roost?

With the Final only days away, referee Arthur Elis was getting mail by the sackload.

'I reckon I'm getting more fan letters than Rita Hayworth!' he said. 'And as you've guessed, a large percentage of them ask for Final tickets. This last week I've had £30 sent to me and a number of open cheques. I wonder if the 400-odd people will believe me when I write back and say I haven't even a Cup Final ticket of my own.'

Chancing their luck, Newcastle applied to the FA for permission to take the FA Cup on tour with them to South Africa – depending, of course, on whether they were successful in their attempt to win it for the second time in a row. The FA agreed, stipulating that an insurance cover of £500 be taken out on a trophy which had never been outside Britain.

A Football Association tour of Europe in the close season had been arranged, and there was speculation that Jackie Milburn might be chosen. Newcastle officials remained very definite that Milburn would travel with his club to South Africa. Stan Seymour commented, 'Why should we imagine the FA selecting Milburn for *their* Continental tour when he was ignored for the more important home internationals? Any suggestion that Milburn will not be going in our party would cause our hosts great concern. We refuse to contemplate any possibility of our centre-forward being nominated in the FA party. He will go to South Africa as he went with his club to America and Canada.'

The Football Association selectors did not choose any player involved in the Final to go with the England party on their Continental tour. Two centre-forwards, Lofthouse of Bolton and Allen of Spurs, were included in the squad. Said Stan Seymour, 'We are delighted but not surprised that Milburn has not been selected and so can tour with Newcastle United.'

The last League match, against Aston Villa, ended with United winning well by 6–1. It was a memorable game for big Frank Brennan, as he scored a great individual goal. He said it was to spite Hughie Gallacher.

Hughie used to write a weekly column for a local paper, and one day he'd written that I was just a stopper centre-half. So that day against Villa, I said, 'Right, Mr bloody Gallacher, I'll show you who's just a stopper!'

The first chance I got, I raced out of my own penalty area with the ball and passed to Jackie Milburn, shouting, 'Hold it!' Jackie hared off up the right wing with the ball, and I bounded up the middle of the park. When Milburn got level with their eighteen-yard-box, I shouted, 'Right, Jackie, *now!*' Jackie placed it lovely for me to run on to and bang it into the back of the net. As I was running back to the centre-circle, I looked up into the stands and shouted, 'That bugger's for you, Hughie!'

Newcastle finished the season in a modest eighth place, but set a new record goal tally of ninety-eight. For the first time in five seasons, Jackie Milburn was not the club's top scorer; this honour went to Chilean George Robledo with thirty-three goals. This was still short of Hughie Gallacher's own record of thirty-six goals in the 1926/27 season, and even further behind Albert Stubbins' phenomenal forty-four in thirty games during 1943/44.

After that game United went down to Brighton, again to stay at the Royal Albion, but Harvey stayed behind for treatment to an injury. The planned leisure itinerary for the week prior to Cup Final Saturday was: Monday and Tuesday free; Wednesday, golf at Roehampton; Thursday, see ice-hockey match; Friday, go to the theatre.

While United were in Brighton, more of Seymour's thoughts appeared in the *Newcastle Journal*:

When I was a player, I constantly looked to the future. I rented two little shops and sold cigarettes and confectionery, later switching to sports outfitters. I can only speak for myself, but I do not think the United board would raise the slightest objection to any player, even today, doing the same as I did, so long as he is his own master . . . and gives his full time to all calls made upon him by the club.

This was a direct indication that Newcastle players could, from that moment, take part-time employment, which up until then had been denied them, as long as it did not entail working for someone else.

An eleventh-hour move was made by the BBC to have the Cup Final televised. Peter Dimmock, Head of Outside Broadcasting, was said to be optimistic. 'We are still hoping the FA will change their mind,' he said. 'Since the last refusal of the FA to allow live broadcasts we have made several suggestions for a compromise. We shall be happy to make any compromise which the FA care to make.'

In Newcastle there was a last-minute scramble for Final tickets. In spite of an unsuccessful application to Newcastle United, the mayor of Gateshead, J. A. Hutchison, received a two-guinea ticket from the chairman of Gateshead FC, Mr W. Tulip. 'I thought it was not beyond Newcastle United to offer tickets to civic chiefs on Tyneside,' commented an aggrieved mayor.

British Railways in Newcastle said that 10,000 fans would be travelling by rail, 2000 in dining-car trains. Over a hundred people applied to travel by air, but lack of capacity limited this to only forty-three. Newcastle's most unlucky director was Dr Bob Rutherford; due to illness this was to be the second Final he would miss.

One young lad who would definitely not miss the game was Joe Mercer's ten-year-old son. Joe's lad Michael had never seen Arsenal lose a Cup tie. When Joe Harvey's son, seven-year-old Ken, who was also going, heard this, he said, 'Too bad!'

With only two days left before the big day, a man walked into a Jarrow pub with a fifteen-shilling ticket which he said he would swap for a set of second-hand football strips for a team he ran. With no takers, he left mumbling something about having it left on his hands. On the Friday night, seventeen train-loads of fans left Tyneside, the first departing at 10.40 p.m. from Newbiggin and Ashington.

Earlier that afternoon the General Purposes Committee of the Football Association had stated that their previous decision not to allow the game to be televised would not be rescinded, and that therefore there would be no television coverage of the Final. They added that a telefilm would be shown on the Monday.

Director Alderman W. McKeag, Lord Mayor of Newcastle, received a telegram from Newcastle, Natal. It read: 'Newcastle, Natal wish Newcastle United best of luck in Cup Final.' One other token of good fortune was that 1901 penny, again carried by United skipper Joe Harvey, as Neil Harris had done in 1924 and Jack Allen in 1932.

On paper there was little to choose between the two Cup Final teams as their skippers Mercer and Harvey, two ex-Army sergeant-majors, swapped yarns on the centre-circle prior to the kick-off. Arsenal's Final line-up was: Swindon, Barnes, Smith, Forbes, Daniel, Mercer, Cox, Logie, Holton, Lishman, Roper. The Newcastle team was: Simpson, Cowell, McMichael, Harvey, Brennan, T. Robledo, Walker, Foulkes, Milburn, G. Robledo, Mitchell.

The game began quietly, with neither attack threatening to crack open solid defences. Suddenly, there was drama! Running for the ball with no one near him, Arsenal full-back Wally Barnes turned sharply then keeled over, clutching his leg. It was a bad injury, blamed on the lush green Wembley turf. Barnes played on, but his bravery wasn't enough and the inevitable departure from the field of the Welsh international left a ten-man Arsenal side to try to stem the tide of black and white shirts threatening their goal. From then on, the game was never going to live up to any of its pre-match build-up. Jackie Milburn, having had one of his quietest games, summed up the feelings of the Newcastle side.

That May afternoon, Arsenal gave one of the greatest displays of courage I've ever experienced on the football field. From the moment Wally Barnes was injured until the end of the match, the Londoners kept themselves in the game – and I say this after making full allowance for the Newcastle United team playing really badly.

There was even a lack of drama about the goal which won us the match, Mitchell put over a centre, and it seemed a lifetime as Robledo's header floated slowly through the air, hit an upright, and glided down over the line.

There was a tremendous roar of excitement from the Geordies in the crowd. Yet there was none of the tension . . . and I for one did not feel the satisfaction of the previous year.

Frank Brennan said almost the same thing: 'It was nothing like the first time. Nothing ever is. First time is always the best.'

For a change, let the ladies have the last word.

Mrs Stan Seymour:	'It was very interesting to be in the Royal Box. I should have loved it for the Queen to be present, though Mr Winston Churchill was a great deputy.'

Mrs Ida Harvey:	'It was a terrible game. Arsenal played the football, and I was mighty glad when it was over.'
Mrs Ethna Brennan:	'It was a harassing game, but I thought we had the better chances.'
Mrs Laura Milburn:	'I was a bundle of nerves. I kept kneading my handkerchief and tearing the corners.'
Mrs Isobel Mitchell:	'I was eating a sweet and smoking a cigarette at the same time, as we waited for that goal which it seemed would never come.'
Mrs Rosemary Simpson:	'It was a lovely scene at Wembley, and a wonderful experience to see Newcastle win.'
Mrs Elsie Robledo (George and Ted's mother):	'I wondered when George was going to get going.'

The *Sunday Express* correspondent summed up this dour match for everyone: 'This victory was as hollow as a kettledrum.'

The 100,000 spectators at Wembley paid over £44,000 to see the game. Newcastle players, by previous arrangement, were rewarded as follows.

> Third round *v* Aston Villa £2
> Fourth round *v* Spurs £4
> Fifth round *v* Swansea £6
> Sixth round *v* Portsmouth £8
> Semi-final draw *v* Blackburn £7 10s
> Semi-final replay *v* Blackburn £15
> Cup Final *v* Arsenal £20

A celebration dinner was again held at the Savoy Hotel, and the Newcastle party stayed overnight at the Great Northern Hotel before coming home on the Monday. Their train was due in at 6.20 p.m., and the whole area adjacent to Newcastle's Central Station stayed closed to traffic from five o'clock. The train stopped at Durham Station for Alderman McKeag to get off and dash the remaining dozen miles on his own. This ploy was to enable him to greet the players in his official capacity as Lord Mayor of Newcastle.

As the train pulled alongside the platform there was a mini-Gallowgate roar from the 500 people the police had allowed into the station. The stone pillars were swathed in black and white, contrasting with the vivid crimson carpet laid out to welcome the team. The engine hissed to a stop beside a huge board which declared: 'WELL DONE, LADS – IT'S STILL WORS'. On the side of the engine was another placard showing the years that Newcastle had won the Cup: 'IT'S STILL WORS – 1910–1924–1932–1951–1952'.

First off the train was Joe Harvey, Cup held on high as in the previous year. He was greeted by Alderman McKeag, now dressed in sable, and United's official mascot Peter Anderson of Byker, immaculate in a black and white striped suit, topper and bow-tie. McKeag made a short speech: 'You have made me a proud man – next year we might make it a hat-trick.' Then the procession set off through the streets of Neville, Collingwood, Grey and Blackett, before entering Gallowgate. The orderly, good-humoured crowd packed the pavements fifty-deep all along the route. Millions of pieces of paper and confetti showered down on the players as office girls once again gave their heroes a jamboree welcome. As the coach pulled into St James's, a great roar went up from the 45,000 crowd who had waited patiently for over two hours.

A smiling Joe Harvey emerged with the Cup still in his hands. Behind him, limping slightly, was Jackie Milburn. Harvey, tired of holding the trophy, passed it on to Bobby Cowell, and grabbed the mascot's topper which he placed at a jaunty angle on his head. The fans loved that.

After parading round the outside of the pitch, the players went up to the directors' box for the obligatory speeches. This time the chant from the women in the crowd was 'We want George,' and the embarrassed 'Pancho' obliged, thanking them for their support. Alderman McKeag had to rush off for the official opening of the Boy Scouts' 'Gang Show' at the Theatre Royal, and missed the now traditional cutting of a huge cake – a miniature replica of Wembley arena – by captain Joe Harvey.

Festivities in Newcastle went on until the small hours, with thousands of people thronging the dance halls and theatres. At the Grand Theatre in Byker, Tyneside's Little Waster, Bobby Thompson, amused the audience with a comic commentary on the match, while Yeoman's Sparkling Terriers reproduced the Final in canine fashion, properly attired in scarlet, and black and white.

In the week following the Final even more letters arrived from South Africa, so great was the demand for tickets for the tour matches. From Southern Transvaal, where United were due on 6 June, came a telegram saying, 'We are greatly thrilled at the prospect of playing England's best.'

Three days after United's Wembley triumph, in a game between the Scottish Miners and the Northumberland Miners, Jimmy Milburn, Jackie's cousin, played well and scored one of the goals that gave Northumberland a 3–1 win.

CHAPTER ELEVEN

South Africa: Weather fine, wish I was back at the Rec

On 11 May the first of the United party left for South Africa on the Pullman train *Northumbrian*. So began a journey that was to take them 20,000 miles, of which 16,000 miles would be by air. For safety reasons the team travelled in two groups, the first being made up of directors Seymour and Taylor together with Harvey, Simpson, Cowell, Walker, Davies, Foulkes and Mitchell; they were to be joined in London by Ted Robledo, who had been spending a short holiday in the capital.

As the train pulled away from the Central Station platform, Joe Harvey waved and shouted, 'All the lads are looking forward to having a grand time over there, and we hope to do Newcastle credit.' Stan Seymour qualified his captain's remarks: 'What we really want to do is show the South Africans what a grand game football is, and help them as much as possible in developing it.'

The second group, consisting of Lord Westwood, Norman Smith and players McMichael, Batty, Brennan, Milburn, G. Robledo, Hannah, Crowe and Stokoe, left two days later. Typically, when the train was due to leave Frank Brennan still had not arrived. Seconds before departure Big Frank ambled up to join the rest of the group. An anxious Norman Smith enquired about Brennan's apparent lack of luggage. Funny man Frank pointed to his breast pocket, out of which peeked a toothbrush. 'I didna forget it, Norman; it's all there!'

When the Newcastle vanguard arrived in Johannesburg, the first man to greet them on the tarmac was expatriate Geordie Frank Melville. Originally from Seymour Street in Newcastle, Frank had emigrated to South Africa in 1921, but he still hadn't managed to lose the distinctive Tyneside twang.

United once more, the team presented Stan Seymour with a pen and pencil set to mark the occasion of the boss's birthday on 16 May. On arrival in South Africa Jackie Milburn, still carrying an injury, was told he would be out for at least ten days.

Twenty-five thousand people turned up to watch the first game of the tour against Southern Transvaal. Unused to the strange atmospheric conditions and lively ball, United were shocked into a 2–0 deficit very early in the game. Two goals from George Robledo and one from Hannah saved the blushes of the 500 Geordies who had come to acclaim 'their' team, and got the tourists off to a good start. Next stop was to be Natal by train, and from there a quick flight to Cape Town for their third match in five days.

The locals back in Ashington were busy keeping tabs on Jackie's adventures on the other side of the world. Laura was probably too involved in the day-to-day running of a home and family to notice a pamphlet issued by the Methodist Church to the effect that the town she was living in had been likened to 'Satan's citadel'. Sixty Methodists from the Cliff College Campaign had descended upon Ashington and held open-air meetings. In a document published after leaving the town, they said: 'Ashington is undeniably club and cinema conscious. We expected a rough-house at our meetings, but what we saw were a few communists and evidence of drink in men and women. But in spite of everything, we managed to bring light into one of Satan's darkest citadels.'

Civic heads were astonished by this outburst and demanded an apology. Soothing balm was administered by the Reverend Morton of the Seaton Hirst parish when he said, 'Much can be said in mitigation. The people live in desperate conditions where sombre houses, dreary surroundings and few amenities make them club and cinema conscious.' (In 1952 Ashington had five cinemas with a seating capacity of 4600, and twenty-two working men's clubs.)

On the Continent England defeated an Austrian team 3–2 in what was termed the 'Championship of Europe'. Centre-forward Lofthouse scored twice and earned himself the title 'Lion of Vienna'. Two days later England beat Switzerland 3–0, with Lofthouse and Sewell sharing the goals. The same day Newcastle beat Western Provinces 4–0, with Milburn, playing his first match of the tour, getting a hat-trick. Newcastle then beat Northern Transvaal 2–1, but Milburn was injured and ruled out for another ten days. He sent a postcard back to sister Jean: 'Weather fine, wish I was back at the Rec.'

The tour was proving to be a tiring one for everybody. With only half of the games played, of the sixteen players in the party only Harvey had played in every game. There was great excitement when the side went to play against Northern Rhodesia, with its large British community. A broadcast of the match went out in both English and Afrikaans. Newcastle beat the Rhodesians 6–1, with unusual names appearing on the goal-sheet. Bobby Cowell scored – albeit from a penalty – as did Charlie Crowe and Joe Harvey. They were fun games, with the United team doing just sufficient to win as well as entertain. United next played Eastern Transvaal, whom Wolves had beaten 13–0 only the previous year. Playing Frankie

Brennan at centre-forward, Newcastle eased their way to a 2–0 victory, with a jubilant Brennan scoring.

The Orange Free State were United's next opponents. The game was played on a Saturday, coinciding with the running of the Northumberland Plate, the Pitmen's Derby, at Newcastle Races, which had been moved to a Saturday for the first time in its 120-year history. A southern raider, little Sovepi, plundered the big northern prize, and Newcastle beat the Orangemen 3–0. United then made it twelve wins in a row when they defeated a South African eleven 3–0 in what was billed as the first football 'Test match'.

The FA, at their annual summer meeting in Llandudno, announced that the Charity Shield match – Manchester United *v* Newcastle United – would take place on 24 September. Other items of information to emerge from the meeting were that the following year's Cup Final was to be televised, together with the second halves of the England *v* Wales and England *v* Belgium matches; that Newcastle's share of the Wembley gate would be £6365, with the other ninety-two clubs in the Football League receiving £1097 from the pool: and that Wolves had been granted permission to present a souvenir, not exceeding £50, to Billy Wright, who had just broken Bob Crompton's record of forty-two games for England.

As a Tyneside team showed the South Africans how soccer should be played, with Newcastle beating Eastern Provinces 5–1, back at Lytham St Anne's South African golfer Bobby Locke was winning his third British Open in four years.

The next 'Test match' was to be played at the Rand Stadium in Johannesburg. In the run-up to the game several of the United squad, including Stan Seymour, had been advertising a well-known breakfast cereal on local radio. There was great laughter as the team approached the ground when a life-size Jackie Milburn cut-out, advertising a different breakfast product, was spotted stretched across the terracing.

The match proved less amusing, however; United suffered their only defeat of the tour, 5–3. Jackie Milburn played in this game – one of only five in which he took part during the entire tour. After forty-five minutes of chasing a lively ball on a bone-hard pitch, Brennan plonked the ball into a bucket of water to get rid of some of the bounce. Milburn sat on it during the interval.

After the game Eric Litchfield, a former United player and now a South African journalist, brought the only taste of sourness into the tour by stating in the Johannesburg *Daily Mail*: 'Newcastle are suffering from delusions of grandeur . . . their form is so bad, Seymour is considering buying replacements. South Africa will never again invite Newcastle United to the Union.'

During Newcastle's tour a series of articles had appeared in the *Sunday Times*, written by Charles Morgan, under the heading 'South African Journey'. This 'frank, objective report' discussed the clash over racial policy and the Union Constitution.

CHAPTER TWELVE

Transfer talk had an unsettling effect

The Newcastle players returned home leg-weary, jet-lagged and in need of a good rest. But Jackie had only a week to get to get to know a three-month-old son he'd hardly seen before reporting back to St James's Park to start all over again. From the opening day of the previous season until the end of the 1952/53 season, Newcastle would have had a soccer spell of twenty-one months with hardly a break. There was concern that the football team would have to pay dearly for their strength-sapping trek in the next campaign. The cost of the Tynesiders' tour, £16,000, had been borne by the South African Football Association, Newcastle had played sixteen games and lost only once.

Trial games were being held at St James's Park and, just as in 1943 when Jackie and Raymond Poxton had seen the games advertised in the paper, an article appeared in the *Newcastle Journal* advising that 'Any youngster who would like a try-out in the several evening games to be arranged at St James's Park should write an application as soon as possible.'

For their first practice match the United players had to wear borrowed boots, as theirs were still 'deep sea' somewhere near the Bay of Biscay. Prices for ground entrance at St James's for the new season went up from one shilling and sixpence to one and nine (terraces then held 17,000), and season-ticket holders had to pay £7 instead of £5.

Accounts issued by the Newcastle directors showed that United had made a profit of £42,637 for the 1951/52 season. This compared with the previous four seasons as follows.

```
1947/48  profit  –  £24,744
1948/49  profit  –  £49,765
1949/50  profit  –  £10,077
1950/51  profit  –   £7,099
1951/52  profit  –  £42,637
```

Newcastle began the new season badly, some would say predictably, by gaining only seven points from their first eight games. Milburn did not get his name on the score-sheet until 27 September – and then it was a penalty – as Newcastle beat Manchester City 2–0. But Jackie very nearly wasn't even a Newcastle United player by the end of September 1952.

Some Newcastle directors had been meeting up with their opposite numbers from various clubs when the question of a player's value was discussed. A Portsmouth official had asked, jokingly, 'What price Milburn?' Equally light-heartedly Lord Westwood, recently appointed to United's board, replied, 'Start bidding at £30,000.'

What had begun as a joke suddenly became deadly serious, and Seymour, when pressed, indicated that a Milburn move was not out of the question. Mr Newcastle had always been a man to play the percentage game: if he thought the odds were in his favour he would let a player go without compunction. He had already done so with Stubbins, Shackleton, Wayman, Taylor and Bentley, all excellent capped players. Perhaps he felt that now was the time to let 'his greatest ever signing' go to another club. True, Jackie's form was not anywhere near as good as it had been in that 1950/51 season. True, he was spending more and more time on the treatment table. True, at twenty-eight years of age Jackie was at least a yard slower than when he had gone flying home in Northumbrian foot handicaps.

There was swift reaction to the news that Milburn was up for transfer to the highest bidder over £30,000. In general the reply from most southern clubs was negative. Tottenham manager Arthur Rowe said, 'We might be interested in Milburn at half that price.' Portsmouth manager Eddie Lever commented, 'We *are* looking for a good centre-forward, but not at that price.' Arsenal's reaction was 'Not interested anyway'. And Fulham's manager, Bill Dodgin, said, 'We couldn't even hope to start bidding at that fee.' Jackie was amazed. On 14 September he said:

I knew nothing about this until I read it in the morning paper. Naturally I discussed it with Mr Seymour, and asked if he thought I should ask for a move, and he said, 'Yes – in writing!' So I wrote a request immediately and went back home to Ashington.

Within twenty minutes of getting home there were calls at the house for newspaper interviews. I could only say that I had no desire to leave United or Ashington, but that there seemed to be no future for me at St James's Park.

I have a nice home, a wife and three children here at Ashington, and until this happened I did not want to leave United. I have only once before asked for a

96

transfer, and that was three years ago when my wife was ill and we thought a move might suit her. I have been sitting wondering if I have been unwise to meet transfer trouble half-way, but don't really see what else I could have done.

Newcastle United board held a special meeting the next day and within half an hour sent out word that Milburn's transfer request had been turned down. Commenting on the events of the last two days, Stan Seymour said: 'I always tell players to ignore newspaper gossip on transfer topics; most of it is imagination. Milburn told me he felt it would be better for him to make a move, and I said if he was of that mind he should put it in writing.'

Newcastle United may have had many problems – to stay in the headlines was not one of them. News spread that other United players were disgruntled and wanted 'away'. Very quickly, both Hull City and Tottenham Hotspur put in bids for George Robledo. Seymour's response: 'No chance!' Robledo countered: 'All I know is what I've read!'

In their Charity Shield game against Manchester United, the Tynesiders brought in another young Ashington lad, Neville Black, an inside-forward who had been showing promise in the reserve side. But it was Milburn's replacement, Vic Keeble, who scored both Newcastle's goals in a 4–2 defeat. Ignored by England against the Irish League, Jackie could only contemplate on what might have been, as the man who had now made the centre-forward position his own, Nat Lofthouse, scored six of the seven goals put past the Irish goalkeeper.

In a game against Manchester City Jackie was injured again, this time seriously. It was diagnosed that he would require a cartilage operation on his right knee, and he was told he wouldn't play again for three months. Shortly afterwards, he entered a Newcastle nursing home. Jackie began receiving get-well letters almost immediately. He reported this in the *Football Gazette*.

Among well-wishing correspondents are two South African football enthusiasts I met during our close-season tour. In their air-mailed messages were tributes to Newcastle United on their displays. They advised me to flex my knee as soon and as often as possible. I did manage to lift my leg on the day following the operation, and when the doctor saw me doing this he said no other cartilage patient under his control had been able to do it.

Whenever I am alone, my thoughts invariably turn to football. One thing which has been worrying me is the falling off of team spirit of late compared with two or three years ago. There is no doubt that it has slumped considerably, and I am not the only United player who realises it.

Vanished almost entirely is that fighting-back spirit when a goal down – a spirit which has turned so many lost causes into victories. Last season we were full of such revivals, and so was the season before in both League and Cup matches.

No one realises more than I do that when things are not going well it is difficult to throw off despondency, but surely then is the time for all-out endeavour. Recent reports of transfer requests may have had an unsettling effect on some players, but this is no new occurrence. Every player should realise that only by doing his best can he be sure of keeping his place.

One of the only decent results for United during the early part of the 1952/53 season was a 2–0 derby win over Sunderland. This was to prove the season's biggest gate at St James's: 60,750.

Following Newcastle United's lead with Milburn, Football League clubs proved that they meant to fight the FA ruling about releasing players for representative matches when Doncaster manager, Irishman Peter Doherty, refused a request by the Irish FA to release their full-back, R. C. Graham, to play for Ireland against England on 4 October.

Jackie, now convalescing in his own house in Ellington Terrace, was able to follow the fortunes of his home team, Ashington, who had progressed to the first round proper of the FA Cup – always something of an achievement for the colliery side. Managed by former Newcastle winger Jackie Dryden, and wearing the familiar black and white, Ashington were drawn away to Tranmere Rovers, British Railways ran a twenty-five-shilling excursion to Liverpool for the army of pitmen who travelled with their team. Sammy Scott, a terrier of an inside-forward, worked a full shift at the pit before joining his team-mates. There was no fairy-tale ending for the tiny club, however, as Tranmere thrashed them 8–1.

Newcastle's League form continued to be inconsistent. At home on 20 December they got their first look at a new goal-scoring sensation when they entertained newly promoted Sheffield Wednesday. Ginger-haired centre-forward Derek Dooley had blasted the Sheffield side out of the Second Division with forty goals in thirty games to create a new goal-scoring record for the Division. He hammered in two more as United crumbled to a 5–1 defeat in front of 37,970 dejected fans.

Jackie's re-entry into football came exactly when the doctors had predicted: on 27 December, twelve weeks after his operation. He played in the middle for the Central League team against Leeds United reserves. News that he was playing swelled the attendance to 10,000 – and it was raining! In spite of a quiet game, he seemed well satisfied and reported:

I'm glad I got a few knocks; it means I can go all out now. I'm looking forward to getting back into the first team, but I don't mind playing in the second so long as I know I am getting better.

It was only the second time in nine years that I have been at home for Christmas dinner – up till then I'd always been playing. On Boxing Day I did a little sprinting at the Rec; I have lived on that ground since I was five.

I've only had seven games this season and scored one goal from a penalty kick; for a centre-forward that's not good enough.

Already there was talk of Milburn leading the attack for the forthcoming Cup tie against Swansea. In fact he was back even earlier than that, playing in front of his own supporters on New Year's Day against West Brom. His inclusion was forced on Seymour owing to an injury to George Robledo. The game was memorable only for being held up owing to a chimney catching fire in nearby Leazes Terrace. Thick black smoke belched across the pitch, making visibility virtually nil; the referee brought the players off the field for two minutes while it cleared. Some wag shouted, 'Set a'had to another bugger,' as United coughed and spluttered to a 5–3 defeat. Milburn, Mitchell and Davies got United's goals.

With one week to go before the Swansea match, Seymour took the players up the coast to Alnmouth to stay at the Schooner Hotel. With Ashington only a few miles away, Jackie decided to go on his own by bus, but he found himself taking the return journey home when he reported a swelling of his right knee. Said Stan Seymour, 'Milburn will be fit for Swansea, but we are taking no chances. He can stay in Ashington and travel into St James's every day for treatment.'

On the Saturday Jackie received a great ovation from the 63,499 fans who turned up to cheer United on their way to what they hoped would be a hat-trick of Cup wins. Getting his first taste of Cup-tie soccer, Bob Stokoe was preferred to Harvey at right-half. Joe commented stoically, 'I was Bob's best man at his wedding and wished him luck then – the same goes now.' Coincidentally, Harvey's opposite number in the 1952 Cup Final, Arsenal's captain Joe Mercer, also missed the third-round tie. In almost a repeat of the West Brom game, the referee brought the match to a halt after only eight minutes. There was no sooty smoke this time, only a grey blanket of fog which had been wrapped around the north-eastern city for several days.

As they groped their way out of the ground, the spectators, who had paid in excess of £8000, were advised by tannoy that the game would now take place on the following Wednesday; strictly cash at the gate. No money was refunded. This was a bitter pill for the Geordie crowd, but far too much to swallow for the Welsh followers who had suffered a 624-mile round trip to see – although most of them didn't – eight minutes of soccer. Just across the Tyne Bridge, Third Division Gateshead were able to complete their Cup tie against Liverpool and prove Geordie eyes sharper than Scousers' in the mist, as they won 1–0 against their more illustrious opponents.

The Swansea team went back to their Whitley Bay hotel, and next day took advantage of the local team's offer to train on their ground at Hillhead. Newcastle took a slightly longer journey up to Alnmouth once again. All twenty-two players were richer by £1, this being the normal fee for a drawn game. Before the replayed game the draw for the next round was made, fortune favouring Newcastle once more with another home tie, this time against Second Division Rotherham.

On the Wednesday another big crowd of 61,064, swelling the Gallowgate bank account by a further £8750, turned up to see United beat Swansea 3–0. Milburn, whose knee had swollen up again, missed the game, and his stand-in, Vic Keeble, scored twice, with Reg Davies getting the other goal. Commenting on Jackie's absence, Seymour said, 'We are still confident Jackie will respond to electric treatment and be ready for action again shortly.'

Rotherham officials weren't at all pleased with the allocation of 1000 reserved tickets which Newcastle sent them, and complained: 'We have 6000 members in our Supporters' Club, and to send this meagre amount is insulting. This match is regarded as the biggest thing ever for Rotherham.'

The Newcastle treatment room on the Monday prior to the Rotherham tie resembled a casualty ward. Only four players reported fit enough to play, and one of these, Keeble, still a soldier, was playing for the Army in a mid-week game. Jackie Milburn was definitely ruled out, but other regulars were expected to be able to play on the Saturday.

Rotherham, a side which included eight pitmen, brought fourteen players in their party for a three-day stay at Tynemouth. Jack Granger, a stylish forward, was being chased by sixteen clubs, including Newcastle. On the right wing was part-time miner Len White, who had recently played for a Football Association eleven.

Newcastle began hesitantly, and at half time there was no score. The awkward-looking Keeble managed to knock in a goal in the sixty-third minute, but in doing so he injured his toe and spent the rest of the game limping. Within five minutes Rotherham were level. This was a signal for the entire United defence, apart from Cowell, to crumble, enabling the visitors to score two more. Newcastle supporters streamed out of the ground well before the final whistle. Granger scored twice and Rickett got the other for the Yorkshire team. After congratulating Rotherham, Stan Seymour said, 'That's that! Now we use the breathing space to build for fresh triumphs.'

The result, which on paper looked sensational, was not a fluke. Newcastle United were not playing well. Was it the long tour of South Africa to blame, or the never-ending list of injuries to key players? Jackie had indicated in his article written in the nursing home that something was wrong. But could bringing new players to the club solve anything?

Newcastle continued their search for new talent, with Seymour visiting Scottish clubs in particular. Soon after their Cup exit, director Wally Hurford went on a scouting mission to the club which had dashed their hopes of a hat-trick of Cup wins, Rotherham. Jack Granger was still the target, but Hurford came back with glowing reports of winger Len White. A few weeks later Newcastle got a rare bargain as White joined them for £13,000.

Fit once more, Jackie was given a run-out at inside-right, a position he had not played since a game against Charlton in 1950. The opposition was Manchester City, and Jackie said, 'I fancy the job this time. I hope to get more opportunity to approach direct on goal.' He was right there, but the one goal he did score was not enough, as Manchester City put the Tynesiders into the relegation zone with a 2–1 victory.

On Saturday 13 February, in a game against Preston, Derek Dooley, Sheffield Wednesday's rising young star, collided with the Preston goalkeeper and fractured his leg. He was rushed into Preston Royal Infirmary, where he was immediately placed on the critical list. On the following Tuesday Dooley's right leg was amputated above the knee. A spokesman for the hospital said: 'Amputation was the only thing we could have done to save his life. It is a chance in a million. Normally, a fracture of this kind is straightforward. Gas gangrene got into his leg, presumably from the soil on the pitch.' At the time of his accident, Dooley was second-top scorer in Division One with sixteen goals.

That Saturday was the first time the football pools had paid over £100,000 to a prizewinner, when Mr J. Coulton, a forty-one-year-old insurance clerk from Battersea, won £109,111. He was so distraught at the news of Dooley's operation that he donated £3000 of his winnings to the Sheffield centre-forward, saying: 'I have great admiration for Dooley; he is a fine chap and a wonderful player. I felt I must do something to help in this tragic business.' On being told that a pools winner had given him £3000, Dooley, still in intensive care, said, 'Aren't I lucky!'

St James's Park got lit up on 25 February when Celtic were the team chosen to inaugurate the Geordie club's new floodlights. Newcastle won easily by 3–0, with the re-called George Robledo scoring all three goals. But League points were still proving elusive – little wonder, when there had been twenty-nine changes in the last seven games.

At the end of March, Wembley Stadium thrilled to another Milburn-like piece of finishing as England Boys shared six goals with Wales Boys. This time the Milburn touch was supplied by his second cousin, fifteen-year-old Bobby Charlton, who scored two goals and battled and schemed with all the finesse of the Milburn clan.

Dozens of League clubs, including Manchester United, Leeds and Newcastle, made a bee-line for the Charlton household in Beatrice Street, Ashington. Jack, Bobby's elder brother, had sampled a year of pit work before following his uncles George, Jack and Jimmy down to Leeds. But it was Matt Busby and Jimmy Murphy who won the day – and the signature – as Bobby was enlisted into the Busby Babes squad.

Jackie Milburn, injured again but on the way to recovery, was asked by Willie McKeag to turn out for the *third* team against Whitley Bay. Word spread that he was playing, and 5000 fans flocked to a little ground in Wallsend to see their idol in action. McKeag was one of a thousand people who couldn't even get in; someone had locked the only turnstile ten minutes before the game started. Two Ashington lads, Milburn and Prior, scored the winning goals, Jackie's effort proving sufficient to get his name on the team-sheet for the first eleven's next match at home to Manchester United.

Frank Brennan was selected for the next Scotland *v* England game. Getting an extended run for England – a luxury not afforded to Milburn – Nat Lofthouse was named as England's centre-forward, and also the Football Writers' Player of the Year.

When the crucial Easter programme arrived, United were still not out of relegation trouble. Other clubs near the foot of the table were Derby, Manchester City, Stoke, Sheffield Wednesday, Liverpool and Chelsea. Things were marginally better for the Tynesiders when they played their last home game, against Bolton, needing a point for safety. In a state of panic, Seymour dropped Bobby Cowell, probably their most consistent defender, because he was too adventurous. Milburn kept his place and made a goal for Hannah in a 3–2 win that guaranteed First Division soccer for the coming season. Not so lucky were relegated sides Derby County and Stoke City. Arsenal finished as League champions. Jackie Milburn played in only fifteen games and scored five goals. George Robledo was top scorer with eighteen goals.

Alf McMichael, Ireland's captain, was refused permission to travel with the Irish international side on a tour of Canada. A statement said that it was in the interest of the player, and that it was better to relax in close season. When it was explained to them that the tour would end in June, United's officials relented and gave Alf and Tom Casey, signed from Bournemouth, permission to travel. Said a relieved McMichael, 'I greatly appreciate Newcastle United's altered decision.'

Newcastle went on to play in a tournament especially arranged to celebrate Coronation year, featuring top English and Scottish clubs. Before the games got under way, Seymour announced that Newcastle had signed teetotal, non-smoking Jimmy Scoular for a club record fee of £25,000. It was also stated that Scoular was to take over the captaincy immediately, and that Joe Harvey's main role in the future was to be reserve and youth team coach.

Scoular was a dour man who did not fit comfortably into the easy-going style of the Newcastle United players, either on or off the field.

Seymour signed Scoular to take over as captain – I don't know why – things were never the same with Joe Harvey out of the team. His credentials as a skipper in comparison to Jimmy Scoular – phew! – Jimmy was a nice fella, but he was the start of the cliques cos he was Scottish, and you got a few of them knocking around together. He was a good player, but he wasn't what we were used to at Newcastle. Mainly we were all just local lads who'd got together after the war.

That year saw a wage rise for the players, from £14 to £15 a week. This was only a maximum, however, and many clubs paid far less. At Newcastle twenty-two players were on the £15 maximum when the 1953/54 season got under way.

With the start only a matter of days away, Jackie had not even begun serious training. He'd taken part in a trial match, but left at half time because of recurring fibrositis trouble. The first game was to be a real appetiser: a local derby against Sunderland. The Wearsiders, living up to their 'Bank of England' tag, fielded three costly close-season signings: Ray Daniel, Jimmy Cowan and Billy Elliott. The gates were open earlier than usual – 12.30 p.m. – to allow the crowds plenty of time to take their place. Pre-match entertainment was provided by the band of 4th and 5th Royal Northumberland Fusiliers.

Milburn was selected at outside-right for the first time in two seasons. Two minutes into the game, Shackleton put Sunderland ahead. Scoular was injured soon afterwards and was in pain for the rest of the match. Milburn, who needed to build up as much confidence as he could on the wing, constantly left the opposition standing with solo thrusts on goal. Although Jackie didn't score, he had an excellent game and made goals for Mitchell and Keeble to win the match 2–1.

With no Scoular, and with Joe Harvey also missing, there was a dressing-room vote as to who should take over as captain. Charlie Crowe, now established as a regular first-team left-half, got the job. Bob Stokoe came in at right-half for the injured Scoular in the next game against Liverpool, which United won with goals from Hannah and Davies. Jackie played very well in both the openers and was in exuberant mood when he said, 'I am as happy as a sandboy on the wing! It's like a holiday after those years in the middle, though I admit that, for a long time, I asked nothing better than to be left alone at centre.'

Newcastle United were beginning to look good once more. They were showing a consistency which left them afraid of no one. For a match against Liverpool, fielding Bob Paisley at left-half, the Geordies were again unchanged, and showed their class by winning easily, 4–0. This was the third consecutive home win, and statisticians had to delve as far back as 1929 to recall such a feat. Playing Bolton at home, United had a chance to stretch that run to four, as Nat Lofthouse stayed behind in Lancashire with his foot in plaster. There was now room for Milburn in the England team if he could capitalise on Nat's absence. But Newcastle chose this game to slide back into their slipshod ways and were beaten 3–2.

On a week's special training at Blackpool, Bob Stokoe missed his footing on the stairway of a big department store, fell down half a dozen steps and wrenched his knee. This injury signalled the recall of Scoular into the side against West Brom at home. The Throstles, playing by far the best football in Division One, trounced United 7–3.

In a balance sheet produced at the annual general meeting, Newcastle showed a loss of £38,619. Transfer fees together with players' wages accounted for £85,970. Constantly heckled from the floor, Alderman McKeag likened the proceedings to an 'inquisition' after being asked to account for a sum of money allegedly paid to a firm of solicitors of which he was a partner.

Stan Seymour, voted chairman of the board for the first time, assured supporters that they 'would get the class of football they rightly deserved'.

During the last two years the club has slowly drifted into its present position, in part because direction has not been consistently single-minded on important issues needing decisive action.

It is my wish that the responsibility of selecting the team should lie with those directors in constant touch with the League side at home and away, as well as, when possible, the form of the reserves. I am prepared to act as chairman of selectors.

As a businessman of the city, I know too well what the success of a United team means to us all. We cannot expect to win honours every season, but we should always be in a prominent position in the football world.

Back to their inconsistent ways, United broke a thirty-two-year-old record – this time for *losing* three consecutive home games – when they lost 3–1 to Spurs. This defeat panicked Seymour into making seven changes for the next game, including moving Jackie Milburn to lead the attack. But shuffling the pack did not produce the required magic to beat Sheffield Wednesday, and after a 3–0 drubbing United found themselves sixth to bottom of a League table they had looked like heading at the season's outset.

Again players were unhappy at being left out of the team, and Hannah and McMichael asked for transfers. The Irish captain's left-back position was now being filled by hard-tackling Ron Batty, who had played the role of understudy for so long. McMichael commented, 'It is not in my best interests as an international to be out of League football.'

Following United's *sixth* consecutive home defeat – 2–0 by Huddersfield – Stan Seymour left the ground after only twenty minutes' play, commenting: 'I hope it will be understood that I shall act in the firm opinion, with the interests of Newcastle always put first, that the club is greater than the individual – any individual. There are some problems on which the public cannot always be informed, but the remedies *will* be found' The following week, in a seven-hour spell, Seymour bought two new forwards: local lad Alan Monkhouse, who had signed for Millwall only to return to the North-East after a few months saying he was homesick, and Ivor Broadis, much-travelled English international who landed at Newcastle via Carlisle, Sunderland and Manchester City. The twenty-nine-year-old cost Seymour £20,000. When asked if that was the end of his recruiting drive, Seymour commented evasively, 'Who knows? It depends on the players.'

In November a representative game was played at St James's Park, and Milburn was picked at outside-right in an FA eleven which was virtually an England 'B' side. The opposition came from the Army. With Walter Winterbottom in the stands, Jackie sparkled, scoring two goals in the FA's 3–1 victory. Unpredictable as ever, Seymour decided to move him back into the middle for United's next match, in which they beat Cardiff 3–0. Ivor Broadis scored two goals on his home debut.

With the Newcastle board relaxing their ruling that players should not have part-time jobs, Jackie with financial help, was able to open a fireplace shop in the middle of Ashington. There was a great deal of modernisation going on in the area as miners' wives got rid of their old-fashioned black lead ovens and fireplaces and began installing an ultra-modern tiled variety. A new town was being built at nearby Cramlington, and Jackie, through his many contacts, was given a large order to supply the builders.

Eric Nichol, a local haulier, recalls moving several of the units from the Station Road shop, but says that whenever he asked Jackie for a hand in lifting the heavy fireplaces, Jackie the businessman would become Jackie the canny Newcastle United footballer, put his hand on his fibrositic back, and shake his head as he refused Eric's plea for help. Jackie's wife Laura bore the brunt of the shop work, but spent much of her time removing her two playful daughters, Linda and Betty, from the showroom window.

England took on Hungary at Wembley on 25 November, fielding three Blackpool forwards: Matthews now aged thirty-nine, Mortensen, and the little man Ernie Taylor, getting a belated first cap for his country. After losing 6–3 to the Olympic champions to suffer their first defeat by a foreign team at home, Stan Seymour waded into the England selectors with: 'Sack the lot of 'em! I've said for years that the England representative teams should be chosen by a panel of the most knowledgeable men in the country. Men like Tom Whittaker, Stan Cullis, Matt Busby, Joe Smith and Jimmy Seed. Instead, England's soccer fate is in the hands of amateurs at one of the toughest jobs in the world. But will they? No! They'll just carry on in their own dictatorial way.'

Seymour must have been impressed with the Hungarian style of playing a centre-forward 'deep' behind the rest of the attack, because that was the way he and new coach Joe Harvey asked Milburn to play in United's next game, against Arsenal. Said one of the Gunners' defenders, 'They tried to play a Hungarian rhapsody!' Newcastle were beaten 2–1, and, after losing their next game as well, dropped the deep centre-forward tactic and moved Milburn back to the right wing.

Newcastle, after being drawn against Lancashire Combination League team Wigan in the third round of the FA Cup, were laid at 12 to 1, with Wolves the 9 to 1 favourites. Wigan's manager said, 'Wigan has gone crazy over the Cup tie against the famous Newcastle United. The boys are eager to intensify training.'

Thanks to their abysmal League form, United went into the Christmas games only five places above bottom team Liverpool, who already looked doomed. Milburn was dropped from the team to play fellow strugglers Middlesbrough, and thanked Seymour for it. It was Jackie's first break in an ever-present run during that season.

I am glad I was dropped. It was a refresher sitting in the stand. I felt I could see how I may be able to alter my game to recover the form I found on the wing in the opening games of the season. There is no danger at me being unsettled at being left out. I expect I'll be in the Central League side against Manchester United next week. But, at twenty-nine, I don't mean to be dropped by United again for a long time once I'm in again.

Sunderland were also in the relegation zone, and when Jackie was dropped into the reserves they made discreet enquiries about his availability. They had a crisis at centre-forward themselves – Trevor Ford had gone to Cardiff – and the Wearsiders resorted to fielding Welsh international centre-half Ray Daniel as a leader of the attack. Although Milburn would have welcomed the short trip from Tyne to Wear, Seymour made it clear that a move was out of the question.

Back in the first team on New Year's Day, Jackie did his Hogmanay first-footing at the expense of Blackpool, scoring both goals in a 2–0 win. Ted Goodier, Wigan's manager, was at that match and afterwards said: 'I know my team will be beaten 11–0 next Saturday, and I changed my mind about bringing the rest of the team today in case it frightened them. The Wigan station-master says he will have a red carpet ready if we get a draw – there are ninety-eight steps!' No-one was fooled by this piece of pre-match kidology. Wigan, as Combination League champions, had already beaten Hereford and Scarborough in earlier rounds, and with their present in-and-out form, United could never feel confident whoever the opposition.

As in previous years, Buxton was chosen for a week's special training before the Cup game. Although at the club for almost two months, Ivor Broadis was still living and training in Carlisle. However, he was able to join up with his colleagues at the Derbyshire spa town. Newcastle chose this game to experiment with the team, and Seymour dropped Bobby Cowell, with Ron Batty switching from left to right full-back. But it was the forward-line formation which was the most astonishing. Milburn, a makeshift centre-forward but obviously more at ease on the right wing, was picked to play inside-left, with Alan Monkhouse brought in to lead the attack.

Wigan gave Newcastle an almighty fright at St James's Park. Broadis scored early in the game, but the Lancashire side came back to lead 2–1. It needed a ferocious Milburn drive to level the game, draw the match and set everyone wondering where the replay would be held. Wigan's dressing rooms had been burned down the previous April, and Bolton Wanderers made Burnden Park available. The Wigan Rugby side also offered their ground, but Wigan FC were adamant that their own Springfield Park, holding 31,000, was to be the venue for the replay the following Wednesday.

For this game Newcastle relied on a side that looked a little more reliable. Cowell came back, and Keeble replaced Monkhouse at centre. An anonymous telephone call to their Buxton hotel sent Seymour scurrying over to Wigan. What he saw horrified him: 'It is terrible. The pitch is bad enough, but the facilities are dreadful. The game should have gone to the rugby ground. It is like a wreck at the back of the pier! I have phoned elderly directors to ask them to stay at home rather than tackle this shambles.' Ted Goodier exploded: 'What do they expect? We lost all our accommodation in a fire. Newcastle are getting spoilt – nobody else has complained.'

Very few of the 6000 tickets for the replay were taken up by United supporters, and only 300 people booked for the special train which left Newbiggin at 6.50 a.m. on the morning of the match. Ticket touts were seen boarding the train at Newcastle Central with boxes full of half-crown tickets which they hoped to sell for inflated prices at Wigan.

In the programme that day was an appeal for Wigan supporters not to barrack Newcastle United on account of an 'eve-of-the-match ground controversy'. The 27,000 crowd did their best to lift the local team after Newcastle had gone into a commanding 2–0 lead. United were very relieved to hang on for a 3–2 victory, which put them through to play an away tie at Burnley. Again not all tickets were sold, and as a football special left Newcastle Central with a box of 300 unsold tickets on board, a British Railways spokesman conjectured, 'It could be the weather.'

The game against Burnley ended as a 1–1 draw, with Broadis getting United's goal. Bobby Mitchell, again taking the role as penalty taker on Milburn's refusal, managed only to stub his toe and send the ball trickling goalwards. In the replay at St James's it was level pegging right until the last ten minutes. The two Ashington men in opposition – Newcastle's Milburn and Burnley's Adamson – collided going for a fifty-fifty ball near the Burnley goal. Jackie went down; Jimmy Adamson pleaded an accident, but the referee gave a penalty. Mitchell made no mistake this time, and Newcastle marched on to round five with a game against League leaders West Bromwich Albion at the Hawthornes.

Shortly after this Scoular was dropped and relieved of the captaincy, with Alf McMichael taking over as skipper. Walker and Davies, who were not getting a regular first-team game, put in transfer requests, and after an encouraging 3–1 League win against Burnley the team set out once more for a week at Buxton to train for their next Cup game at West Brom.

Vic Buckingham, West Brom's manager, commented: 'We realise that our Cup opponents are capable of very good displays, but we shall not be worrying about what they can do. We think this is to be *our* year in League and Cup.' Buckingham's optimism proved to be well founded, as his team went into a 2–0 lead. United fought back and were dominating the game when the final whistle blew with the score at 3–2 in West Brom's favour, ending the Geordies' 1954 hopes of a return to Wembley. Said Seymour, seemingly undismayed by the display: 'We are proud of the fight the boys made and the shock they gave a very good opposition. We shall field the same team against Charlton on Thursday.'

By the middle of March the North-East's big guns – Newcastle, Sunderland and Middlesbrough – occupied three of the last five places in the First Division. Liverpool, five points adrift, were virtually assured of going down; it was a simply case of who went with them. For the home game against Sheffield United, Alan Monkhouse was brought back and scored a hat-trick. Milburn got a goal, and United were practically safe after a 4–1 win.

Bob Stokoe was the next player to ask for a transfer. He had already tried to get away at the end of 1953. This time he was unhappy about being played at centre-half as Brennan's deputy when the big Scot had been injured. 'I am prepared to sign for about any First or Second Division side' he said, 'so long as it is understood that I move as a right-half, the position for which I was trained. On general grounds, too, I should like to try my luck elsewhere.' Seymour's reply was: 'Stokoe has forced our hands by his agitation for a move, and he is on the list.' It was thought that a price of around £10,000 was asked for Stokoe. The next week, against Derby County reserves, United fielded five unhappy players who had asked for transfers: Stokoe, Hannah, Foulkes, Batty and Davies. Vic Keeble got a hat-trick that day as the 'stiffs' won 3–1.

It was around then that Albert Stubbins was driving through Ashington and spotted Jackie's fireplace shop. He got out of the car to say hello to his old friend, and ended up as Ashington's centre-forward! Albert, still on Liverpool's retained list at a price of £3000, was 'talked into it' by a persuasive Jackie anxious to see

107

his home-town team lifted from the bottom of the North Eastern League. Albert said later:

It wasn't the first time I had been propositioned by Jackie. In 1952 we were on the point of opening a restaurant in the middle of Newcastle. We even had a name for it – The Goalmouth – which we thought was very apt. It came to nothing because of lack of finance. But anyway, he talked me into this Ashington job, and I was there for about a season before I went over to the States to be their national coach.

This was one of many instances when Jackie Milburn took on the role of unpaid Public Relations man for a team he cared about. Many years later he was to make a similar proposition regarding the Newcastle United manager's job.

Mathematically Newcastle could still be relegated, but in a game played over the Easter period they beat Sheffield Wednesday 3–1 to assure their status for another year. Ivor Broadis, the only north-eastern player chosen for the English 1954 World Cup squad, was unable to get into the Newcastle side that day.

As a very disappointing season for the Tyneside club came to a close, West Bromwich Albion, who had ended Newcastle's FA Cup hopes, went on to beat Preston 3–2 in the Final, but failed to do the 'double' as Billy Wright's Wolves took the Championship. Middlesbrough was the unlucky north-eastern side to slide into the Second Division together with Liverpool, obviously missing Albert Stubbins who, in his first game at centre-forward for the Colliers, scored one of his typical twenty-five-yard goals to level the score and gain a vital point against Anfield Plain. Newcastle finished fifteenth in the League, with Jackie Milburn the top scorer netting sixteen goals from thirty-nine games. In the close season England, with Stanley Matthews, now approaching his fortieth birthday, at outside-right, were beaten by Uruguay 4–2, in the quarter-finals of the World Cup.

Having shown a massive loss on the season, the Newcastle board adopted a penny-pinching attitude and dropped Ronnie Simpson's wage to £13. This so antagonised the Scottish goalkeeper, who had missed only three games in two seasons, that he made the following statement: 'It would appear that I am singled out of all the regular League team players for this wage cut. If I do re-sign for next season I will ask for a transfer.'

Two other players, Foulkes and White, the latter now working part-time in a Tyneside pit, also took pay cuts. As usual, Seymour was able to justify the board's action: 'We are adopting an incentive scheme whereby players whose play warrants top money will get it, whether in the first or second team.'

Before the new season got under way, Derby County stepped in with an offer for an unsettled Bob Stokoe. Events were to dictate that a Stokoe move was out of the question. Frank Brennan was not included in the Probables side against the Possibles in a trial match. The black and white side that day was: Simpson, Cowell, McMichael, Scoular, Lackenby, Crowe, Milburn, Broadis, Keeble, Hannah, Mitchell.

Seymour rushed up to Scotland in an attempt to sign Partick Thistle's centre-half, Jim Davidson. A Scottish international twenty-six-year-old Davidson was the target of several English clubs. When a figure of £20,000 was mentioned, Seymour backed out of the bidding. Frank Brennan was mystified at this undignified scramble to sign a centre-half. At over 300 games, the amiable Scot had played far more matches for United than any of his contemporaries. 'I am quite fit and hoping for another five years in first-class football,' said Frank. 'I am signed up for the coming season and have made no move towards leaving Newcastle United.'

Two of United's best-loved players celebrated their 250th appearances for the club, in a match against West Brom: Jackie Milburn and Bobby Cowell. Frank Brennan came back into the team as Newcastle completed an early double over Aston Villa, winning 2–0 with goals from Milburn and Mitchell.

After seven games had been played, Newcastle United shared first place in the League with Wolves and Manchester United. There was a growing feeling in the North-East that this Newcastle side, playing attractive and efficient football, could be in line for further honours. This proved wishful thinking as Newcastle, back to their most infuriating, threw away a 2–0 lead over Leicester to lose the match 3–2. Stan Milburn played left-back against his cousin Jackie, and gave away a penalty. Frank Brennan, obviously upset by all the speculation over his future, chose this day to play one of his most untidy games for Newcastle, sending Seymour hurrying off on another talent-spotting exercise.

One Geordie who made the journey home that weekend was Charlie Wayman. The popular little goal-getter joined up with Middlesbrough, in an attempt to lift them from the foot of the Second Division. The Boro also came across to Tyneside with an open chequebook to try to secure Brennan to bolster a woefully weak defence. Frank refused to go. With Milburn tried again at centre-forward, and without Brennan, United lost a derby match at Roker Park by 4–2, sending the Wearside team clear at the top of the First Division.

Seymour lost no time in enlisting a centre-half, and paid £22,000 for twenty-two-year-old Scot Bill Paterson, who had been playing for Second Division Doncaster Rovers. Said Rovers' manager, Peter Doherty, with typical Irish blarney, 'Bill Paterson will gain Scotland caps with Newcastle United.' On Paterson's signing Seymour conjectured, 'Stokoe has the chance to fight for the wing-half place he desires.'

In an eventful match at home against Spurs, United's defence, with Paterson making his debut, was all over the place, and the game ended in a high-scoring 4–4 draw. United's goalkeeper was hurt and Jimmy Scoular took over in nets; Charlie Crowe scored only his second goal for United in 132 League appearances; and Spurs right-back Alf Ramsey, after the game, said, 'This is the worst playing surface in the First Division.'

As part of Paterson's transfer, Newcastle took a team to Doncaster for a mid-week friendly. During the game Ivor Broadis, during a brief respite, quizzed Doncaster's Robin Lawlor about their ex-centre-half, telling him how much Newcastle had paid. The shocked Irishman replied, 'It's the biggest robbery since the Crown jewels!'

A Newcastle United Shareholders Association meeting, chaired by Mr E.C. Pringle, said that a letter should be sent to club directors requesting the appointment of a full-time manager. It was felt that it should not be the duty of a club chairman (Stan Seymour) to act as manager as well. A query also arose regarding Middlesbrough coming to ask for Brennan's signature when the player knew nothing about it. It seemed that both clubs had agreed on a figure of £12,000. Mr Pringle stated: 'This Newcastle team can put us in the Second Division. Why don't they appoint Joe Harvey as team manager and coach?' At Newcastle United's official AGM, Stan Seymour countered: 'We have been on the lookout for a manager for two years – we want the right man when we get one.'

Bill Paterson was dropped into the reserves for the next game, and Seymour explained: 'He is not doing himself justice, and will benefit from a spell in the reserves while he settles in. Brennan will be in the team if the trainers are satisfied with his condition.'

Having seemingly backed down over the Brennan issue, on 9 December Seymour gave further ground to the Shareholders' Association by appointing a new manager, Dougald Livingstone. Coaching in Belgium at the time, Livingstone still had one year of a five-year contract to run, but was expecting permission to leave for Newcastle within a month. Seymour gave Livingstone's brief as being: '. . . confined to coaching, supervision of training and all matter pertaining to play'. Joe Harvey was to stay on as coach, with Norman Smith as trainer.

Working on a three-year contract, Livingstone did not present outstanding credentials, apart from coaching abroad. He had played right full-back for Sheffield Wednesday against Newcastle and Stan Seymour back in the twenties. He had been born in Dumbarton: '. . . from over the border, and my wife is a Mackenzie! I cannot but think that Newcastle have players who should achieve better results than they have been doing. I shall take up my post full of confidence and enthusiasm.'

The draw for the third round of the FA Cup was made and Newcastle were to play away at Plymouth, currently lying next to bottom in the Second Division. The call-over from the Victoria Club showed Newcastle as 20 to 1 outsiders. Nevertheless, United's official spokesman, Seymour, commenting on the draw, said: 'We should win all right, for the lads will know they are in for a fight, but it is a bad draw for Newcastle United supporters. We shall travel on Monday before the game, staying at a hotel outside Plymouth where there is a nine-hole golf course and other facilities to keep the players entertained and assist training.'

Perhaps it was the euphoria of being back on the Wembley trail again, but Newcastle turned in their best performance of the season in beating Arsenal at home 5–1, with goals from Keeble (2), Mitchell (2) and Milburn. However, the game before the Cup tie, against Sheffield United, was lost 6–2, and once again it was a Newcastle side struggling to find some semblance of consistency that left for Torquay on the Monday. Scoular and White, both injured, were left behind.

The fact that only 20,000 tickets had been sold by Plymouth reflected the conviction in the area that Newcastle were as good as through to the next round. Four train-loads of Geordies left for the West Country early on the Friday before the game. Charlie Crowe – up till then United's regular left-half and captain – was pulled out of the match with an ankle injury. In the team for a first Cup game came young Stan Keery. Seymour commented: 'This present side of ours can go a long way in the Cup again if they tackle this hurdle energetically, and get reasonable luck in the draw.' Dougald Livingstone said: 'On the form I saw Plymouth show against Middlesbrough last month, we can scarcely fail to win.' Jimmy Scoular, fit again and restored to the team captaincy, was also optimistic: 'We are a very happy team and a hopeful team. We refuse to be disturbed by the rout at Sheffield.'

Against Plymouth, United fielded a strange-looking line-up. Milburn was tried at inside-left in spite of having played fifteen straight games on the right-wing, from where he'd scored ten goals. Centre-forward Keeble scored the only goal of the match, sending a 28,685 crowd home convinced they'd just witnessed a form of legalised daylight robbery. A defensive Seymour admitted: 'We stole this match. Our lads gave a very poor show. They looked early on as if they would win easily, but they eased the concentration.' In spite of this dismal showing, when the draw was made for the next round with Newcastle at home to either Brentford or Bradford City, money was poured on to the Geordie team to take £10,000 out of the bookies' pockets. Newcastle's odds tumbled to 11 to 1.

Jimmy Rae, Plymouth's manager, well aware of the Brennan situation and looking for spare players, sounded out Newcastle officials about getting big Frank on a year's loan. On being told of the offer, Brennan said that he was not prepared to go to Plymouth. Said Seymour: 'Brennan is now on the transfer list at a very modest fee, because we do not consider that he fits in with our scheme for the encouragement of younger players.' Frank retorted: 'I have yet to be told by Newcastle that I am on the list. I don't wish to give up playing at thirty one, but intend to continue living in Newcastle and carrying on business in the city.' Washing his hands of the matter, Seymour's last words were: 'The matter is entirely in the hands of team manager Dougald Livingstone. Any suggestion that Brennan is not playing because of his business activities in Newcastle is entirely wrong and unfair.' (Brennan had recently opened a sports outfitters shop in Newcastle, and was tendering for contracts in direct opposition to Seymour.)

On 26 January the Newcastle board issued a statement to the effect that Brennan had never been for transfer, and that he would be retained by Newcastle and given the match practice needed for him to continue with his valuable service to the club.

The whole Brennan episode had cast a huge shadow over the Gallowgate ground. But there was never a doubt that the Geordie team had the character to forget the in-fighting and concentrate on the imminent Cup tie against Brentford. The London team's manager, Bill Dodgin, was a much-travelled Gateshead man whose brother Norman had figured in a fine Newcastle team during the war. Another local connection from the same era was Pegswood-born centre-forward George Stobbart. 'Stobbs', who had knocked in fifteen goals already that season, joked: 'I'm hoping that I've got a trick or two up my sleeve which may put Bob Stokoe off once or twice.' Dodgin said: 'I am bringing my lads up to Whitley Bay for a few days. Brentford people are thrilled by the prospect of meeting the Magpies in the Cup – it has whetted their appetite for a sight of top-quality play.'

The Manchester referee was put on the spot even before the game began. He had to spin a coin to see which side changed from their traditional black shorts into white.

I only played under two managers: George Martin and a fella called Dougald Livingstone. You know what Livingstone did one day . . . it sickened me. The most educated left foot I ever saw in my life was Bobby Mitchell's. The manager had us coaching at Fenham, and he drew a chalk mark on Bobby Mitchell's left boot, demonstrating how to side-foot a ball to the rest of us. 'That's exactly the point where you catch it,' he says.

'Whey, the lads, like Frank Brennan and them, were looking at me, and we couldn't believe it! I mean . . . that's kids stuff.' I says: 'Hey, that's me finished with him. That's the end as far as I'm concerned.' Everybody started to laugh about it, because they said Mitch's left foot was bloody dynamite! He could do anything with it . . . he could open a can of beans with his left foot, and . . . this chalk mark!

Livingstone came from Sheffield Wednesday; he was the coach, and he'd been in Belgium. He was a nice fella, but a school teacher type. We were hard-bitten pros by the time he got there – he came in 1954 – and you expect somebody to be, not entirely ruthless, but the boss. You couldn't look up to fellas like this, and it caused cliques in the camp which we had never known. Up to 1952 we had never known any cliques – gangs of three or four knocking about together, and this lot ignoring that lot. All this sort of seeped in then, and it was never the same when Joe Harvey left.

Martin and Livingstone were the only two managers we had, because Seymour more or less ran things. It was run on promises. The club was run on promises. 'Come on, lads, you win this one and I'll get the groceries in for you.' Promises – just promises. The managers picked the team, but if the directors thought it wasn't right, they changed it straight away.

Charlie Crowe remembers that Livingstone's coaching techniques bordered between the ludicrous and the dangerous. One visit to a gymnasium ended up with half the team being injured after jumping over hurdles and clambering up ropes suspended from the ceiling.

Local bandleader George Evans, resident at the Oxford Galleries, composed a new waltz for his Geordie dancers. Entitled the 'Wembley Waltz', the lyrics of the song described the progress of Newcastle United in winning their two previous FA Cup Finals. George himself sang the song when the band were featured on the BBC North of England Home Service. The last two lines of the song went:

> *'We waltz to Wembley to see a bit of football,*
> *and watch Newcastle waltz off with the Cup.'*

In the Cup tie against Brentford, goals, which had looked an impossibility before half time, flew in after the interval. Newcastle scored three in a five-minute burst, including a rare goal from Mitchell's right foot, eventually winning 3–2 in a scrappy match. As the first team waltzed their way into the next round, Frank Brennan was plodding his size elevens on the turf at Wallsend in a run-out for the thirds against Heaton Stannington. After the game he said: 'So far as I am concerned, the whole thing is ended.'

The Brentford party packed up to leave for London, taking with them the white shorts which United had bought for the game but which were eventually worn by the Bees. Dougald Livingstone stated: 'The London lads are welcome to them as a souvenir of the game. They nearly made one of the day's sensations, but we are still on the Wembley trail.'

Newcastle were drawn away to Nottingham Forest in the fifth round, and were immediately made third favourites at 9 to 1 to win the Cup. Forest were in seventeenth position in the Second Division, and Newcastle hadn't played them since losing 2–0 in the 1947/48 season. Forest manager Billy Walker was not dismayed by the draw: 'On what I've seen of Newcastle they are nothing out of the ordinary, and I think we can beat them on our own pitch.' That pitch was only 400 yards away from Notts County's ground, who were also due to play at home in the fifth round on the same day. With County's record gate standing at 49,000 and Forest's at 44,166, the streets of Nottingham were destined to be packed that Saturday.

Before then, United's board had a vote of no confidence passed against them by the Shareholders' Association at Newcastle's City Hall. Estimated voting was 2000 for and only three against. Another motion passed that evening was that a Newcastle United supporters club be formed. Some suggestions made were more hilarious than practical, including: 'Rake some of the muck away from the one and ninepenny end, or supply supporters with thigh boots.'

United were faced with team problems, with English international Broadis fit again but unable to command a place because of the good form of Davies and Hannah. Proving a very good buy, Len White had played centre-forward twelve times already that season, scoring eight goals from that position. Jackie Milburn roamed across the forward line playing every position except outside-left.

Prior to the Cup game, Newcastle went to the Norbreck Hotel at Blackpool. Manager Livingstone stated: 'We have to get away from Newcastle; there is a foot of snow on the St James's pitch and the Fenham training ground. Conditions are more favourable at Blackpool. The team will not be decided till later.' The Friday night before the game, the Newcastle party went to see 'Jack and the Beanstalk' – on ice!

Livingstone brought back Bobby Cowell, who had been dropped for the previous game; Len White was included at centre-forward; Keeble got into the team at inside-left, to the exclusion of George Hannah who immediately asked for a transfer: 'I don't think it is fair that I should be dropped after playing in four games of which three were won. I scored winning goals in two of these games, including a Cup tie.'

Newcastle had Milburn to thank for scoring an equaliser four minutes from time in a game that they had looked like losing only a minute before. Forest's left-winger, Peter Smith, who had been off the field for twenty minutes following a terrible tackle from Scoular, returned to score what looked like a winner with only five minutes of the game remaining. From the re-start, Jackie Milburn, so often a champion of lost causes, beat a couple of defenders, rounded the goalkeeper and slid the ball slowly towards the empty net. 'It was agony watching that ball crawl towards the net with Forest right-back Hare racing to cut it off,' said Jackie after the game.

Livingstone blamed the icy ground for United's lukewarm performance: 'Some of our boys were not too well suited by the conditions at Nottingham. Our replay team will not be named till I've seen the pitch.' Stan Seymour was happy to get another chance: 'I am satisfied we can be in very good form for Wednesday's replay. We did not play well, but we are still in the Cup, whereas Chelsea and Spurs went out to lower-class clubs.'

Thirty men were employed at St James's Park in an effort to get the pitch fit for the Wednesday, but the sudden fall of an extra six inches of snow set the game back until the following Monday. By then the draw for the sixth round had paired United with Huddersfield.

On 24 February the Newcastle United Supporters Club was launched. Newly elected secretary J. Schofield of Heaton stated: 'Our aim is to spread and stimulate interest in Newcastle United.' He also said that he hoped it would lead to a closer acquaintance with the Newcastle club 'from Stan Seymour down to the youngest player.'

For the seventy-eighth derby game with Sunderland, United had Broadis, Hannah and Casey returning to the side. Keeble was played at centre-forward, with Milburn moving back to the right wing. Sunderland were without two of their stars: Len Shackleton was dropped into the reserves to play Blackhall Colliery, and Billy Bingham, their Irish winger, was injured. The Sunderland line-up for the match was: Fraser, Hedley, McDonald, Anderson, Daniel, Aitken, Kemp, Fleming, Purdon, Chisholm, Elliot. Newcastle United's side was: Simpson, Cowell, Batty, Scoular, Stokoe, Casey, Milburn, Broadis, Keeble, Hannah, Mitchell.

A massive 61,550 crowd watched Sunderland win 2–1, with Milburn getting United's goal after moving back into the middle. It was a dismal show, and the team had to lift itself or face another quick Cup exit. In the replayed Cup tie with Forest, it looked as though Newcastle had shrugged off that Sunderland beating when they went into a 2–0 lead at half time with goals from Mitchell and Keeble. Forest clawed their way back to level the game, sending it into a goalless extra time. Having already decided that the next venue would be chosen by the spin of a coin, Forest chairman Jack Brentnall spun a half-crown, Stan Seymour shouted 'heads' and kept the tie at the Gallowgate ground.

United shuffled their forward line around yet again for the second replay, bringing in Alan Monkhouse at centre-forward; switching Milburn to inside-left; and bringing in Casey and Hannah to replace Broadis and Keeble. Monkhouse more than paid his way by scoring the two goals that beat Forest 2–1. But it was Milburn's match as he wandered across the park, the complete footballer, emerging to torment defenders with devastating bursts of speed as he laid on both goals.

A shattered Forest centre-half, McKinley, said after the match: 'My only worry about these games was that Newcastle would play Jackie Milburn at centre-forward.' Forest captain Tom Wilson agreed: 'Only one man beat us, and he is Milburn.' A heading in the following day's *Newcastle Journal* confirmed: 'Milburn United Scrape Through'.

The Nottingham manager, Billy Walker, was convinced that Newcastle United had played with twelve men: 'They must have had a good-luck fairy in their side! Never in my life have I known a team carry as much luck as Newcastle have done against us. We have all used the saying "third-time lucky", but it baffles imagination that a team can be so third-time lucky as United were after being so first-and-second-time lucky against us.'

The Newcastle board was very lucky, with the total attendence at the two Cup ties at Newcastle being over 75,000, paying £11,500 to get through the turnstiles. Newcastle players collected £12 each for the three Forest matches, which had lasted a total of 330 minutes.

With the sixth-round tie at Huddersfield only days away, Newcastle's manager was still undecided about the team's format. 'I prefer to watch the men in training another day or two before choosing the cup team.' Joe Harvey, returning from a spying mission on which he had seen Huddersfield lose 4–0 to Preston, reported: 'If that Huddersfield form is true, Newcastle should win well; but I have my doubts.'

Newcastle again made Blackpool's Norbreck Hotel their base before the match, availing themselves of the soothing waters of the hydro and the bracing greens of the golf course. Ex-pitman Len White playing only the second game of golf in his life, joked: 'I'm playing a lot better now that I've taken the wrapper off the ball!' The night before the game, the players went to Blackpool Tower to watch a boxing match.

Huddersfield, who had lost their last five League matches, faced yet another changed United forward line: White, Broadis, Keeble, Milburn and Mitchell. Once more the Tyneside team looked thoroughly beaten, trailing 1–0 until Milburn teed one up for a gleeful Len White to drive home and book Newcastle's ticket for another replay. Two north-eastern teams had already claimed their semi-final places: Sunderland, beating Wolves 2–0, and Third Division York, winning with the only goal of the game against Notts County. Manchester City made up the trio waiting to see who would complete the semi-final quartet.

Newcastle, dangerously close to the bottom of the League, still attracted 52,380 supporters to see them get the better of Huddersfield at the second attempt. Both goals in a 2–0 victory were scored during extra time, Mitchell scoring the first before Keeble made sure of that vacant semi-final place.

The draw kept the two big north-eastern clubs apart, kindling hopes of a Newcastle *v* Sunderland final. United's game against York, at Hillsborough, looked the easier game to forecast, but Sunderland, near the top of the table, were made joint favourites in the betting: 2–1 Sunderland; 2–1 Newcastle; 9–4 Manchester City; 14–1 York.

Tickets for the semi against York went on sale at 5 p.m. on Tuesday 22 March, and touts were soon selling half-crown tickets for £1. Mrs Nellie Storer was the first to arrive, at 7.30 a.m. She was met by a snowstorm and a fleet of hot-dog sellers who did brisk business throughout the day. As the time drew near to open the turnstiles, men arriving from work took over from their wives, many of whom had endured a four-hour blizzard.

Newcastle went back to the Golden Mile at Blackpool prior to their semi-final, combining training with pleasure. After emerging from a variety show, Charlie Crowe was hustled to the phone to hear that his wife, Ruth, had presented him with twin boys, Charles and Simon. An excited Charlie, catching up with the rest of the team, cigarette in mouth, did an impression of Jimmy James, much to the amusement of the real Mr James who was chatting to Stan Seymour.

Maintaining their dubious record of drawing all their semi-final matches at Hillsborough, Newcastle scraped a 1–1 draw with York, Vic Keeble getting the all-important goal which took the tie to Roker Park. Ahead from the third minute, United made no mistake in the replay, running out 2–0 victors with White and Keeble scoring the goals. There was a price to pay: Jackie Milburn – ever present in Cup games – pulled a groin muscle and was sidelined for a fortnight.

Newcastle was now faced with a massive backlog of matches and a daunting ten games in twenty-three days. Even with Milburn out of the side they began to get back into a rhythm, beating Everton 2–1 and sentencing Sheffield Wednesday to a swift return to the lower division with a 5–0 hammering. Over the Easter period the Geordie side recorded their first treble since 1907 when they again beat Everton, winning 4–0, with two goals apiece from Mitchell and Milburn, now fully fit and restored to the centre-forward role. That brace notched up Jackie's eighteenth goal of the season, thirteen of which had been scored from the wing.

Jackie was stood down for a game against Chelsea, as Livingstone persisted with his experimentation process. 'We shall make changes regularly over the coming rush of matches,' he said, 'in order to give men a rest and to seek the most effective line-up for Wembley.'

In effect, what the manager was doing was creating uncertainty in the minds of all the players, none of whom knew if his name would be on the team-sheet for any given match. Gone was the comfort and self-assurance enjoyed in 1951, with each man guaranteed a definite place in the Final. It was a recipe for suspicion and unrest within a side which had once thrived on its camaraderie.

With Wembley only two weeks away, a decision was reached by the Players' Union that a petition be placed before the next Football Association and League meeting. Signed by 2500 players from the ninety-two clubs, it voiced disapproval of the present contract whereby:

Above: Just off-target against Arsenal at Highbury

Left: Some famous Arsenal names faced United in 1952 Final

Below: Another Newcastle celebration as United bring the Cup back home

Half-time, Johannesburg style, as Stan Seymour and Jackie talk tactics during the 1952 tour of South Africa

Cup mania again as United fans clamour for tickets for United *v* Huddersfield, sixth round tie in 1955

The making of a legend! The 45-second goal against Manchester City in 1955. It's still a record in a Wembley Cup Final

Jimmy Scoular's turn this time to hold the Cup aloft. Trainer Norman Smith takes the fans' salute in preference to manager Livingstone

A rueful Charlie Crowe eyes the Cup that cheers

With Don Revie standing next to him, Jackie Milburn lines up for his last international against Denmark in 1956

Jackie signs his autobiography *Golden Goals* for three Newcastle schoolgirls in November 1957

Left: The Milburn family move to Hollywood ... Northern Ireland

Below: Windsor Park saw Jackie score some memorable goals for Linfield in his three seasons as player/coach

Malcolm Brodie of the *Belfast Telegraph* types Jackie's Linfield resignation, in 1959

Between jobs, Jackie watches Newcastle play in 1960. Far left is a 15-year-old Bobby Moncur, later to captain United and Scotland

Ladies in waiting, Cissie Charlton, Nance and Laura Milburn, before Jackie's Testimonial game in 1967

Ashington packs its backstreets for the Charlton brothers in July 1966

Harvey, Crowe and Milburn tread the fitness trail again in 1967

Old pals, Joe Smith and Raymond Poxton, share Eamonn's secret as Jackie is caught on 'This is Your Life' in 1981

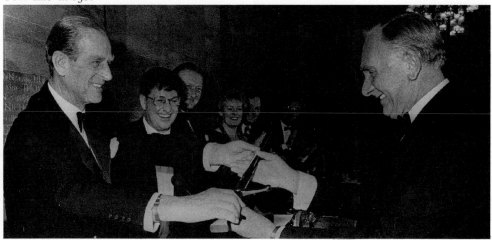

One of many honours for Jackie later in life was this handsome sword presented by the Duke of Edinburgh

Always first in with his copy, Jackie was a *News of the World* journalist for twenty-three years

Milburn and Harvey reflect on: 'What happened to the lads who chased a dream?'

Every game was a giggle for Jackie Milburn and a whistling Bobby Cowell, including this relaxed charity match at Rothbury in 1965

March 1988, and it's the last shift at Ashington colliery. Ex-pitman Jackie Milburn is on hand to share a joke and a few memories

The Football League clubs are permitted to retain our services by offering a retaining wage of £332 per year. In addition, they can, without offering a wage, place us on the open-to-transfer list at a fee unknown, and until this fee is paid we are unable to play for a Football League club. The present system should be abolished. Players should enjoy the same freedom to earn as much as possible and freedom to change our club when our contract expires.'

In reply, F. Howarth, secretary of the Football League, stated: 'It would ruin the League competition if players were able to go where they liked without restraint at the end of their contract.' He pointed out that the Ministry of Labour Committee in 1951, had expressed their opinion in favour of the League on that issue.

On the same day, still attempting to safeguard his own future, thirty-one-year-old Jackie Milburn acquired a twenty-nine-seater luxury coach, christened the 'Ashington Flyer', which he later used in the private-hire business.

Back in the League, Newcastle played a Blackpool side which had trounced United's Cup opponents Manchester City 6–1 the previous week. Ivor Broadis was brought into the side, which ostensibly gave him a last-minute chance to gain a Cup Final place. Broadis already knew, however, that he had no chance of playing in the Final. He had been in the club office and had chanced to glimpse a paper lying on secretary Ted Hall's desk. It was headed: 'Open-to Transfer', and at the top of a list of names was 'Ivor Broadis'.

The match against Blackpool was drawn 1–1, but the fans were more interested in the postcards which were distributed at the turnstiles. Once filled in with names and addresses, the cards were to be used in a massive lottery to decide who was to get Cup Final tickets. If that was to prove an administrative pain for the board, it was nothing to the headache the players gave them as they trooped off the St James's pitch after the final whistle. They demanded a substantial increase in their personal allocation of Cup Final tickets.

On Tuesday 26 April, the headline on the front page of the *Newcastle Journal* announced: 'Directors Say: Press Your Demands and We Play Reserve Side at Wembley'. Hadn't we heard that threat before?

The board met the night before and decided to issue the ultimatum to the players who were trying to sidestep a Football Association ruling that only twelve tickets be allocated to players. What exacerbated the issue was the appearance of a column in a Sunday newspaper stating that Manchester City players would receive between forty and fifty tickets. The FA stipulation had been a direct result of an enquiry held in 1952 concerning the distribution of Cup Final tickets by Newcastle United and Arsenal.

As in 1951 and '52, Newcastle United had another eve-of-Final crisis to overcome, but even the ticket issue was nothing to what had been happening behind closed doors at Gallowgate. Livingstone had chosen his Cup Final team and presented it to the board ten days before the game. There was uproar from the directors when it was noticed that the name of Milburn was *not* included! The manager's chosen forward line read: White, Davies, Keeble, Hannah, Mitchell. If

Livingstone's stock had ever reached any great heights within the boardroom, it definitely fell far below zero with his proposal to send a Newcastle United team to Wembley without Jackie Milburn.

The whole episode highlighted the folly of bringing in someone from outside the region to manage a club where tradition prevails, even to the exclusion of rational common sense. Without the benefit of first-hand knowledge of what makes the North-East a 'hotbed of soccer', an outsider could never hope to get the necessary 'feel' of what was right and what was not even worth considering. Obviously Livingstone wasn't aware of the combustible nature of a Milburn and a Newcastle United mixed in the right proportions. If he did know, and still dropped Milburn, then it was a grievous fault, and grievously was he made to pay for it. His team selection was summarily despatched to the waste-paper basket, and within forty-eight hours Livingstone himself was banished from his own office into the cubby hole set aside for match-day referees.

CHAPTER THIRTEEN

1955
Cup Final, it was like playing at home

In an article written the week before the final for the *Journal*, Ivor Broadis, in a sombre mood, stated: 'Come mid-summer, I shall no longer be a Newcastle United player. I have been informed by Mr Livingstone that I am on the transfer list. That's football! At the season's end, you are either "retained" or you're "for transfer". I am for transfer – it's as simple as that!'

No mention was made to the press about the possible omission of Milburn, and as the team left for Brighton prior to the last game of the season at White Hart Lane, the following Cup Final team was announced: Simpson, Cowell, Batty, Scoular, Stokoe, Crowe, Milburn, Davies, Keeble, Hannah, Mitchell. Len White was chosen as travelling reserve. Jimmy Scoular, by now reinstated to the club captaincy, made a statement the same day: 'We have accepted twelve tickets, under protest.'

The Tottenham manager, Arthur Rowe, with the London club still needing one point to avoid relegation, dropped full-back Alf Ramsey in favour of Charlie Withers for the game against Newcastle. In a poor match which saw the Geordies slow hand-clapped for operating an off-side policy, Spurs won 2–1, playing against only ten men after Crowe was taken off in the first half after falling awkwardly in a tackle with Harry Clarke.

Brighton physio and masseur Sam Cowan, attached to the Sussex County Cricket Club, was enlisted to treat Charlie Crowe's badly twisted ankle. But on the Wednesday of Cup Final week it was decided to send for Tom Casey to join the party at the Royal Albion Hotel in Brighton. Crowe recalls:

On the Friday morning, the ankle was still very stiff and puffy. Stan Seymour asked me for a decision by mid afternoon. After turning and kicking the ball, Norman Smith said to me: 'It's not right, is it, Charlie?' It was then that Jackie Milburn whispered: 'You can still play, Charlie. Me and the rest of the lads will "carry" you if you break down.' But I knew it wasn't right, and told Seymour.

Apart from the debate about Crowe, further drama was enacted when Reg Davies came back from watching Brighton play Aldershot on the Wednesday night, looking very flushed and obviously running a temperature. A local GP was called in and diagnosed laryngitis. A thermometer confirmed a temperature of 102, and poor Reg was immediately confined to his bed. Next day it was announced that Len White would play outside-right at Wembley, with Jackie Milburn switching to inside-right. White, so disappointed at being dropped from Livingstone's original selection, didn't know whether to be elated at getting into the team or sorry for Davies missing out at the last minute.

Don Revie, Manchester City's centre-forward, was awarded 'Footballer of the Year' on the Thursday night. He paid tribute to his team-mates: 'Without their help I would not be here, and though Manchester City football has been called the "Revie Plan", it is the plan of all the lads.'

Eleven Newcastle United wives and one girlfriend – Casey wasn't married – left to spend the Friday night in London. They were in good company: 15,000 Geordies followed their team to Wembley, 9000 of them by rail, among them Matty Heslop of Gateshead sporting an eighteen-inch black and white topper decorated with photographs of all the players.

Laura Milburn was the first of the players' wives off the train at King's Cross, and when asked to predict the result she tipped Newcastle to win 3–1. Bobby Mitchell's wife was taking no chances and carried a lucky piece of coal in her handbag, while Elsie Cowell stuck with her familiar Cornish Pixie. 'It's brought me luck so far,' she said. The women were all booked into the Wyndham Theatre to see Sandy Wilson's *Boy Friend*, and had Saturday morning free to do some shopping in London's West End.

The Newcastle players had been invited by the BBC to take part in a live broadcast on the eve of the Final, but Livingstone cancelled, saying: 'I find that some of our players tend to be made very nervous over the television process.' A fee of £25 had been arranged to *share* among the players. Various Newcastle United members gave last-minute quotes to the national press:

Stan Seymour:	'At Wembley we will put the hat-trick seal on five wonderful years.'
Jackie Milburn:	'It seems like playing a tie at home!'
Bobby Mitchell:	'We've drawn the south dressing-room – we came from there to start all this against Blackpool, and we will finish the job.'

Bobby Cowell: 'We've been non-favourites in the last two Final wins, and Manchester City carry the extra weight tomorrow.'

At Newcastle airport on the morning of the match there was a Wembley airlift, with two Dakotas and a Viking taking off carrying 104 fans, all of them convinced that the name of Newcastle was inexorably linked to Wembley: it was where Newcastle went to *win* the Cup! As the planes taxied up the runway, the weather forecast for the London area was issued by the Air Ministry: more sunshine and blue skies.

At ten minutes to three on Saturday 7 May 1955, the following teams lined up to be presented to Prince Philip, who at one time had commanded the frigate *Magpie*: Manchester City – Trautman, Meadows, Little, Barnes, Ewing, Paul, Spurdle, Hayes, Revie, Johnstone, Fagan; Newcastle United – Simpson, Cowell, Batty, Scoular, Stokoe, Casey, White, Milburn, Keeble, Hannah, Mitchell.

As a match the 1955 Cup Final was very nearly a fiasco for the 100,000 spectators, despite four great goals. The game flared immediately when Jackie Milburn, left completely unguarded, flicked his head at a Len White corner kick, the ball whipped past Bert Trautman's upstretched left arm, dipped under the crossbar, and Newcastle United had as good as won the Cup in only 45 seconds! After this unforgettable start ('I'll not wash my hair till August') and having made his point, Jackie Milburn was never seen in the game.

As a spectacle the Final was spoilt when, in the eighteenth minute, at precisely the same time and spot as Wally Barnes had been injured in 1952, Jimmy Meadows, chasing the ghost of Bobby Mitchell, over-reached himself and wrenched his knee and lower-leg ligaments, sustaining an injury which was to put him in plaster for six weeks.

In an open-air meeting at Greenside, County Durham, Clement Attlee was stopped in mid-speech by a fan enquiring the score: 'One nil so far – let's hope they keep it up,' was the Labour leader's jovial reply.

The ten men of City equalised just before the interval when Johnstone headed in a short pass from Hayes. The half-time whistle went with only one team playing cultured, stylish football; that team was Manchester City. And yet by the fifty-eighth minute the game was all over bar the shouting, United having taken the lead with a goal from an impossible angle scored by Mitchell, followed by another from George Hannah. Playing the game at walking pace after that, United bored the crowd by inter-passing for minutes on end, keeping close possession until bursting goalwards, testing the German goalkeeper who did well to keep the score down to 3–1.

Back on Tyneside the Newcastle streets, which had been absolutely deserted for an hour and a half, suddenly burst into life as people streamed out on to the pavements, waving black and white flags and shouting greetings to each other. It was Newcastle United's first TV Final, and fans had been glued to their chairs in front of new sets bought specially for the occasion. Poor unfortunates in north

Northumberland, served by the Kirk o' Shotts transmitter, had to make do with a televised Scottish cricket match!

After the match the Queen turned to Stan Seymour and said: 'You've broken a record, haven't you?' Indeed, Newcastle United's three Wembley wins of the fifties made wondrous soccer history. In winning the 1955 Final they became the only team to win at Wembley on every occasion they'd been there and the first to play in ten FA Cup Finals, and equalled the record of Blackburn and Aston Villa in winning their sixth Final. Jackie Milburn's headed goal created yet another record: it was – and still is – the quickest goal ever scored in a Wembley Final. It was that one goal which made Newcastle the glamour club of the post-war years and created a golden moment for its scorer. If anything in life is certain, that unexpected header – as rare as a black diamond – was one of the prime factors in the creation of the legend that is 'Wor Jackie'.

That night the Newcastle party celebrated in style once more at the Savoy Hotel, dining on salmon, steak, asparagus, and soufflé Surprise Vulcan. Just after midnight the first train bringing elated supporters back to Northumberland arrived at Ashington railway station. On his way to work in foreshift, a miner, bait-tin dangling from his leather belt, shouted across the road to one of the emerging fans: 'Had a canny day, Geordie?' A burly man, swathed in black and white rosettes, replied: 'One of the best, marra – one of the best!'

On the Sunday morning, the Newcastle players and their wives were under siege in the Great Northern Hotel. It seemed as though every pressman in London wanted a quote. A *Women's World* correspondent managed to get exclusives from a female point of view. 'Next year I hope the Queen might be asked to make the presentation out in the middle of the field,' said an optimistic Laura Milburn. 'What a thrill if the wives could be there too. That would be worth the trip!' 'It's not even as if husbands tell us anything about it,' said Jean Stokoe. 'They're hopeless!' Elsie Cowell had a special reason for wanting United to win the Cup. 'We have three children and we have two Cup-winners' medals. I wanted to be able to take home a third this weekend for the other child.' As usual, it was Jackie Milburn who was given the last word: 'The wife has collected so many parcels doing her shopping that we'll have to chuck the strips out of Norman Smith's skip and use that!'

It was 'Sunday Night at the London Palladium' as the world-renowned theatre played host to both Cup Final teams. In a show which lasted four and a half hours, entertainment was provided by: Tommy Trinder, Max Bygraves, Alma Cogan, Dickie Valentine and Jimmy Wheeler. The long night ended with the blushing Geordies being cheered from pits to gods as they spun around on the giant turntable on the stage. In an era when the adventurous spirit was so often stifled, this was to be the last great successful quest for this particular Newcastle United team.

In monetary terms Newcastle collected £8000 from Wembley's £49,881 gate money, and £25,000 from the full 1954/55 Cup series. Chairman Stan Seymour announced: 'We shall ask the Football Association for permission to make a special gift to our players to mark the records they have established.'

The last time we won the Cup in 1955 they had a do in the Oxford Galleries for us – a Cup Final dance. Everybody was there. We were told to take the wives. The place was packed. At the interval, everything was stopped. The football club were making a presentation to the players' wives.

They went up in rotation to get their presents, which were handbags! Of course, you know how handbags are full of paper on the inside to make them look full. Whey, when everyone was coming back they were howking away inside the bags – there wasn't a bloody thing in any of 'em!

As a matter of fact, when George Hannah's wife was coming off the stage the bloody handle came off her bag. Ask the wife – she'll tell you. We discovered, within the next couple of days that Newcastle (this was wor present for winning a Cup Final) had bought a job-lot of handbags for seventeen pounds! And that was what we got for winning the Cup. Oh, it's unbelievable! We never got a penny. The lads never forgave the club for that!

Here, Jackie's memory had let him down: it was after the 1951 Final that the handbags came out. Their reward for winning the '55 Final was a bon-bon dish, silver plated! The nature of the trinket itself is immaterial; it was the final bitter insult. Milburn and the rest of the players were sick. Never had a team done so much and finished with so little.

We won three Cup Finals: '51, '52, and '55. We were promised the moon by Stan Seymour: 'You win, lads, and you'll get the groceries' – the usual! We never ever got a single penny, and my total wages for winning three Cup Finals – with the tax paid – was £73 16s. That's for winning three! Three Cup Finals! Whereas now they're on ten thousand a man, or something like that.

When I started to play for Newcastle the basic wage was £8 in summer and £10 during the season; then it was £10 and £12. And you had £2 for a win and £1 for a draw. In the England team you got £20 for turning out. There was no bust-up over money till the George Eastham affair. I wish it had happened sooner.

At the end of the 1954/55 season Newcastle finished in eighth place in the League, and Milburn and Mitchell shared top honours for scoring the most goals with nineteen each. Mitch's nineteen strikes from the wing beat the previous club record held by Stan Seymour.

The now familiar welcome accorded to the victorious team on their return to Newcastle was described by Jackie in his weekly column for the *Sunday Sun*:

The Welcome Home was terrific! It was a bit embarrassing for us, but it was very heartwarming. I have never heard so much noise in my life. Like myself, you supporters are *fanatics*. This has been the queerest season that the Magpies have had since I joined them in August 1943! It certainly has been a season of contrasts, and in a way we are pleased it is over till August.

Bob Cowell, Mitch and myself have set a record of winning three FA Cup-winners' medals with the one team, and we are forever grateful to all our colleagues who have helped us. We three are very lucky and very proud.

Newcastle's United were successful in the 1950s because they were the team with the big-time experience. Tom Whittaker, manager of Arsenal, in a telegram to the Cup winners, saluted their exploits: 'Congratulations on a magnificent performance: a feat we will never see equalled again in our lifetime.'

CHAPTER FOURTEEN

Things were never the same after Joe Harvey left

The Newcastle board had arranged for a ten-day close-season tour of Germany, but when news was flashed around the world that United had won the Cup yet again, Brazil stepped in with an offer to accommodate the Geordies. But it was too late to change plans already made, and the Newcastle party took off from Woolsington Airport on 23 May, bound for Hamburg. The first public indication that friction existed between board and manager came when it was noticed that Dougald Livingstone was not travelling abroad with the team.

At Hamburg they were met by their German interpreter, Wolfgang. It transpired that Wolfgang – now nicknamed Wilf – had been a prisoner of war at Gilsland in Northumberland, staying on until 1953. Whenever he was asked a question by one of the Geordies, his stock answer was: 'Whey aye, man'. While confined in the Russian embassy waiting for visas which would enable the party to travel across the various zones, Cowell and Simpson amused themselves – and intrigued the Ruskies – by having a quick game of pitch 'n' toss.

The first game of the tour was won 3–2 against a Berlin eleven, with Milburn getting two goals and Keeble one. The match turned into a bit of a rough-house, but that was nothing compared with their next game against Nuremburg. It was to be a game of personal tragedy for three-time medallist Bobby Cowell. Indirectly, the blame could be laid on Newcastle's captain, Jimmy Scoular, who had a running battle throughout the game with the German left-half, Uckow. So frustrated was the German at the treatment meted out by hard-man Scoular – his boast was that he never started anything but always finished it – that during a stoppage when

Bobby was arranging a 'wall' for Ronnie Simpson, Uckow jumped with both feet at the Newcastle full-back's calf, causing the Newcastle man to be carried off the field.

Lying in agony in his hotel bedroom, leg in plaster, Bobby was visited by a furtive Jackie Milburn carrying a large bottle of brandy. 'It's to ease the pain, Bob,' said non-drinker Jackie. 'And to help you to get to sleep!' Early in the morning Norman Smith arrived, to find the pair rolling drunk. It was the last laugh that Cowell and Milburn would share together as team-mates, for the thirty-three-year-old County Durham lad never kicked a ball again, for United or anyone else.

After that, no one was interested in the remnants of a tour in which four games were played: two won, two lost. The team arrived back with about four weeks remaining before training was due to begin. Jackie Milburn chucked his boots in the garage and drove out in his motor coach in search of business. That was the theory, anyway, although what normally happened was that he ended up chauffeuring the entire United team around the countryside of Northumberland, usually ending up in Seahouses where the Milburns had a caravan parked in a farmyard.

By mid July manager Livingstone, still living in a city hotel, knew his fate when the house he had been promised – vacated by Ivor Broadis who had been transferred to Carlisle – was given to Bob Stokoe and his wife. Not long afterwards, chairman Wilf Taylor gave a press conference and stated: 'Newcastle United and Dougald Livingstone have parted by mutual consent – and that's all there is to it.' Livingstone was a little more frank: 'The real reason why I have left Newcastle,' he said, 'is that since United won the Cup last May, duties have been taken away from me until there was nothing left for me to do. It began four days after the Cup Final when I was told I would no longer select the Newcastle team.' Livingstone, who had been on a £1500 salary, still had almost two years of his contract to run. No mention was made of compensation.

Club stalwart Joe Harvey also packed his bags, and left to take a £1250 per year manager's job at Barrow. Seymour had reservations: 'I cannot dispute Harvey's feeling that it is a chance to gain valuable experience; he will receive full benefit on the condition that he does *not* play again.' Joe had already requested moves – in 1951 to manage Carlisle, and in 1953 when he was Workington's first choice. Both requests had been turned down. Newcastle were without a club manager once again but, as in the past, Stan Seymour took the reins and the title of director/manager. One of his first duties was to drop Frank Brennan's wages from the maximum £15 a week down to £8. Brennan had played only six League matches in the previous season. Later that year, big Frank moved into the North Eastern League with North Shields.

Milburn, who started the season at outside-right, was moved into the middle for the Charity Shield match with League champions Chelsea. Only 12,802 people were interested enough to watch the home side win 3–0. Jackie gave a great individual performance, prompting Ken McKenzie of the *Journal* to describe him as 'a giant among pygmies'. Seymour, after having seen his side lose their third

126

Charity Shield match in a row, stated: 'These affairs should be done away with. The small crowd showed what they thought of the fixture.'

Jackie continued to play well, and in a home game with Charlton scored a fine hat-trick, giving notice to England selectors that the time was ripe for a recall to the national scene. That same day, 17 September, a twenty-year-old from Grove Hill, Brian Clough, made his centre-forward debut for Middlesbrough in a 1–1 draw against Barnsley.

Milburn's excellent showing in London had obviously not gone unnoticed, and the following week club secretary Ted Hall was banging on the Milburn front door. 'Pack your bags, Jackie,' he said. 'You are playing for England in a practice match tomorrow night at Tottenham.' Hall then rang Stan Seymour from Jackie's house to tell him the news: 'Jackie is to take injured Stan Matthews' place against Denmark next Sunday in Copenhagen.' The immediate reaction from Jackie was: 'A wonderful piece of luck for me! I'm quite happy regarding playing outside-right, either for England or Newcastle, and only hope this first international of the season proves successful.' England players had recently had a pay rise from £20 to £50 a match.

In Copenhagen on 2 October, just before the game got under way, Ebbe Schwartz of the Danish Football Federation said: 'We hope to lose gracefully.' The England team was: Baynham, Hall, Byrne, Clayton, Wright, Dickinson, Milburn, Revie, Lofthouse, Bradford, Finney. England won convincingly 5–1, with Revie and Lofthouse scoring two goals apiece and Bradford getting the fifth. It was an outstanding display by Revie, who masterminded the England victory. Milburn, in spite of moving into the middle late in the game, had left his shooting boots at home, and some of his strikes at goal were wild and desperate. In a game in which he had wanted to do so well, Jackie Milburn, who had exploded on to the international scene in 1948, ended his England career eight years later, going out not with a bang, but a whisper.

Bob Stokoe remarked: 'I believe Jackie finished off with thirteen caps, and we have to appreciate that there weren't as many international games in those days as there are now. But that was nowhere near what his particular career had deserved. Walter Winterbottom was in charge of the England team, and we *were* in Newcastle, which everyone else in football thought was in Scotland!'

England's long-serving captain Billy Wright, who played with Jackie on several occasions commented:

His personality was good. He was very quiet, very shy, but once you got to know him he'd got a bit of devil in him. Underneath he was a typical Geordie. He fitted in well – it was difficult. He came in when you had the stars: the Swifts, the Lawtons, Mannion, Matthews, Finney. When you played with the stars you gave them the ball and then let them get on with it. And so Jackie, playing for Newcastle United, didn't have that cos he was playing with a team. When you came to England you had to try to give your team game, like when you were playing for

Newcastle. But it was very different when you were playing with stars, and I think Jackie found that a bit difficult.

Newcastle completed a marvellous Christmas programme, taking maximum points from three games to move up to sixth place in a League table currently led by Manchester United. Best of the Tyneside Yuletide presents had to be United's 6–1 thrashing of Sunderland. With the Magpies easing off in the second half, Jackie Milburn went berserk with his team-mates, urging them to 'remember the 9–1'. He was referring to a record 9–1 defeat at the hands of the Wearsiders in 1908.

But again it was the narrow focus on Wembley's twin towers as Newcastle faced Sheffield Wednesday in the third round at Hillsborough. United shared in another record by taking part in a floodlit Cup tie – the first to be played in the history of the FA Cup. Wednesday dressed up for the occasion in shiny satin blue shirts with white collars and sleeves. The Magpies kept it simple, wearing a white shirt and black shorts. Despite standing top of Division Two, the Sheffield side wilted under the bright lights and United ran out 3–1 winners, Jackie getting one of the goals.

When the draw for the fourth round was known – Fulham away – Newcastle were installed as 14 to 1 third favourites. The game was due to be played on 28 January, but only days beforehand Bobby Cowell was told what he had refused to believe for the last six months: that he would never play again. The sickening news came as no surprise to Stan Seymour: 'We had known all along that Cowell would not play again, but felt that the realisation would be easier for him if it came gradually. Bobby is on full money for the rest of the season, and before he is off the Newcastle payroll he will have good reason to feel confident regarding his future.' Later that year Cowell was given a testimonial match at St James's Park, the proceeds of which amounted to just over £4000. The Cowells used over half of this to buy the United club house they were living in, and then Elsie and Bob began looking for work.

Two days before the Fulham Cup tie, the cockney club's director, Tommy Trinder, was in fine form. Wearing a black and white strip with a slogan saying 'You Lucky People' on the back, he quipped: 'I wear this in one of my sketches – it gets a lot of laughs. We hope to rise to the occasion, and all our lads vow they can. Our inside-right, Bobby Robson, has a double incentive to play a blinder – he comes from Durham, you know.' Relaxing at Brighton, young Robson, a Geordie who had been snatched by Fulham from Langley Moor Juniors, was trying to get over an injury problem: 'I feel nearly sure I can make it in time. Sure, I'll take a risk – wouldn't you, if you came from less than twenty miles from Newcastle and had a chance to play against the Cup holders?'

Fulham, fielding youngsters Bobby Robson, Johnny Haynes and Jimmy Hill in their forward line, were hit by three United goals in forty minutes, the first a fifteen-yard strike from Milburn. Chamberlain (3) and Hill (1) replied as the London team fought back to lead 4–3. The ungainly Keeble ('You couldn't bend a piece of wire that shape,' joked Brennan) charged Fulham goalkeeper Black over the line for the equaliser, then headed in the winner with less than ten minutes to go, making the final score an incredible 5–4 in the Magpies' favour.

Newcastle played Second Division Stoke city in the fifth round, and in front of 61,540 fans won the match 2–1 with goals from Mitchell and a young Bill Curry, who had played only a handful of games for United. Newcastle and Sunderland were paired for the next round – the first Cup meeting between the two Geordie rivals since before the First World War.

Before then Fred Howarth, Football League secretary, gave the news that the Football Association Council had decided to pay 4 per cent of the net receipts of all international games played in England to the players' Provident Fund. 'We now have every expectation that we shall get back to 10 per cent of players' earnings given to players on retirement from football. We have never had any pleasure in reducing the percentage.' The Football League, giving the excuse of 'falling gates' and 'rising costs', had made two reductions: first to 9 per cent, and in the current season to 7½ per cent, in the scheme which had guaranteed retiring players a set sum since the Fund had been established in 1949.

For the Sunderland Cup tie at St James's Park, Newcastle, who were now the bookies' Cup favourites at 4 to 1, fielded: Simpson, Batty, McMichael, Stokoe, Paterson, Scoular, Milburn, Davies, Keeble, Curry, Mitchell. Referee R. H. Mann of Worcester had a ticket problem: 'I wrote to Newcastle United asking for a ticket for my fiancée, but had not received a reply before leaving home,' he complained. British Railways and both clubs advised the 61,500 who did have tickets to get to the ground on time.

Many supporters didn't bother going to the ground: they headed straight for nearby Leazes Terrace and clambered upon tiled roofs to get a better view. What they saw was an inept Newcastle display which culminated in a 2–0 win for Sunderland. Milburn and Mitchell, joint top scorers the season before, were crowded and harried, clipping the Magpies' wings and leaving the Wearsiders flying high into the semi-finals. No Newcastle solace was drawn when Sunderland lost their chance of a 1956 Cup final place, beaten 3–0 by Birmingham.

Jackie Milburn's season, which had started so badly with the departure of close ally Joe Harvey, and then promised so much with selection for the England team, ended as miserably as it had begun with Newcastle losing nine of their last ten games. Vic Keeble took over Milburn's mantle as King of Newcastle United's goal-scorers with twenty-six goals, while Jackie, giving serious thought to retirement, decided to risk another season.

The season 1956/57 was never going Jackie Milburn's way, and he was overshadowed by young part-timer, Alec Tait, who scored a hat-trick in a 6–2 defeat over Sunderland. It was again Tait who took Milburn's place in a pulsating third-round Cup-tie replay with Manchester City, the Bedlington youngster scoring a Milburn-type special, beating off four defenders in a run which took him from way inside his own half, before beating Trautman with a superb shot.

Newcastle won that game 5–4, but gave best to Millwall at the Den in the next round. That early Cup knock-out all but finished United's season, and they narrowly avoided relegation in seventeenth position. Again Jackie's name did not figure as top scorer, the honour going to Reg Davies with thirteen goals, this meagre total factual proof of the Magpies lack of goal-scoring power.

Bob Stokoe reflected: 'Jackie hadn't been doing very well – the team hadn't. Players like Lennie White, Vic Keeble and others had come into the club and were beginning to score goals, and Jackie's goals had sort of dried up a little bit. And in the end, I think he just got to the stage when he had to get away.'

CHAPTER FIFTEEN

OK Ireland. You win – I'll stay forever

On 13 June 1957 the unthinkable happened: Newcastle agreed to let Jackie Milburn go as player/manager to Irish team Linfield. When the news was announced in the press, there was an 'ah-yes-we've-heard-this-one-before-but-it-will-soon-blow-over' attitude from the Geordie public. Hadn't he been going to London in 1948? Didn't Hunslet, that Rugby League team, offer him £3000 to play with the funny-shaped ball in 1951? Wasn't it Lord Westwood who, had asked clubs to start bidding at £30,000 in 1952? And hadn't it been Sunderland, in 1953, who had almost done the impossible by getting Jackie to change his black and white strip for a red and white variety? Oh, no – this was all the same load of rubbish!

The first person to know that Jackie really was leaving Newcastle United wasn't even in football at all; he was in the Army! Ashingtonian Ray Brotherton was doing his national service in Belfast when Newcastle came across the Irish Sea to play in a friendly match at Windsor Park, home of Linfield. As Jackie ran out on to the pitch that day, Ray and a gang of other Geordies shouted across to him: 'Howway Jackie, show them waat you can dee.' Recognising the Geordie dialect, Jackie came over to the soldiers, shook their hands, and told them to hang around after the game so that he could have a chat. True to his word, Milburn emerged later and immediately invited the lads to have a look around Windsor Park. As his guided tour was ending, Jackie turned to his fellow Geordies and said: 'It's a great place, isn't it. Don't tell anybody – but I'm going to sign on to play for Linfield next season.' Ray didn't keep the secret entirely to himself, but wrote and told his father. Said Ray: 'On the strength of that story, my father got more drinks in Ashington clubs than he'd ever had in his life!'

In spite of verifying that he was leaving, Jackie, as usual with two or three irons in the fire, almost backed out at the last minute. He was attending a training course that summer, which on its completion, would assure him a position as physical instructor with the local education authority. Said Jackie: 'I am a very lucky man to have the choice of two such good opportunities, but that doesn't make it any easier to decide.'

This wasn't the first time – nor would it be the last – that John Edward Thompson Milburn had had to make a crucial decision which would affect his entire future. A PE teaching appointment in the area, besides giving him a job for life, would afford him the opportunity of still playing part-time for Newcastle – if they were willing – and would also provide a pension when the time came for him to retire. But what had always been Jet Milburn's *raison d'être*?

. . . it was always football . . . I only ever knew one thing . . . it was football all the time with me . . . I knew nowt else.

But why Ireland? Jackie's Irish connection went all the way back to 1945. The first time he had scored with his head for United had been on a tour of Ireland, in a game against Linfield. His first representative game for England had been against the Irish League at Liverpool. Shortly afterwards had come his first full England cap; and, of course, it was at Windsor Park – home of Linfield – that he had scored his first goal for England.

Newcastle United had always found Ireland to be a very fruitful hunting ground in their search for talent. McMichael, Hannah and George Eastham had all been picked up for a relatively small outlay. It suited the Newcastle board to have 'their' man in charge of an Irish team, with immediate access to players from every club in Ireland. But what finally tipped the scales in Linfield's favour?

Money! Pure and simple! Quite honestly, that's all I went for. Plus the fact that the club had plumeted, and I was getting to the age . . . I felt there was too much responsibility on me shoulders. You had to score goals. And if they weren't coming, you were taking the can back. Things were never the same after Harvey left. You just felt . . . depressed and despondent. Things were never gonna get any better. Mebbe I was being a bit selfish thinking that way, but you felt the responsibility was far, far greater than it ever had been before. You just wanted to get out of it!

The papers were packed with it when I left. They were packed with angry letters and one thing and another, asking us to stay on. You see, we were earning fifteen quid a week. Linfield offered me twenty-five quid a week, and a thousand pound for signing on. Whey, I had never seen that sort of money! Plus the fact that when I was at St James's, we had a kid called Jimmy Coulter, came from Northern Ireland, from one of the lesser clubs – he got two thousand pounds for signing; George Eastham came across – he got money; George Hannah came – they reckon he got two thousand pounds. We had never seen that kind of money! And these lads were part-timers from Ireland, coming across and bragging about how much money they had in the bank.

You might think it's sour grapes, but it wasn't. If you've never seen that sort of money, what the hell do you do? So I just thought at the finish, the responsibility on me for scoring goals is getting a bit hard to bear; plus the fact I'm gonna be at least ten quid a week better off; I'm gonna have a thousand pounds in the bank, which I'd never had in me whole life, and you've got three kids. You're getting towards the end of your tether; at thirty-three years of age you don't know what's gonna happen in the future – cos the only thing I ever knew was football.

Linfield approached me – I didn't say nothing! They had come across and asked Newcastle about me. They asked for an interview, and when they said: 'We'll give you twenty-five quid a week and a thousand pound in your hand,' whey – I was gonna be a millionaire! Cos I had never had anything like that. And I was fifteen seasons at Newcastle. So I agreed immediately.

Jackie does himself less than justice by saying that money was the main reason he left Newcastle. Those who knew him well would readily confirm that he cared little for the tangible symbols of success. Like the rest of the United team of that era, he was never a great socialiser, content to stay in most nights with Laura and the kids. His pleasures were simple; reading Raymond Chandler novels; listening to Nat King Cole records; having sing-songs around the piano with the family, then listening to the songs played back on a tape recorder which had been given to him by an admirer. He had given away most of his mementoes. His Newcastle shirts had gone to charities for auction – that is, the ones that weren't commandeered by his father Alec, who had found them ideal for wearing down the pit – and his England strips went the same way. Indeed, one England number-nine shirt travelled the Atlantic to America. The thirteen England caps he had won were kept in a large hat-box, either under the bed or in the garage.

The second reason Jackie gives for leaving – his lack of goals and the attendant worry – is a more valid one. In his last season at Newcastle he had scored only twelve goals in thirty-two appearances. Apart from the 1952/53 season in which he underwent his cartilage operation, this was the least that Jackie had scored for United since the war. He found it difficult to come to terms with the critical crowd's reaction. He wasn't used to it:

I'd never had that before – never had any bollockings – and when it did happen, you didn't know how to react. I would rather have got into me shell and hid somewhere, or pretended I was injured!

But even the criticism and abuse which came his way towards the end of his playing days at Newcastle, together with the increased money he would be earning, in themselves would not have been sufficient to lure him from the little niche that he had carved for himself on Tyneside. There had to be another more fundamental reason, something which his genuine humility would not let him admit even to himself: Jackie Milburn, ex-coal miner, was ambitious! He knew that, at thirty-three, he couldn't have more than two or three seasons left as an efficient player, but wanted desperately to make good as a manager. He looked around him and saw many of his contemporaries doing well in managerial positions after hanging up their boots: his old mate Joe Harvey, now at Workington; Joe Mercer, now managing Aston Villa after a spell at Sheffield United; his ex-England team-mate Alf Ramsey, setting unfashionable Ipswich on fire. The list was impressive.

Little wonder, then, that Jackie thought the role of a manager was not beyond his reach. Hadn't he known managers at Newcastle who had come and gone because they weren't up to it? Perhaps if he served a five-year apprenticeship, just as he had at the colliery, then he would emerge with sufficient qualifications and experience to take over at St James's Park. The thoughts that rattled around in his head would have filled the Gallowgate End twice over!

There was bitterness in the parting, which was not apparent in Stan Seymour's comment in the *Daily Express* on 14 June: 'Right up to the last moment I was wishing Jackie would change his mind. He has been a Newcastle United player since he was nineteen, and always he has lived up to the great tradition of the club – a gentleman both on and off the field. If he does half as much for Linfield as he has done for Newcastle and England, nobody will have any regrets.'

Officially, the move was a straight player-exchange deal. Newcastle had been after Linfield inside-forward Jimmy Hill for two years. In 1956 Seymour had gone across to buy him, but had come back with George Eastham instead. Linfield secretary Joe Mackey said: 'There was no money involved – it was just a matter of swapping players.' This, in fact, was not true, but it was a proviso made by the Newcastle club that no information should be given to the press regarding fees involved. How would the Tyneside board look if it became known that they had placed an exhorbitant fee on the head of one of their most loyal servants? There was great sorrow when Jackie Milburn left Newcastle, but it would soon have turned to anger if the truth concerning the deal had been made official at the time.

The only trouble, the only thing I didn't like was the fact that Newcastle wanted a £10,000 transfer fee, which was taking all the money away from the club I was gonna manage, and a player in exchange – Jimmy Hill. They skint the club I was gonna manage! That riled me at the time: the fact that the club, Linfield, were on the bottom through having to pay this fee. Normally they were the best team in Ireland.

Jackie joined Linfield on a five-year contract at £1300 a year but, contrary to the general belief at the time, *not* in a managerial role. A Linfield representative said: 'We have secured Milburn from Newcastle United as player-coach. Any question of management of the club is a question for the future.' Although not confirmed, it was thought that a promise of a managerial post had been made to him for when his playing days were over.

As Jackie, his family and pet parrot Polly were settling into their new home on the outskirts of Belfast – telephone number Hollywood 2343 – there were already rumblings of dissatisfaction back on Tyneside. Geordie supporters were wondering if their champion would receive anything in the form of cash appreciation from United as a testimonial reward for fourteen years' service to Newcastle United.

The football club chairman, Wilf Taylor, ruled out the question of them paying any benefit: 'I had a long discussion with Jackie before he decided to accept the Linfield appointment. One of the issues I raised was that if he finished his playing days with Newcastle United it was very probable indeed that some form of testimonial, and probably a special match at St James's Park, would officially be arranged for his benefit.'

Stan Seymour confirmed this: 'I told Jackie that management ruling would not allow a benefit game being granted except where a man was ending his footballing career as a player. To my regret, though, we and the board wish Milburn every success. He has decided to leave the North-East for a career which is always a colourful but arduous managerial profession.'

This upset almost the entire population of Tyneside, and letters of protest were written in hundreds to the local press. The Newcastle board was pressurised into making a statement to the effect that Newcastle United were unable to stage a testimonial match for Milburn as 'he is now a registered player with another club and out of our control'.

Jackie had no set plan to put Linfield – once the richest club in Ireland and with a floodlighting system which alone cost £17,000 – back at the top of the Irish League. After spending a couple of weeks assessing his players at the beginning of August, he said: 'Well, for a start, I'm cutting out the "lapping" business and concentrating on fast sprints. Most of the players hang on to the ball, but they are catching on to the value of a quick pass and moving into the empty space.'

He played his first game for Linfield against Distillery. Optimistic Linfield fans predicted that a stream of golden goals would flow from his boots, making the Blues an unbeatable super-team. It was foolish idle chatter, and Jackie did well to pay no heed to it, choosing instead to listen to Distillery boss Maurice Tadman, formerly of Plymouth. It was he who told him that soccer in Ireland would be no holiday, and it might take Jackie all of six weeks to settle down into anything like his best form.

When he stepped out on to the compact Distillery pitch, he knew critical eyes would be watching his every move. For once the big occasion proved too much for him, and Jackie had an abysmal game. He tried too hard to be both captain and coach on the field, shouting encouragement to his team of part-timers, and so stifling his own natural game. Distillery put a man on Milburn to shadow him all over the park. This was six-foot policeman Joe McKinstry, who blotted the Geordie out of his first Irish game.

After that Jackie resolved to let his feet do the talking, and within a couple of months, as Tadman had predicted, his goal-scoring touch returned, much to the relief of the Linfield fans. Once he was able to shrug off a leg injury, he started to bang in goals with something of his old consistency. From then on, whenever he got the ball, a buzz went over the ground in anticipation of one of the spectacular goals that were his trademark. In a tribute to Jackie, the Linfield fans committed near-heresy when they rewrote the 'Blaydon Races; and gave Geordie Ridley's tune a new set of lyrics:

> I saw a smiling face today,
>> the face of Joe Mackey,
>>> he said the greatest thing he ever did
>>>> was signing on Wor Jackie,
>>>>> First Wor Jackie wasn't used
>>>>>> to playing in strange places,
>>>>>>> 'til Linfield bought a gramophone,
>>>>>>>> and played the Blaydon Races.

> Up on the Spion Kop
>> the Blues supporters gathered;
>>> waving high the City Cup
>>>> blended with the heather
>>>>> the Glens were leading three to two
>>>>>> the Blues were none the wiser,
>>>>>>> 'til Jackie Milburn got the ball,
>>>>>>>> and scored the equaliser.

Milburn's first cup semi-final in Ireland was in November 1957. He had something to prove this time, as the opposition was once again to be close rivals Distillery. But on this occasion on the more spacious Linfield ground, Jackie Milburn was able to show the Irish people just why he was so revered in his native North-East. Linfield won the game 7–1, and Jackie scored four spectacular goals to put his side into the final of the Gold Cup. Delirious Irishmen went so far as to compare his fourth goal to his 'Ernie Taylor backheel' special at Wembley in 1951. This game certainly silenced the critics who were saying that Milburn was just another washed-up Englishman who had come across to finish the twilight years of his career in the backwaters of Irish football.

That same month, Jackie was back on Tyneside signing his new autobiography. *Golden Goals*, published by Stanley Paul of London. Again Milburn had scored, this being the first book ever written by a Newcastle United player.

George Follows of the *Daily Herald* speculated:

And Newcastle United? They are going to be all right. They now have a friend, who served them faithfully for fourteen years, to help tell them exactly who is who and what is what in this rapidly improving Irish Football. Boardroom echoes say that Newcastle's new chairman, Alderman William McKeag, legal, almost-regal talking solicitor, will push for the appointment of a new manager and strip Stan Seymour, the old pro, of his director-manager's power. Dare Jackie Milburn believe he was the man for the job?

The £10,000 Linfield outlay was soon recovered as attendances soared to record levels at the games Jackie Milburn played at Windsor Park and around the province. The Irish doubters were silenced as Jackie, now recovered from that troublesome leg injury, hit eighteen goals in a seven-match spell, showing electrifying bursts and devastating shooting that would be talked about for years. After a few months on Irish soil, Jackie observed:

A lot of people tried to kid me that the game was very slow and easy over here. They are hopelessly wrong! There are some great players and quite a few of them could walk straight into First Division football, I think it is much harder here than in England. The tackling is very keen, and it is ridiculous to run away with the idea that it is slow-motion stuff. I have been very impressed by the sportsmanship. I can honestly say that since I started playing in the Irish League I haven't had one dirty tackle. This is a champion place! My wife and I are very happy here and the kiddies love it.

Apparently, no signs yet of homesickness from Jackie, and the pundits back on Tyneside proved to have been patently wrong when they had predicted he would be back within a year. Yet Jackie did come back – again and again! Every chance he got he would take the first available flight (one time he shared a plane with pigs) in order to come back to see his ex-colleagues in action. Many Irish League games were played on a Friday night, leaving the weekend clear for Jackie's Irish Sea hopping.

An Irish cup medal was denied Jackie at his first attempt, as Linfield took on Ballymena at The Oval in Belfast. He had been out of the side through injury for a month, and in a one-sided 3–0 defeat he broke down once again, limping through the entire match.

At the end of a very successful season, Jackie was selected by a panel of sports writers and referees as the Irish League 'Footballer of the Year'. He obtained a unanimous vote which established him as one of the most popular players in Ireland. Typically modest, he said: 'I feel really proud. It's a great honour for me, but also for my club, Linfield.' Jackie finished as the League's top scorer with a prolific fifty-five goals.

Right from the kick-off next season Jackie showed that, even at thirty-four, he was playing as well as ever, by leading Linfield to a 9–1 win over Crusaders, scoring an incredible double hat-trick in the process. Back in England on the same day, playing in an all-Manchester derby game, eighteen-year-old Bobby Charlton scored from the penalty spot, beating City goalkeeper Bert Trautman to clinch a 1–1 draw. Linfield ended the season by winning the League Championship, and Jackie went one better with his record goal-scoring tally by netting fifty-six goals.

If everything in Jackie Milburn's Hollywood garden was lovely, back in the North-East of England, Newcastle were in a right tangle. They escaped relegation only on goal average in the 1957/58 season – also the year that Sunderland failed to pull off one of their famous Houdini acts and got their first ever taste of Second Division soccer.

In June 1958, flamboyant Charlie Mitten arrived at Newcastle as manager after Stan Seymour had stepped down. Ex-player/manager of Mansfield Town, Charlie was McKeag's darling and in his eyes could do no wrong. Even so, barely a year had elapsed before Mitten threatened to leave over a disputed contract.

Mitten got his own way, and with a three-year contract at an enhanced salary now in his pocket, became a frequent visitor to Windsor Park. It was shortly after this that Jackie, who had completed barely two years of his five-year contract, made his first request to leave Linfield. He went to the trouble of getting Malcolm Brodie, sports editor of the *Belfast Telegraph* to type his resignation for him, and handed it to the Linfield board on 20 July 1959, saying: 'I have definitely made up my mind and I see no point in changing it. The family is to start a business in Newcastle and I am to help with it. This is an opportunity to get into business which I cannot afford to turn down.'

Tom Harvey, Linfield's chairman, commented: 'If Milburn has definitely made up his mind to retire from the game, we cannot prevent him. We could not even stop him from taking a coaching appointment. We will, however, protect ourselves as far as possible by retaining him so that he cannot play for any club in England.' Two days later, after numerous Linfield deputations to his house, Jackie withdrew his request. As League champions, Linfield had qualified for the European Cup, to be played in 1960, and had a plum draw against Swedish champions AFK Gothenburg. Said Jackie: 'I haven't changed my mind about quitting. I am still going into business in Newcastle. But in fairness to Linfield, I have decided to play in the European Cup.'

What prompted Milburn to ask to be released from his contract? Was it sheer coincidence that his request to leave was prefaced by the arrival in Ireland of Charlie Mitten, Newcastle's manager? Jackie was to admit, much later, that it was at Mitten's invitation that he tried to sever his ties with the Irish club.

One thing that Mitten did during his brief but colourful stay on Tyneside was to persuade Swansea's Ivor Allchurch that Newcastle wasn't all that much further north than Wales! The little Welsh international after signing for United, formed a lively trio with Eastham and White, probably the best set of inside-forwards in Division One.

Milburn's pal Bobby Mitchell, only two months his junior, was still a United regular, and with Jackie himself brought back, playing on the right wing, Mitten would have assembled a forward line to gladden the heart of the most discerning Geordie supporter.

If that, indeed, was Mitten's offer, why did Jackie suddenly decide to stay? There was Linfield chairman Harvey's threat that he would not be released to play for another League club and that he would be left to rot on the retained list, which had happened to Albert Stubbins, Raich Carter, and countless others. Obviously that was the main deterrent, but further bait was dangled in the shape of an offer for him to manage a seventy bedroom hotel in Bangor.

When Jackie decided to stay on at Linfield it was only to be until after the European Cup games against Gothenburg. Linfield officials initially agreed to this, but after a series of interviews, some of which lasted until the early hours, they finally convinced Jackie that his future in Ireland was as secure as it was anywhere else. Robert Howard, of the *Reynolds News*, rang Laura to ask if she was glad to be staying. 'I'm glad I know what I'm doing,' was her caustic reply.

Writing a column for the *Daily Express* only a few weeks after asking to leave, Jackie Milburn showed what a complex character he really was when he wrote under the banner heading: 'OK You Win – I'll Stay Forever'.

Some people say I am not happy at Linfield. Get this straight – for my money, Linfield is the happiest club in the world. If possible I would like to stay with them for all time.

Why then did I ask to have my contract ended? I intended to go back to Newcastle to set up a family business just as security when my playing days finish. It's as simple as that!

My wife has packed three or four times to go on a house-searching mission. I can tell you, if the Linfield officials had not been so persuasive I would be in Newcastle this very minute.

It was at this point that Jackie, completely unsolicited, admitted that he had been offered the chance of playing for Newcastle again.

Then I thought if I went to Newcastle I might not get a game, and if that happened I would cut off my leg!

Another important item helped me to change my mind. Since I first toyed with the idea of asking for my release, I have joined the hotel business in Bangor. I thoroughly enjoy the business – nearly as much as football! The proprietor wants me to take over eventually when I have everything at my finger tips. And that just clinched it.

But Jackie didn't think long term like that at all. For all his protestations that he was looking to the future, he never admitted to himself that the gloomy day would ever arrive when he had to retire. Even at thirty-five he believed that he was still good enough to get back into English League football. This had been verified in the representative games he'd played against the English while he was at Linfield. He had revelled in these games, pitting his skill and speed against the best players in England.

Yet, when Jackie spoke of 'staying in Ireland for good', he meant it *at the time*. But realistically, he could no more have spent his days behind the counter of an Irish hotel than he could behind the goalposts as a ballboy at Roker Park. Why, then, did he say it? Throughout his entire career, Milburn was completely honest in his intentions, but being a gentleman, he could never say or do anything which would offend in any way. And it was here that conflict was bound to arise. It was this trait – many would say a Milburn hallmark – which was one of his failings:

the inability to analyse and be critically decisive at the precise time that he was faced with a problem.

Perhaps there was another reason why Jackie wanted to leave Ireland: the religious aspect. Towards the end of his first season at Linfield, Jackie admitted to the *Weekly News* that he had been getting threatening letters in a vicious attempt to frighten him. One letter hinted at some of the very unpleasant things which could happen to him if he scored a goal in a particular game. Another was signed 'From one of those who took care of Jimmy Jones'. Jones, Belfast Celtic centre-forward, had been injured during crowd trouble in 1951.

Jackie shrugged off any suggestion that he might be intimidated: 'Frankly, I was quite expecting something like this. I've had several such letters before, and they invariably arrive just before a Cup tie or other important games. I just throw them in the fire.' Brought up as Church of England, Jackie admitted that he had 'lost all religion' when his father died of a brain haemorrhage, caused by a fall at the colliery, at the early age of fifty-four. In all the interviews he gave at the time, he did not even hint that he felt threatened by the religious tension which existed in Belfast. This was the private face of Jackie Milburn, keeping his thoughts to himself. At a distance of almost thirty years, did he view things any differently?

We loved the place and the people, but unfortunately there was a lot of religious trouble over there which I hated. I detested it. Linfield were all Protestants, and you had Belfast Celtic who were the Catholics. We weren't brought up in these circumstances.

Oh, they made threats about this and the other, what they would do. Somebody said they would throw acid in Laura's face – whey, what can you do? Plus the fact that we didn't really know anybody out there; not like at home. Laura came in one night saying she'd been out for a walk in Belfast and decided to pop into someone's house for a cup of tea; then she suddenly realised that she didn't know anyone.

Jackie began the 1959/60 season at Linfield by taking on another job – as a freelance journalist with the *Newcastle Journal*. He left no doubt in people's minds that he was missing the big time, by writing: 'I envy you north-east soccer fans today – the day of the big kick-off! For what I have missed more than anything since my departure from Tyneside has been the electric atmosphere created by the crowds at First Division football.'

Jackie's European Cup debut looked like an instant replay of the 1951 FA Cup Final. He scored two terrific goals at Windsor Park in the first leg, and although the Swedish side pulled a goal back, there was Irish optimism that a 2–1 lead could be sufficient to put Linfield into the hat for the next round, and so make history as the first Irish side to qualify for a further round.

The Linfield party arrived in Gothenburg at 7 p.m. on Tuesday 22 September 1959 to stay at the Palace Hotel. Together with six directors, the team made an impressive appearance in Sweden's western capital, but all eyes were on Milburn, who was subjected to VIP treatment. For once his luck ran out, and Linfield never managed to get into a game which they lost 6–1, much to the dismay of the seventy-five Linfield supporters who had flown into Sweden from Belfast.

If they were disappointed then, the Irishmen had plenty to cheer about on 1 May 1960 when Linfield beat Ards 5–1 to win the Irish Cup for the twenty-seventh time in their history. Jackie had now helped Linfield to take every Irish trophy to Windsor Park in the three years he had been there. In a statement to the *Sunday Dispatch* Jackie said: 'This is one of the proudest moments of my life. My stay in Ireland has been crowned with the top badge of all – an Irish Cup medal.' In spite of being out for lengthy spells through injury, Milburn scored thirty-four goals during that season.

Jackie began the 1960/61 season impressively and was soon scoring goals. But it was while playing in two representative games for the Irish League that he confirmed to himself, and an audience of football managers from all around Britain, that the Jet was still capable of flying. The first game was against the Scottish League at Windsor Park where he played very well, but it was in the second, at Blackpool in October against the English Football League, that Jackie displayed all his old flair as leader of the attack.

It was in Blackpool that he was 'sounded out' by a number of club officials with regard to his position at Linfield, and if he needed any further encouragement to return home, these latest enquiries provided it. On his return to Windsor Park after the Blackpool game he handed in a written request for a move, on the grounds he had used twice before at Newcastle: 'my wife's ill health'.

I have made two requests to leave Linfield in the past fifteen months, and even though I have tried my best to fulfil the duties expected of me, I must confess that due to an unhappy frame of mind this has been somewhat difficult.

We are coming back primarily for my wife's health, for she has already had three nervous breakdowns in the last three years. It is obvious we would be much happier living in England. I would like to stress that I have not applied, nor have I had the offer of a job elsewhere.

For the Linfield club Tom Armstrong, committee chairman, said: 'We did not want Milburn to go, but thoroughly understood the situation in which he was placed.' Jackie was big news all around Britain once again when he announced in the Newcastle Journal on 26 October:

I've no plans whatever for a job, and for the time being will be going to stay with my mother in Ashington. My sole reason for wanting to leave Belfast is my wife's health. Linfield were not all that keen to let me go, but in the circumstances let me have my release. I finish with them on Thursday – then I'm on the dole!

We hope to move to Ashington fairly quickly, and will certainly be there in about two weeks' time. Once I've got the children fixed up at school I'll look for a job – and I don't mind what I do or where I go.

Jackie's mother, Nance, found herself a target for newsmen, and when probed about her son's future, she told a Journal reporter: 'I suppose he will have to do the best for himself and his family.'

On his return to the North-East in mid-November, Jackie wasted no time in pulling on his football boots again. He got a great welcome from a crowd of enthusiastics at Croft Park, Blyth, when he turned out in a charity match. After scoring four goals against a TV celebrity side, Jackie beamed as he ran off the pitch.

This is the happiest day I have had in three years. It is not only playing football again with the lads I know, or the cheers of the youngsters. It is just being back home in the North-East.

I have had so many offers of jobs, I don't know which way to turn. There are offers from all over the country, many from friends in the football world, and I intend to see every one of them. But I am really worried.

Favourite to get Jackie's signature was his home-town team at Ashington. The Colliers' manager, ex-Newcastle player Davy Davison, was confident that the local hero would be signing for them '. . . in time for Saturday's match at Scarborough. By joining us, Jackie will earn a Saturday match fee at least as big as he could get with Newcastle United [£20], and he will make as much in weekly wage from the excellent job we have offered him.' The job Davison alluded to was in the tobacco trade as an area representative.

If the Colliers were favourite in most people's book, they definitely weren't in Jackie Milburn's! Too often had he seen and heard the harsh treatment meted out at Portland Park to players who failed to perform to the high standards demanded by the Ashington pitmen.

I was at Portland Park one Saturday, and an old friend of mine, Len Duns, a lovely footballer who used to play for Sunderland, was playing for Ashington. Whey, you know what it's like when you lose that extra yard of pace . . . the crowd are jeering and shouting. So I says to meself, 'Hey, there's no way that I'm going to subject meself to that; not from me own!' So I turned them down.

Jackie felt that there was no need for him to take a step down the ladder into non-League soccer. He was convinced – and hadn't that game at Blackpool proved it – that he was still capable of winning a place with a Football League team. There was one major stumbling block: his Provident Fund money. The Provident Fund was a sum of money set aside to aid players in a variety of circumstances, one of these being premature release from a League side. On leaving Newcastle United Jackie had been awarded £900 from the Fund, but there was a proviso on its acceptance that he could not return to the English Football League. From his talks with Charlie Mitten and other interested parties, Jackie had been led to believe that if he paid back the money in full then he could re-register as a player in

England. With this in mind he had already applied to the Football League authorities, even before leaving Ireland. In effect, he was shown the red card!

An *Evening Chronicle* article on 29 October, stated: 'A Football League spokesman today revealed that Jackie Milburn cannot return to League football in view of an agreement with the Inland Revenue authorities which provides that Provident Fund money is tax free. The League feel that any attempt to repay money would jeopardise the whole scheme.' With this one ruling, Jackie had everything that he had hoped for – to pull on a black and white shirt again for the one team he loved – denied him. On 1 November 1960, realising there was no longer any need for secrecy or subterfuge, Jackie issued this statement to the *Newcastle Journal*:

I applied to the Football League for permission to play League football again in England only because Newcastle United manager, Charlie Mitten, urged me to do so. Mr Mitten told me that I could still play successfully for United and that he would be glad to re-sign me if I could secure my freedom to play in the League again. With this encouragement I wrote to the League hoping that all would be well if I repaid the £900 I received from the League Benevolent Trust. Now I learn that the League refuse my request.

That's disappointing, for with a few weeks' training it would have been a great thrill to try doing a little more for United, along with my old pal Bobby Mitchell. It looks as though that dream is ended, but I do want Tyneside to know that it was the Magpie call, at Mr Mitten's suggestion, which drew me.

Asked the next day by the *Journal* if Newcastle United were interested in Milburn in any capacity whatsoever, Mr Charlie Mitten, the manager, replied: 'Definitely not'. Amid the speculation, Stan Seymour took the opportunity to write a 'Welcome Home' article in the *Evening Chronicle*, managing to give himself a pat on the back in the process:

Jackie is assured of a great welcome as the little clubs of Ashington, South Shields, Berwick Rangers, and Horden Colliery Welfare endeavour to secure his services in the autumn of his career.

I am particularly interested in Jackie for I have signed many a cheque for many a player and seen a football fortune come and go into Newcastle United's bank account, but my greatest bargain ever was when I secured 'Wor Jackie' for St James's Park.

Often as I sit down in the dumps – and that is very frequently these days – I recall the deeds of Jackie. Those wonderful triumphs which helped to give us victory three times at Wembley. And to think I found such a gem for nothing!

Seymour had good cause to 'sit down in the dumps'. After systematically culling one of the most exciting teams in the country, the Newcastle United board was again at the sharp end of another controversy, this time over their refusal to grant George Eastham a transfer. Unable to get a game, George took a part-time job working for a friend in Reigate. He was adamant that he wanted to join a club based in London. As the United directors boarded up the shutters in anticipation of a long drawn-out siege. Eastham staggered them – and the football world – by issuing writs on six directors: Hurford, Mackenzie, Taylor, McKeag, Seymour and Rutherford. For good measure he also sued manager Mitten, the Football League and the Football Association, alleging that he was being prevented from carrying on with his trade as a footballer.

Although all this took place just before the 1960/61 season got under way, it was not resolved until 1963 when Mr Justice Wilberforce gave a judgement in favour of Eastham and against Newcastle United, because of 'unreasonable restraint of trade'. The case set a precedent, and as a result of that one decision players were now free to negotiate their own contracts. Newcastle United had scored yet another 'first'; but it was one record they did not relish.

Jackie Milburn had to forget Newcastle United's problems and concentrate on his own. He was positive about one thing: if he couldn't play in the Football League, there was no chance of him settling for non-League soccer in the North-East. His pride wouldn't let him. Walter Nunn, Ashington FC's chairman, said at the beginning of November: 'We have been told by our manager that Jackie Milburn is not coming to us. He is going south.' Manager Davison confirmed in the *Newcastle Journal*:

Jackie turned down an offer that would have been worth £40 a week to him. He said that the north-east football fan was more knowledgeable about the game than anyone else, and after a couple of bad games he might get the bird. I told him not to be ridiculous. For all his great skill as a player, Jackie seems to have an inferiority complex about his ability.

Jack Charlton: I was surprised when he went away to Ireland in the first place. I thought he would have taken a position somewhere here in England. But, like with me now, people keep saying: you can have the job in Ireland for the rest of your life. But things change in football; what's great today is not necessarily great tomorrow. And we all came to the situation – it was probably the same with Jackie – when you feel that the general public, not the Press, are beginning to change their attitude towards you. Then it's time to move on. So he got offered the job in Ireland and he went. He was very highly thought of there, and still is.

But Jackie was a north-east lad, and I don't think that he ever enjoyed being away from the area. I would have thought that the best time for him to have taken a manager's job in the north east was when he came back from Ireland. Whether he would have made a good job of managing Newcastle United . . . maybe he would have done. But you are always judged on your successes, not your failures!

Two other non-League clubs were after Jackie: Boston in Lincolnshire, managed by Ray Middleton, and Yiewsley in Middlesex, managed by Bill Dodgin, brother of Norman and a former colleague of Jackie's while at Newcastle. Both clubs wanted Milburn in the first instance as a player. Fate intervened and decreed that Jackie go to the southern club. Jackie's mother Nance, a widow now for six years, had decided to go to Slough to live with a woman friend who had moved from Ashington a number of years earlier. On inspecting his atlas Jackie discovered that, by sheer coincidence, Slough was only five miles from Yiewsley. And so, within a couple of weeks of coming back from Ireland, the Milburn family packed their bags and set out for the stockbroker belt of Middlesex.

Why Yiewsley? The fact that his mother would be there was obviously a factor. Another major consideration was the set-up at Yiewsley, population 28,000, with a ground capacity of 40,000. The Yiewsley chairman Arthur Whittit, a car manufacturer, had also offered Jackie a job with his organisation. But more than any of these it was the distance he was putting between himself and the prying, critical eyes of his fellow Geordies that won the day for the Southern Counties team. On Jackie's arrival, Whittit commented:

Milburn will get a tremendous welcome here. He should soon feel at home, for I come from Sunderland, Bill Dodgin is from Gateshead, and some of our players had games with Newcastle United and Sunderland. Make no mistake, Yiewsley FC have a bright future. Don't forget that London Airport is in Yiewsley. We are right in the centre of things.

We have only been a professional club for two years, but may well be in the Football League eventually. Milburn will also have a key job in my car business. We make Citroëns here and also the Monarch, a new sports model. Jackie will have lots of scope, and his mother will be happy living at Slough.

As in Ireland, Jackie's first game went badly as Yiewsley lost 4–0 against Bexley Heath in a Southern League game. He stated afterwards:

My first match wasn't the great success it might have been. The result doesn't mean anything. I met the lads for the very first time today, and we are going to be a great team. I'm already looking around for a house to buy. My job as sales manager for Mr Whittit's coach-building firm starts on Monday, and I am looking forward to it very much.

This will be my last club! I am going to settle in Yiewsley and I know I am going to be happy here. It would have been nice if I could have gone back to my old club at Ashington, but I had to find a southern club because my wife's health could not stand the north-eastern climate.

Within a month of Jackie's arrival, Bill Dodgin, whose managerial career had once taken him across to Italy's Sampadoria club, moved on, leaving Milburn to take complete control of Yiewsley as player/coach. Jackie was not overworked as a coach at Yiewsley. The players were all part-time, and attended for training only in the evening. Never one to sit still, Jackie was soon doing five jobs a week! He was a Yiewsley player and their coach; he found time to do the groundsman's job as well; he accepted an offer from Harry Johnston, ex-Blackpool and then managing Reading United, to coach the Reading players once a week; then one day he received a letter from Carmel College, a private school for Jewish boys, asking him to go along and have a word with the headmaster.

What happened there was, I got this letter asking us to go to this college. It wasn't all that far from where we were living. And I was wondering what they were after. So when I got to this place (lovely grounds – smashing), I was shown into this big room. The walls had panelled wood, I think.

Have you ever had a spiritual experience? Cos that's what I had that day. At the other end of the room was this stained-glass window, tremendous it was. The sunlight was streaming through and falling on this figure which I couldn't quite make out because of the blinding sun. I heard this deep voice coming from the figure saying: 'Come in, Mr Milburn. I am very pleased to meet you.'

So then the figure moved out of the light and came forward with his hand outstretched. And, hey, if ever anybody had asked me to describe what God looked like, this man, to me, was the spitting image! He just had this whole . . . aura. Black robe . . . long beard. He said: 'My name is Rosen, Rabbi Kopul Rosen. Can I call you Jack?' Whey, I just mumbled something or other, and then he went on: 'I have seen and admired your play many times, and I knew you would be just the man to coach our boys. What do you say, Jack, will you help us out?'

I was flabbergasted! I really was. Here was this Jewish rabbi asking me, born and bred in a little pit village at the back of beyond, to work in this marvellous place. Unbelievable!

Anyway I promised that I would come for six months, which I did, coaching football and running. But shortly after I'd started, he says: 'Jack I want you to stay here at the college as a housemaster, teaching physical education full-time. I will educate your son Jackie free of charge and will find accommodation for you and your family.

Whey . . . you wouldn't credit it, would you! I told him I'd like a bit time to think it over, and he put his hand on my shoulder and says: 'Best make it quick, Jack, I only have six weeks to live.'

In a pamphlet published in 1988 to commemorate the school's fortieth anniversary, Helmut Schmidt, a former pupil and now a teacher at the college, related this account of Jackie's first introduction to life at Carmel College.

Those who were present at Rabbi Rosen's last football match in November 1961, whether as players or spectators, will never forget the carefully staged comedy, the sudden drama, and the subsequent tragedy.

From his early days, Carmel's first headmaster had always maintained an active interest in football and footballers. Once on the ball he could run fast and tackle his opponents energetically . . . as headmaster he always captained the staff team against the 1st XI.

. . . One outstanding master in his field was smuggled into the school unannounced. How Kopul loved an occasional leg-pull! How he anticipated with glee the long faces of the surprised boys watching the dramatic rout of their football eleven.

It was on the day of the annual staff match against the boys that the arrival was announced of a new gardener who would be playing in Rabbi Rosen's staff team . . . poor old fogeys, they soon looked exhausted. Half time drew near . . . yet the bearded captain looked anything but dismayed and even managed a wistful smile.

The whistle went for the second half and the staff team seemed a little more lively. Before anyone knew what was happening, the new gardener had sent the ball from the half-way line as if it was a guided missile straight into the top left of the goal. Players and spectators were stunned! A lucky shot no doubt, as rare as eight draws on the pools. Why should fortune deny her favour to a gardener once in a while?

. . . The boys had hardly recovered from the unexpected blow when from a distance of twenty yards another rocket hit their goal. The boys rightly decided to pay more attention to that inside-forward and keep him covered. They tried to tackle him when he advanced with the ball. He just danced and rotated around them in a spectacular show of football ballet. No, there could be no question any longer of chance or luck. Here was a virtuoso who fired his shots with the calculated, deliberate precision of a champion of first-class football.

The football fans of the Vth Form who had watched with utter surprise the dramatic turn of events racked their football brains. They knew the style and looks of all the top footballers in the land and no longer had any doubt about the true identity of the 'new gardener' they had been privileged to watch so closely and free of charge.

They were in the presence of none other than Jackie Milburn, the great Jackie Milburn. Good heavens, the goalscoring legend of Tyneside who had helped Newcastle United win the FA Cup three times in five years. The school could now be told by the headmaster at the end of the thrilling match that Mr Milburn had agreed to coach Carmel's young footballers for two terms.

What followed during the next few weeks was as unexpected as being struck by lightning on a cloudless day. Kopul Rosen was found to be dying from an incurable disease. Never would the school see its headmaster so energetic and happy again as when he played his last football match with Jackie Milburn in his team.

Kopul Rosen's sons, David and Jeremy, remember that same day just as vividly as Helmut. David, himself a rabbi now at the P. Sapir Jewish Heritage Centre in Jerusalem, was only ten years old at the time but recalls: 'Milburn started off that game alongside my father in midfield. He didn't seem to be up to much until he got this signal at the half-way line and gave this cracking shot . . . I warmly remember him training us, and recall how honoured and chuffed we felt being trained by him.'

Rabbi Jeremy Rosen, now minister at the Western Synagogue in London, relates:

My father warned us in advance that he was bringing a friend to bolster up the decrepit staff team. On came this quiet, reticent fellow . . . at first he ambled around the field, and then we heard my father call out: 'OK Jack, let 'em have it!'

He was standing somewhere on the half-way line, and with a gentle balanced swing he kicked the ball straight into the net . . . in two more astonishing runs he took the ball from one end of the field to the other, equalled the scores, and then, just as casually, waved goodbye! My father was roaring with laughter when he told us the man was Jackie Milburn.

It was indeed my father who wanted Milburn to join the staff. He offered him the job . . . He died of leukaemia in March 1962.

I have a personal memory; he told me that he thought I should get a Blue when I went up to Cambridge (I was due to start in September '62). I told him I would not be able to as I would not play on Saturdays for religious reasons. He replied: 'Don't be ridiculous, lad. You mustn't let a little thing like that get in your way!' We all loved him very much.

CHAPTER SIXTEEN

At Ipswich, Ramsey gave me no help

Jackie stayed with Yiewsley until January 1963. At the beginning of that year he had told the *Evening Chronicle*'s Victor Reeve: 'I'm still dreaming football! There's nothing I like better than a hard match. When I left Newcastle I gave myself five years to make it as a player/manager. That time's up.'

Jackie could afford to sound optimistic. He knew then that he was on a short-list of two for the job of Ipswich Town's manager. Alf Ramsey was due to leave Ipswich officially on 29 April to take over the England squad in the run-up to the 1966 World Cup. It was the only manager's job Milburn had ever applied for, and he was one of over sixty applicants. Ramsey had transformed a mediocre side, leaping through the divisions to become one of the most consistent teams in the country. Ipswich had set a record of Third, Second and First Division champions in five years, but the team was now crumbling, players were past their best, and there was less than £40,000 in the kitty to put the side back together again.

Jackie was the first to go in front of the Ipswich selection panel at noon on 28 January. After leaving, he and Laura went to the pictures. Candidate number two was an old adversary of Jackie's – Reg Flewin, former Portsmouth centre-half, and then managing Stockport County. He emerged smiling after an hour, and flash bulbs popped in anticipation. The Milburns came out of the Odeon and went back to the ground, where Jackie paced nervously around the frozen Portman Road pitch. John Cobbold, old Etonian, and one of the brewing giants, Tolly Cobbold, walked over to greet him with: 'You've got it, mate. Congratulations!' Asked by

149

waiting newsmen whether Milburn would get a contract, chairman Cobbold replied: 'He can have one if he wishes.'

Milburn admitted: 'I'm a bit windy about following Alf Ramsey, but who wouldn't be? I've watched Ipswich twice already, but I'm not saying what I thought of them. It's easy to be the best player in the world sitting in the stands as I was.' To which Cobbold replied: 'I'm not going to live with ghosts. After the era of Alf, we're starting again. Of course it's a gamble. It must be a gamble taking the man out of non-League football management and putting him in charge of a First Division club. But don't forget, Alf Ramsey had never done any managing either. If Milburn wants money he will find as much available at Ipswich as in any other club of its size. If he wishes to sign players he may sign.'

The next day a euphoric Jackie told a *Journal* reporter: 'I don't want any contract. I think it's up to a man to prove himself.'

Jack Charlton: I think he made a mistake going to Ipswich! It was always thought of as a little town somewhere outside of London. Under Alf Ramsey, they played a particular type of game. They won the First Division on a method of playing with no wingers, and two men up front in the middle. Well, that altered the game completely, and opponents were forced to play two centre-backs to cope with it. And they went through the divisions playing this type of football. They won everything! But once they'd won the Championship, there was no way they were going to repeat that because people now knew how they were going to play. And once we had adjusted our game, it was difficult for them to change to something new.

When Jackie and Laura Milburn got back to their house in Crowborough, Berkshire that night, there was a telegram waiting: 'Congratulations on appointment as Ipswich manager; great news. Bobby Stokoe.' (Stokoe was then manager at Bury.)

'It's marvellous how friendly all the old Gallowgate lads remain,' said Jackie. 'Now I'm dreaming again of bringing an Ipswich team to play Newcastle in the opening match next season – in Division One, of course.' Those last few words were significant. Newcastle, now managed by former skipper Joe Harvey, were struggling to keep afloat in the Second Division, and Ipswich, League champions only the season before, had only a handful of clubs below them in the First Division with barely a dozen games left to play. Part of the Ipswich deal was that Ramsey would stay on until the end of the season in an advisory capacity before taking up his England post.

The move to Ipswich was probably the worst decision ever made by Jackie Milburn. The fact that he had turned down the Carmel College offer, with all its attendant built-in safeguards for his future, scotched his pleading 'security' as his number one priority. The Ipswich job was as safe as a splintered pit-prop!

If Jackie had taken his time, put his foot on the ball and had a good look around he would have realised that this was one game he had no chance of winning from the start. Even the fact that Ramsey was hanging on until the end of the season meant that Jackie was on a loser. If Ipswich stayed up, Ramsey would get the praise, and if they dropped, Milburn would be left to pick up the pieces.

It was hard going! Ramsey didn't help by hanging around the club so much – he lived in Ipswich. The players were still going to him for team talks. But what could you do? John Cobbold was the chairman then. Him and his brother Patrick ran things between them. They were your typical English public school types. Always playing practical jokes, making apple-pie beds for the players, squirting plastic tomato-sauce bottles at each other on the train. Daft things like that, but not things I was used to.

Ramsey, never a good communicator, made things awkward from the start by refusing Jackie access to club files on players. As team talks were 'off-limits' to the Geordie newcomer, it was doubly difficult for him to build up any kind of relationship with the players. Somehow Ipswich stumbled through their remaining games, and more by good luck than good management saved themselves from creating history by being the first side to win the League and be relegated the following season. But the reprieve was to prove only temporary.

Jack Charlton: When Jackie went to Ipswich, it was completely the wrong time. They had changed the face of British football, but their method had been discovered, and the players they had were getting to the end of their career. Ipswich was due for change, but it was going to have to be radical, and when Jackie didn't bring about that change, you couldn't get a bet on them being relegated the next season, which they were. But I always felt it was a bad move for Jackie to go to Ipswich.

The first season I was there, we only just managed to avoid dropping into the Second Division. I was forever on the phone to Joe Harvey, cos he was United's manager by then and they were in the Second. We were always commiserating with each other. I used to travel thousands of miles looking for new players. I tried to buy players for buttons. Twenty players I bought for £20,000. Most of them turned out to be good buys.

After a lifetime in which Lady Luck had been more than generous, Jackie was staggered as the defeats inflicted on the East Anglian side sent his team spiralling down the League table. On Boxing Day 1963, Fulham cracked ten goals past his goalkeeper. 'Every time Johnny Haynes got the bloody ball, they scored!' said Jackie ruefully. Tony Garnett, sports editor of the *East Anglian Times* commented:

Jackie Milburn was the nicest fella in the game, but his team didn't know how to defend! There was a ten-goal defeat and a nine – he bought a goalie from Raith Rovers who had just let in a record number of goals as Raith got relegated from the Scottish first division. It didn't seem as though he could make his mind up; sometimes he went to a ten-pin bowling alley on a Friday afternoon, and him, the

151

manager of the bowling rink and me sorted out the team for the next day. But he inherited a rough lot of players at Ipswich.

In March 1964 the sleepy rural town of Ipswich was hit by a couple of bombshells. The first trouble flared as Town lost at Stoke, confirming their relegation. Milburn held an emergency meeting with his team after the game to confront them with local newspaper allegations that players had been seen indulging in late-night drinking and appearing in brawling incidents. The players denied that any such conduct had taken place. A players' spokesman said: 'We challenge anyone to bring forward any evidence at all of unruly behaviour by any of us.'

With relegation certain, Jackie shook the Ipswich board with his reaction: 'I'll resign, if that's reckoned to be the answer!' John Cobbold took collective responsibility for the crisis.

Milburn has made mistakes – we all do – but for him to resign is not the answer to our problems. The last thing I want to see is Milburn go. Everyone likes him, and I would not accept his resignation if it were offered. If he is to blame for our lack of success, then so am I. Trouble is being caused, just when we need determined pull-together, by an unjustified smear campaign, and we will get to the bottom of it.

The strain of soccer management manifests itself in various ways. Jackie, head throbbing, sat alone for hours on end watching football matches being enacted on the ceiling of a darkened room. Joe Harvey, when he first came back as Newcastle's manager, was convinced he had seen ghosts on the St James's Park pitch. From the touchline he would watch one of his old team of the fifties do something silly with the ball. Joe would be just about to bawl him out when he realised it was one of his own young players.

At the beginning of the 1964/65 season, with Ipswich firmly anchored at the foot of the Second Division, having gained only one point from four matches, Jackie Milburn handed in his resignation. John Cobbold said: 'My board will fully discuss the matter tomorrow, and until then there will be no further statement.' Jackie made this statement to the press:

I am very sorry to be leaving Ipswich, but after a great deal of thought I have decided that it is in the best interests of the club – and the club must come before any individual. This is my only reason for leaving. I am sure that a change can do nothing but good at a time like this.

I have not lost confidence in myself as a manager, but results speak for themselves. Either you are lucky in football management or you are not. But there is no doubt in my mind that I worked as hard as anyone could during the time I was at Portman Road. The strain and worry of the past year has been enormous. There have been times when I have been up all night thinking about the club's problems. This could easily be accepted over a short period, but it is different in

152

view of the fact that the club has struggled ever since the day I arrived. My health is beginning to be affected . . . As to what I shall do now, I just don't know. I should like to stay in football, but will have to wait and see what happens.

Jackie didn't wait in Ipswich but headed straight back to Ashington. This was his true home: the place he should never have left. It was incongruous that Jackie should ever have been anywhere else. To put Jackie Milburn into a southern environment was like trying to pour a bottle of Newcastle Brown Ale into a cocktail glass! The South was never going to be big enough to accommodate a man of Milburn's considerable stature.

Jackie bunked down once more with sister Jean at Ellington Terrace, and next day went for a relaxing game of golf at Morpeth. Keith Swailes, a local teacher and an old acquaintance, spoke to him that day while out on the course. Keith recalls how ill he looked, as Jackie related to him the trauma of the last few days. The first priority for Jackie was to get the family back to the North-East and establish a base somewhere. Keith's house at Morpeth was standing vacant at the time, and he offered it to Jackie until something more permanent came along. Keith says: 'The very next day, Laura was up measuring for curtains.'

Just as when he had left Ireland, offers of employment landed on the Milburn doorstep. Two years earlier, a circular from the Football League had rescinded the rule governing re-entry to the League of players who had drawn Provident Fund money. Jackie was forty, but still fit enough to command a place in most of the north-eastern sides. Bobby Mitchell, only two months Milburn's junior, was now player/manager of Third Division Gateshead. There was speculation that Jackie would team up with his old mate, ensuring bumper gates at the Redheugh Park ground. Jackie failed to confirm his interest, however, and the rumours came to nothing.

On Tuesday 15 September 1964, less than a fortnight after walking out of Football League management, Jackie Milburn made headlines again on the sports page of a national newspaper. That particular date was special for a couple of other reasons: Alec Douglas-Home set the date for the forthcoming general election, and Fleet Street welcomed a new daily newspaper: the *Sun*. No page three lovelies yet awhile, but three new additions to its staff: Noel Whitcombe, ('Whose gay column will appear regularly'); Clement Freud ('I've just bought a horse called Bullfrog'); and Jackie Milburn ('In the first of his series of exclusive articles for *Sunsport* readers').

Jackie was no newcomer to the national press. At various times he had written articles for the *Daily Express*, *News Chronicle*, *Weekly News*, *Titbits*, *Newcastle Journal*, *Evening Chronicle* and *Sunday Sun*. But what he had written was what he did best: astute comments on individuals, and observations about the game of football in general. This *Sun* appointment was something new. Was Jackie being groomed for the 'exclusive' – for which read 'controversial'?

There was no chance of Jackie being involved in anything 'dirty'. His character was unblemished, and though the pedestal wobbled slightly after his Ipswich walk-out, there was little fear of him toppling in full view of his followers. The armour was rusting slightly, but the legend inside was as pure as ever. So what was the lead-in, the 'angle' as Milburn himself might have called it? The answer had to be Alf Ramsey. The new England manager was being less than helpful to the press. A dour, dominant figure, belying his affected accent and slight stature, Ramsey was not a media man. Not only would he not speak to newsmen, he ordered his players to do likewise. What comments he did make were curt and unhelpful. He resented being 'hounded,' as he called it. The England players loved and respected Ramsey. The English press loathed him, because they could never get to him.

And this was where Jackie Milburn threw the media a lifeline. Hadn't he just quit the club that Ramsey had guided from the obscurity of the Third Division to win the League Championship in the space of five years? Wasn't it this record which had prompted the football authorities to give Ramsey the England manager's job with a free hand to do as he pleased – something totally denied Walter Winterbottom? And wasn't that same club Ipswich, who now looked destined to fall whence they had come after only eighteen months under the guidance of Wor Jackie?

Surely there was a story here if Milburn could be persuaded to tell it. Wasn't Jackie smarting just a little after a less than illustrious episode as a First Division manager? Lying in tatters was his: 'It didn't matter where you were at the time, you just wanted to be the best.' Somehow, Jackie was made an offer he couldn't refuse, and the following article was printed in the first-ever edition of the *Sun*:

Ramsey Gave Me No Help

It's twelve days now since I quit Ipswich Town. Since then I've said nothing about the business. Maybe some people thought I just crept out of Portman Road, too much of a coward to face my critics. But people in the north-east know me better than that. I never shirked an issue when I was playing with Newcastle United and I don't intend to start now.

The critics have had their say. Now I want mine. I've never been a muckraker in my life – the game has been too good to me for that – but there are some things that must be said about my disastrous 18 months with Ipswich.

I want to get one thing clear right from the start. Ipswich are a good club and the directors are gentlemen.

But I accuse Alf Ramsey! He gave me neither help nor encouragement when I took over from him. I worked with him for ten weeks and the only advice I got was that I'd have to become thick skinned to make a go of it.

I inherited from him a team that was over the top and going downhill fast. I knew it, the directors knew it, and most disastrous thing of all, the players knew it too. Ramsey's attitude to me didn't help either. In the first few weeks I was there – Ramsey stayed on even though he had been appointed England manager – I was never invited to a team talk!

I asked him about players' reports, about their scouting files, and all I got from

Ramsey was the name of one Scottish full-back and the address of a part-time scout in Scotland. Later, when Ramsey had left to take his England job, he visited us and I asked whether, during his travels looking for future England players, he could recommend any to us. Alf replied tersely: 'No'. I thought at the time: 'Well, that's a fine attitude from a man who is supposed to have a soft spot for his old club and the man who is asking all League clubs for help and assistance.'

. . . Ramsey's attitude convinced me I was on my own . . . in a ruthless jungle . . . a far cry, indeed, from the warm, human people I'd been brought up among, the folk who had gone out of their way so much to help me during my life in the north-east.

We kept in the first division somehow . . . as everyone knows, we dropped the following season, but it was a year too late for me. If we had gone down the previous season, at least I could have started rebuilding in the second division instead of trying to do the impossible in the first.

We dropped because we weren't good enough, and there wasn't much money to buy new players. When Ramsey left, we got rid of nine players, and only one of them was thought good enough to stay in the League. So I had to buy mainly young players at a small price but players I thought could do a job in the future for me . . . if we could afford the time to give them grooming in the reserves. The inevitable happened. I had to push them into the first team before they were ready. But that didn't bring relief, and so we went down.

I'm convinced, though, that I have given my successor the nucleus of a good team – players like Gerry Baker, Jack Bolton, Joe Broadfoot, Mick McNeil and Frank Brogan. The club says the next manager will have money to spend; that's news to me! At Ipswich I've left the basis of a good team, a scouting system, and a youth policy.

(*Interview with Frank Clough*)

It wasn't a typical piece of Milburn writing, and obviously Frank Clough had stretched its most controversial aspects to the limit, but it was indicative that, if Jackie Milburn felt an injustice had been done, he could be just as critical as the next man.

CHAPTER SEVENTEEN

A bit o' this and a bit o' that

And so Jackie returned to the North-East to do 'a bit o' this and a bit o' that'. As well as writing his regular feature column for the *Sun*, he took on a public relations appointment with J. R. Jennings, a Tyneside scrap merchant. He enjoyed 'getting his hands dirty' and mucking in around the scrapyard, but what he really loved was getting back into his cherished St James's Park.

His good friend Joe Harvey had worked the oracle with United and steered them back into the First Division at the end of the 1964/65 season. Jackie used any excuse to visit the club, seeking stories for his column. Harvey recalled how Jackie used to be at the ground every Thursday before he arrived, and when he entered his own office Jackie would be sitting at the desk with cups of coffee already made for both of them.

If Joe didn't have a story for him – or couldn't be bothered to invent one – Jackie would return in the afternoon, staying on until he had wheedled some kind of information from the Newcastle boss. Harvey began to get paranoid at Jackie's persistence. One day he rang his wife Ida and implored her to go out to lunch with him: 'That's the only way I'm going to get bloody Jack Milburn out of my hair for a couple of hours.' The pair agreed to meet at Gosforth Park golf course for lunch, and when they arrived a waitress indicated that there might be a fifteen-minute wait. Joe and Ida decided to have an aperitif, and made for the bar. As they approached, Jackie's head popped up above the serving hatch, and in his most cultured Geordie accent he enquired: 'And what will sir and madam be having to drink?'

In the early months of 1967, Joe did have some news for Jackie: it was about Milburn himself. Due to pressure from the Newcastle United Supporters Club, the board had granted Jackie a testimonial match. It was due to take place on 10 May, the day before this forty-third birthday. Supporters Club secretary Len Coates had written to the Newcastle board asking if they would give permission for a testimonial game for Milburn to go ahead at St James's Park. United's secretary, Dennis Barker, had informed him that a slot was available at the end of the season. Said Coates: 'I'm delighted at the news. . . . Jackie deserves this reward after such a long time.'

Jackie was elated and worried at the same time. Happy that he would get the chance to tread once more on the ground that he had made his own so often in the past, and worried in case no one would remember him – and even if they did, that they would not bother to come to see him play again. It was the Milburn inferiority complex working overtime. 'Ever since I left United,' he said, 'I have thought of one final fling before the fans who were so good to me. Scores of players over the years have told me they would turn out, but I never thought I'd be taking them up on it.'

Taking no chances with his fitness, Jackie enlisted the help of old team-mate Charlie Crowe. Two nights a week the veterans trained at St James's Park, working out in the gymnasium, doing circuits and lifting weights. After an especially punishing session one evening, Charlie advised his more zealous friend that he had had enough and that he was off for a shower.

As they got outside the gym and into the car park, Jackie suggested that they have five minutes' shooting practice with Charlie acting as goalkeeper. Charlie shrugged his agreement, and walked across to the white posts painted on the brick wall. It was 7.30 p.m., and with the light beginning to fade Charlie never saw the ball which Jackie struck towards him. It flew past his ear, banged into the brick wall and rebounded to Jackie before Charlie had a chance to take up his position. Charlie jumped out of the firing line and shouted at Jackie: 'Hey, man, you could've killed me there!' Crowe laughs about it now, but is positive: 'If that ball had struck me in the face and my head had hit the wall, I would have been done for.' Walking out of the car park that night, with Jackie Milburn still hitting balls at the wall with either foot, Charlie was convinced that a football had never been hit with greater power or more precise accuracy.

A great deal of hard work went on behind the scenes in organising Jackie's big night. One Milburn fan, George Embleton, took a week off work to sell tickets. Stan Seymour junior helped enormously in organising the teams. The 14th/19th Lancers brought a Centurion tank over from Germany where they were posted, so that Milburn could officially name it 'Wor Jackie'. Naturally, he smashed a bottle of Newcastle Broon rather than champagne over the gun turret during the christening ceremony. (The tank was the second object to be blessed with the name of Jackie Milburn. In the fifties, Mr W. J. Stables of Wark had named a species of orchid after his hero.)

In a statement the afternoon before the match, Joe Harvey told *Evening Chronicle*'s John Gibson:

I'm really looking forward to getting in that dressing-room tonight with the old team. I've never known a better atmosphere than the one we had. Ernie Taylor is coming up from Manchester, Tommy Walker from Oldham and Jack Fairbrother from Nottingham especially for the reunion. The only one missing is George Robledo. I've told Jackie the arrangements: I'll lead the team out and he can score the goals – just like the old days!

And what an array of talent there was that rainy evening in May when Jet Milburn raced on to the pitch, arms aloft, acknowledging the 45,404 cheering Geordie fans. Two games were played, the first a twenty-minute each way romp between 'Guest Stars' and 'Newcastle's Wembley Heroes'. The line-up of teams was: NEWCASTLE WEMBLEY HEROES – Fairbrother, Cowell, Corbett, Harvey, Brennan, Crowe, Walker, Taylor, Milburn, McMichael, Mitchell; GUEST STARS: – Thompson, Craig, Hardwicke, Anderson, Hardisty, Lewin, Wardle, Shackleton, Ashman, Broadis, Finney.

Typically, the game began with a piece of pure theatre as Milburn was allowed to run through completely unchallenged to score in fifty seconds – only just outside his Wembley record. That goal set the pattern for the rest of the game, dominated for long spells by the presence of vintage Shack, who had the crowd begging for more.

Played only marginally more seriously, the game which followed included some great footballing names, past and present: JACKIE MILBURN'S XI – Marshall, Irwin, Clarke, Elliott, Kinsell, Iley, Herd, Davies, Milburn, Martin, Robson. (Craig for Milburn after 25 mins); INTERNATIONAL XI: Waiters, Armfield, Brennan, Crerand, McGrath, Stiles, Suddick, Eastham, B. Charlton, Puskas, Mulhall. The game produced four goals, one of which was scored by Jackie, the others coming from Eastham, Charlton and Puskas. After only twenty-five minutes play in the second half, the match was abandoned because of incessant heavy rain. That the thousands of fans had turned out on such a dreadful night proved how much they loved Jackie Milburn. If ever he had any doubt of what he meant to the Geordie public, that particular night put the record straight once and for all.

Daily Mail sports correspondent Doug Weatherall has no doubts:

I think in a way he was unique. Unique in that he was the local boy; he was the one who lived out all our dreams. And there were happy endings to what he attempted to do. They *did* go to Wembley! They *did* win the Cup! He *did* score those marvellous goals at Wembley, and great goals to get them to Wembley.

If anyone had created the Milburn story, people would have said it was too far-fetched. Fact was far more exciting than fiction in football.

The Magpie supporters were as generous with their hard-earned cash as they were with their applause, and Jackie Milburn walked away that night richer by £8200. The cheque was handed over at an official ceremony a few days later, and Jackie was able to sit back with his old friends and watch a filmed recording of the games. 'One of the proudest moments of my life!' was the way Jackie would remember that night.

It was nostalgia time once again in 1973 when arch rivals Sunderland, now managed by Bob 'The Messiah' Stokoe, played Leeds United in the FA Cup Final. Jackie and Laura received special invitations to be guests of the official Sunderland party. It wasn't quite the same for Jackie, but he relished the occasion for his old team-mate, and no one in the crowd was happier than he when Ian Porterfield scored the only goal of the match which sent the trophy back to the North-East, albeit the wrong side of the river Tyne. To show his gratitude, Jackie bought Bob Stokoe a red, black and white golf bag.

But the following year it was Newcastle United's turn to reach the Final. Joe Harvey had built up a great side, which included Malcolm Macdonald at centre-forward. Supermac was held in the same high esteem as all Newcastle United number nines who can score spectacular goals. Like Milburn he had the speed, flair and ferocity of shot which made him capable of winning matches off his own bat.

Jackie was now writing full-time for the *News of the World* covering all of Newcastle's games. As Hughie Gallacher had done before him, so Jackie took it on himself to give the young Newcastle players the benefit of fourteen years spent in a black and white strip. Malcolm Macdonald recalls:

Jackie was a Sunday newspaper journalist, and yet he had one of the greatest PR positions in Newcastle United that I've ever known – particularly when it was unpaid and nobody had actually given him this job.

But he was always there. Always in contact with the players. Always helping. He wasn't wanting to do the dirty stories, the nasty stories; he wasn't wanting to criticise anybody. In his writings he wanted to be constructive with regard to the players and the teams that he talked about.

But when he was actually there – and he was there an awful lot – all the time he would talk and help – how to overcome players' problems, advising them. And on a Friday or Saturday, as players came in, Jackie in his own quiet way, would have *his* team talk in the foyer before we went in for our proper team talk with the coach and the manager. But we'd probably remember more of what Jackie had told us by the time we got on the pitch than what anybody else had said.

At the time Newcastle reached their first Final since Jackie's forty-five-second goal in 1955, the Tynesiders' recent FA Cup record looked little short of a joke. After those glorious fifties, some of the teams who had laughed all the way into the next round after beating Newcastle were: Millwall, Scunthorpe United, Peterborough United, Bedford Town, Swansea, Carlisle United, and probably the biggest upset of them all – Hereford United. Even the 1973/74 Cup campaign had started precariously with Newcastle held at home to non-Leaguers Hendon Town. It took a St James's Park pitch invasion to get them through a fifth-round battle with Nottingham Forest. But Newcastle United had struggled before and still managed to get their hands on the Cup.

One would have thought that with an earlier Cup Final record second to none, the Newcastle United board would have seen fit to invite the players who had served them so well to be their guests on this great occasion. But, insular as ever, no invitations were given, and Jackie Milburn made his own way to London to see the Final. He probably wished he'd stayed at home, as Newcastle United were crushed under a Liverpool steamroller, with goals from Keegan (2) and Heighway (1) flattening poor Joe Harvey's hopes of another Newcastle Cup victory.

As a match reporter, Jackie Milburn's face became a familiar one in the press boxes at Ayresome, Roker and St James Parks. Fellow journalist Doug Weatherall remembers:

Jackie couldn't say a nasty thing about anybody! He offered something through his columns of warmth and experience, and when he mixed with footballers he used to give them hints. As a colleague, his was a lovely face to see in the press box, cos he was such a charming man. 'Are you all right, bonnie lad?' he used to say. He was always first there at the match, and it was always a delight to see him.

One of the highlights of Jackie Milburn's life came in 1980 when he received the news that he was to be given the Freedom of the City of Newcastle, an award bestowed on only the all-time great north-eastern sons. He shared the news with his mother, who had moved back to the Ashington area. Nance took it upon herself to buy Jackie a shirt and tie, which he promised he would wear at the ceremony. Shortly after making that purchase Jackie's mother died, but according to him: 'Once she knew I was going to be made a Freeman, she died a queen.'

A fellow Geordie who was honoured in the same ceremony was Cardinal Basil Hume. 'I did not meet Jackie Milburn until long after he had completed his playing days,' he recalled. 'In my memory as a boy, it was always of the tremendous turn of speed he had – he was electric and he electrified the crowd.'

In 1981 Jackie, in collaboration with John Gibson, wrote: *Jackie Milburn's Newcastle United Scrapbook*, and indirectly from its publication Thames Television arranged to use Jackie as the 'victim' in *This is Your Life*. Hearing from Laura that there was no chance that Jackie would be coaxed down to London, the TV producers arranged to lure him into the Tyne Tees studios in City Road on the pretext of taking part in a sports programme. Typically embarrassed by the whole affair, Jackie had to sit and watch a lifetime's effort squeezed into twenty-five minutes by the show's genial compere Eamonn Andrews. His old pal Len Shackleton refused to appear. 'Purely on principle,' he said. 'It wasn't meant to be a snub on Jackie – we got on great. I just don't like the show.'

Another honour to come along that year was when Jackie was chosen by the then England manager, Ron Greenwood, in his team of 'Players who have made an important contribution to the history and drama of the FA Cup'. The Football Association, to commemorate the Centenary Cup Final, had a dozen silver cigarette cards printed in a limited edition of 2000, which sold at £260 a set. The North-East was well represented in the following side: Trautman (Man City), Spencer (Aston Villa), Hapgood (Arsenal), D. Blanchflower (Spurs), Wright (Wolves), Moore (West Ham), Matthews (Blackpool), Carter (Sunderland), Milburn (Newcastle United), B. Charlton (Man United), Finney (Preston). The reserve chosen was Duncan Edwards (Man United). By 1984 the North-East was in the middle of a miners' strike, and Ashington's mining families were split asunder with brother against brother and father against son, as the 'lions led by donkeys' were reduced to eating from soup kitchens and living on handouts from local grocery shops. It was the bad old days of the twenties and thirties all over again. The strike tore the heart out of Ashington as the pits, once employing 5000, closed one by one.

Still with black and white eyes, Jackie got himself involved with the Newcastle board in their attempt to find a manager to replace Arthur Cox, who had walked out in 1984 after getting United back into the First Division following another six-year spell in the doldrums. The man who was chosen was Milburn's second cousin.

Jack Charlton: Jackie kept phoning me up, asking me to come and do the Newcastle job. I'd resigned at Sheffield Wednesday and taken a year off. I was a bit unsettled in football – in management – at that time. Since I was sixteen I'd had nothing else all my life. I took six months off when I left Middlesbrough and I suddenly found out there was more to life than seven-days-a week football! I was at Sheffield Wednesday for five years, and then I resigned and took a year off, because I'd been offered a lot of other work. I did a lot of television, making a series of 'Round Britain' and another on angling. I did all sorts of things, and I enjoyed my year, and had no real intentions of going back into football, although I knew eventually I would have to get back into the game because the jobs I got were because I was known through football. But I had the year off, and I did very well: I was very busy!

I knocked Jackie back a couple of times. I said: 'No, I don't want the job. I'm OK! I'm doing very well as it is.' At that time Kevin Keegan had just left. And Cox had left, with a lot of talk being made about how there wasn't enough money to buy any new players.

I was opening a double-glazing factory in Consett, and Jackie said: 'Well, at least come and talk to them,' so I did. Jackie fixed it for me to meet the directors at a golf course in Durham.

Jack Charlton, I got him the job at Newcastle. I rang him up and said 'Hey, Jack, we're short of a manager – do you fancy it?' He said, 'Oh, I don't know.' 'Think about it,' I said. I got him out of bed: he'd just come back from a holiday, I think. I said, 'Think about it, and I'll give you a ring later on.'

So I gave him a ring at six o'clock that night, and he said, 'Oh, whey, I'll come up and see

161

what they've got to say.' So I rang Rob MacKenzie at Morpeth – one of the directors – and Seymour. Champion! They were over the moon. I said, 'Well, when can I fix it?' He said, 'Any time.'

McKeag's got a golf course at Durham. He said, 'If Jack's interested, tell him we'll go there and meet him.' To keep him out of Newcastle, you see, at this golf thing at Durham – which they did. And Jack was over the moon, delighted to get the bloody job, and of course they were over the moon with me getting him.

Jack Charlton: To be honest, I got the impression that they were desperate for someone to do the job, because they had just been promoted, and wanted to stay in the First Division, and with Kevin Keegan leaving, they didn't feel that they were strong enough to stay up.

So I said: 'OK, I'll do the job for a year, and then I'll see how I feel.' And I did the job and it was all right. But they really didn't have any money to spend. What a lot of Newcastle fans don't understand about the finances, is that Newcastle can't draw money at the bank because the ground doesn't belong to them: it belongs to the city! And players don't come on to your balance sheet. In those days, to buy an average player you're talking about a quarter of a million pounds. So my job was to keep them in the first division with the players they had, and whatever I sold I could use to spend on new players. I think the figure available was £200,000 for a whole season.

It's a strange place to manage, is Newcastle! And the first year is when you've really got to get down and sort the job out. You've got so many games in an area like the north-east, but in order to improve the team you've got to get around to see the players that you might be interested in, so you've got a lot of travelling to do. I was up and down the motorway like a yo-yo, and I nearly drove off the road a couple of times coming back from matches, only to read in the paper the next day that I wasn't available because I'd gone fishing!

The Press in the north-east drive you mad! Lawrie McMenemy came up to manage Sunderland at the same time, and I remember him saying: 'Oh, I can handle the Press!' And I says: 'Lawrie, you'll find it difficult up here. They won't write what YOU want them to write; if you don't give them anything, they'll write something anyway!'

I tried very hard to keep Chris Waddle! I got him a cap for England! I told Bobby Robson to play him in Belfast. And from the day he came back from that game I knew he had made a deal with somebody, but he wouldn't say. And it wasn't till the end of the season that it came out that it was Tottenham! But you couldn't talk to Chris: he just wouldn't talk to you about contracts or signing and staying.

Jackie knew all about the Waddle deal! Him and Joe Harvey were the two I could sit down with in the office, and pour out all my troubles to: the difficulties of the job. I used to talk over this player or that player. Everybody thinks that ALL players want to play for Newcastle, which is not the case! Getting players to go there is very difficult. For a start, most of them are married, and they go to their wives and say that Newcastle are interested. Well, at that time Newcastle was a depressed area, and the wife would say: 'No, I'm not going!' or 'Where's Newcastle?'

Everybody thinks Newcastle United has an unlimited supply of money, and that isn't true! Supporters keep saying that directors should put money into the club. I don't know many directors who have *ever* put money into clubs! But Newcastle directors have certainly done as much as anybody else. It always seems strange to me up here that directors have always been the ones who got the blame. There's nobody worked harder for Newcastle United than the directors: they love the club! They never interfered with the way I ran Newcastle – not for one day!

But I wanted to get out after that first year! You find yourself getting trapped into a job, but I did that year, and I didn't have a contract: I never have a contract with anybody! I needed to leave – I wanted to leave! Like I say, I had spoiled myself when I had that year off. And I never settled: I begrudged the time that the game was taking away from me. And I tried to explain this to Jackie, but he couldn't understand. None of the north-eastern people could understand why nobody wants to be the manager of Newcastle United! We argued long and hard about it! I think, to Jackie, Newcastle was *the* job in football. It was very hard for me to resign and leave.

When Jack walked out that day, I could have hit him. There were a few organised hooligans wanting to get rid of Jack. I don't know why. And they started to get at him during this match. It was a pre-season friendly. And they started to shout for Jack, and there was only . . . what . . . twenty or thirty . . . The rest of the people understood.

Jack Charlton: It wasn't because the crowd got on to me! They had a go at me for not signing Eric Gates, and Lawrie signing him for Sunderland. He'd signed him on the Saturday morning before we played a pre-season friendly with Sheffield United. I'll never forget Jackie's face when I went downstairs after the match, and I resigned straightaway.

After the match came out, I said: 'What are you going to do?' Jack says, 'I'm finished with this bloody . . .'. I said, 'What do you mean?' and I rushed across because I knew if any of the press had heard they would have been starting to print it. He started to shout then: 'Oh, I'm finished! I'm packing my bags on Monday morning.'

Jack Charlton: It upset Jackie greatly! But then that whole weekend blew up, and I went away to the farmhouse in the Dales to get away from everybody who was going to be chasing me, and I said I would come back on the Monday morning. And it was difficult over that weekend not to change my mind. In spite of what Jackie may have thought, that whole episode provided me with the excuse I needed for getting away. It was my get-out, and if I didn't take it, I was going to stay. I maybe should've left it until we'd got into the season, but there was a time to do it and that time was then!

163

On the Monday morning I went back and spoke to Joe Harvey. Joe was sat in his little office which was next to mine on the other side of the car-park, and I says: 'What do you think, Joe?' And Joe said to me: 'I would leave! Once they get on to you here, there's a certain section will never let go. I've had it all myself, but I never had anywhere else to go. So, if you've something else, you do what you think is best. But I agree with you.' That's what Harvey said.

And it was only a few hooligans! I don't know . . . when you're in this game you get criticised all your life. You expect it. It keeps you going, man. Keeps you alive!

Now over sixty, and beavering away at his weekly column, Jackie had still more moments to savour, more accolades to embarrass him. In February 1987, to celebrate its twentieth anniversary, the Newcastle Sports Council awarded Jackie a shining Wilkinson Sword for his services to sport in the city. Receiving the sword from the Duke of Edinburgh, Jackie said it was one of the greatest honours he had been given in his career.

A few months later, in May, Jackie was the overwhelming winner of a competition run by the *Sunday Sun* and the North-East Football Writers' Association to find the North-East's greatest post-war player. To win the award of a silver salver Jackie had beaten off the challenges of some of the most famous footballers to come out of the region: Wilf Mannion, Len Shackleton, Brian Clough, Kevin Keegan, Charlie Hurlie and Peter Beardsley. He even received votes from Sunderland supporters!

After more than 130 years of drawing coal, the inevitable happened in March 1988 when the miners of Ashington colliery worked their last shift. Jackie was invited to be on hand for the photographers as the men stepped out of the cage for the last time. 'I was fifteen when I first went down Ashington pit as a trainee fitter,' he told reporters, 'and, to be honest, I hated it every time I had to go underground. Imagine what years of breathing that coal dust can do to your health.'

Woodhorn Colliery, where miners had once threatened to strike because of Jackie, had been closed for a number of years. Now ironically a museum, one of the first exhibitions to go on display was of Milburn memorabilia, standing proudly next to the paintings of the Ashington Art Group, itself now defunct because of lack of interest. Only one founder member, Oliver Kilbourne, aged eighty-five, still remained.

Jackie retired from his *News of the World* job on 8 May 1988, three days before his sixty-fourth birthday, bidding a final farewell to his readers.

Today, with a million happy memories, I wave goodbye to my greatest pal: football! I've made a living out of the best game in the world – as a player, talker or writer – ever since I can remember. Lady Luck has smiled on me most of the time, but now, through minor health reasons, I'm calling it a day. And I wonder what it is going to be like now I'm not involved in a game that's been my whole life.

By then the Milburns had moved back to the top end of Ashington, near his 'second home', the Rec. Now with time to spare, Jackie often went across to the ground where he had run his heart out as a boy, and just lingered beside the deserted football field, staring into space, as though reliving some of those far-off days.

'. . . and you just wondered how a man who had been idolised by thousands of people could feel so alone . . .'

My interview with Jackie Milburn – 'player, talker, writer' – was nearing its completion as the front door opened and his wife Laura came smiling into view. After a few minutes of brief introductions, he gave her the kind of look that bears witness to forty years of good marriage, and said: 'Champion! Haddaway put the kettle on.'

CHAPTER EIGHTEEN

All of my life's been football

1943   Stan Seymour to Frank Watts, Newcastle United's secretary: 'There's the forms; I've signed Jackie Milburn, a future international.'

1949   Ken Malcolm, *Sunday People*: 'The player of inspiration gives as great a delight as rain in the desert. Milburn has this quality to a rare degree.'

1949   Sherrif Hill, *Newcastle Evening Chronicle*: 'Today I met Jackie Milburn, our own international, and confirmed my opinion that there is not so modest a sportsman in the country.'

1949   Roy Peskett, *Daily Mail*, on Milburn's hat-trick for England *v* Wales: 'Step forward Jackie Milburn to be congratulated on as brilliant a centre-forward display as I have seen for years.'

1950   Scott Hall, *Sporting Chronicle*: on Hearts *v* Newcastle charity game: 'Even the Hearts fans talked excitedly about Milburn's mazy dribbles and wonderful footwork.'

1951   Henry Rose, on Burnley *v* Newcastle: 'Milburn gave a display which has helped to restore one's faith in English football. Of the seventeen centre-forwards I have seen this season, I name Milburn number one by a mile!'

1951   Jack Milligan, *Daily Graphic*, on Milburn's second Cup Final goal: 'The Goal of the Century, was the unanimous verdict of 100,000 fans who watched

Jackie Milburn, Newcastle United's flying centre-forward, score from Taylor's backheel.'

1951 Eric Thompson, *Daily Mail*: 'The Cup does something to Jackie Milburn. Usually, he is an ordinary kind of guy, but he is probably the fastest man in football today. He has the personality which marks the greats of old.'

1952 Phil King, *Sunday Dispatch*, on Huddersfield *v* Newcastle: 'Jackie Milburn looked every inch an England centre-forward with his rapier-like thrusts.'

1953 Ivan Sharpe: 'On the field, Milburn always looks like a thoroughbred. He moves that way. I regard Milburn as one of the best centre-forwards in the history of the game.'

1955 Ken Mackenzie, *Newcastle Journal*, on Milburn's 1955 Cup Final goal: 'It was out of the blue for Wor Jackie to snatch one of his rare headed goals in 45 seconds.'

1956 John Arlott, *News Chronicle*, on Newcastle's Cup tie against Sunderland: 'The spectators who manage to get into St James's Park before the gates are shut will see the greatest of modern cup players: Jackie Milburn, one of the most popular footballers in Britain. There is about Milburn the stamp of the old Corinthians, the first men to typify English football. Some of his old speed has gone, but it has been replaced by developing craft; above all, he retains every scrap of his keenness and match-winning shots.'

1957 Stan Bell, *Newcastle Evening Chronicle*: 'Jackie Milburn, hero-worshipped by every Geordie football fan, has played his last game for Newcastle United. His request to join Linfield, the Irish League club, has been granted.'

1957 Stan Halsey, on Milburn's Irish debut against Distillery: 'The trouble was that Jackie was too much a manager to be magician in this match.'

1957 Jimmy Scoular, *Newcastle Journal*: '*Golden Goals*, that's the title of Jackie Milburn's book that is making history for the Magpies.'

1958 Ken Mackenzie, *Newcastle Journal*: 'Jackie Milburn, former Newcastle United and England player, is to lead the Irish League attack in Dublin.'

1958 Hastings Macguinness, *Belfast Herald*, on Linfield *v* Crusaders: 'In scoring six goals, Jackie Milburn gave his finest individual performance since he came to Windsor Park from Newcastle.'

1960 *New of the World*, on Linfield *v* Ards Irish Cup Final: 'This completed the medal collection of Jackie Milburn who has helped Linfield to take every Irish trophy to Windsor Park in his three-year reign at the club.'

1960 Frank McGhee, *Daily Mirror*, on Linfield's debut in European Cup: 'A name out of the glorious past to most fans, but over in Ireland, Jackie Milburn is the man of the moment.'

1960 *Daily Mail*, 10 November: 'On a day when Football League players are considering strike action, Jackie Milburn, 36-year-old Newcastle and England centre-forward, is considering whether to join Southern League club, Yiewsley.'

1963 Mike Langley, *Daily Express*, 29 January: 'Jackie Milburn, three times a Cup winner with Newcastle United, hung up his boots last night and became manager of League champions, Ipswich Town.'

1964 *Newcastle Evening Chronicle*, 24 March: 'Jackie Milburn, former Tyneside idol, now manager of Division One "bottom dogs", said last night he would resign if that was thought to be the answer.'

1967 Ken Mackenzie, *Newcastle Journal*, 10 May: 'Tyneside fans will say a golden thank you to Jackie Milburn when he has his testimonial match at St James's Park tonight.'

1981 Thames Television producer to Laura Milburn: 'Do you think Jackie would agree to be the subject of *This is Your Life*?'

1981 Cardinal Basil Hume: 'I did not meet Jackie until the occasion we were both made Freeman of the City of Newcastle. He was proud and so was I.'

1987 *News of the World*, 1 March: 'Jackie Milburn, Newcastle's most famous sporting celebrity, took a standing ovation at a Sports Council dinner when the Duke of Edinburgh presented him with an award given annually for "Outstanding contributions to sport in Newcastle".'

1987 *Sunday Sun*, 17 March: 'Newcastle United legend, Jackie Milburn, has won the award as "The north-east's greatest post-war player".'

1988 Keith Moor, *Newcastle Journal*, 25 March: 'Football legend, Jackie Milburn, yesterday turned out to help blow the final whistle on Ashington colliery.'

1988 Jackie Milburn, *News of the World*, 8 May (the last headline he wrote for his column): 'Newcastle's Gascoigne Magic Has 'Em Reeling.'

1988 Alan Oliver, *Newcastle Journal*, 13 October: 'Jackie Milburn made his final journey past his beloved St James's Park today. His memory will live on, and when they talk about the all-time greats, his name will always be the first mentioned.'

JACKIE MILBURN

	His complete record at St James's Park League, Cup & Wartime games								Record of England Caps		

<table>
<tr><td colspan="2">LEAGUE</td><td colspan="2">FA CUP</td><td colspan="2">WARTIME</td><td colspan="2">TOTAL</td><td></td><td>Goals</td><td>Match result (England first)</td></tr>
<tr><td>App</td><td>Gls</td><td>App</td><td>Gls</td><td>App</td><td>Gls</td><td>App</td><td>Gls</td><td></td><td colspan="2">1948–49</td></tr>
<tr><td>1943–44</td><td></td><td></td><td></td><td></td><td>24</td><td>12</td><td>24</td><td>12</td><td>v Ireland</td><td>1</td><td>6–2</td></tr>
<tr><td>1944–45</td><td></td><td></td><td></td><td></td><td>32</td><td>12</td><td>32</td><td>12</td><td>v Wales</td><td>0</td><td>1–0</td></tr>
<tr><td>1945–46</td><td></td><td></td><td>2</td><td>2</td><td>39</td><td>14</td><td>41</td><td>16</td><td>v Switzerland</td><td>1</td><td>6–0</td></tr>
<tr><td>1946–47</td><td>24</td><td>7</td><td>3</td><td>1</td><td></td><td></td><td>27</td><td>8</td><td>v Scotland</td><td>1</td><td>1–2</td></tr>
<tr><td>1947–48</td><td>39</td><td>20</td><td>1</td><td></td><td></td><td></td><td>40</td><td>20</td><td>v Wales</td><td>3</td><td>4–1</td></tr>
<tr><td>1948–49</td><td>34</td><td>19</td><td>1</td><td></td><td></td><td></td><td>35</td><td>19</td><td></td><td colspan="2">1949–50</td></tr>
<tr><td>1949–50</td><td>30</td><td>18</td><td>2</td><td>3</td><td></td><td></td><td>32</td><td>21</td><td>v Portugal</td><td>0</td><td>5–3</td></tr>
<tr><td>1950–51</td><td>31</td><td>17</td><td>8</td><td>8</td><td></td><td></td><td>39</td><td>25</td><td>v Belgium</td><td>0</td><td>4–1</td></tr>
<tr><td>1951–52</td><td>32</td><td>25</td><td>7</td><td>3</td><td></td><td></td><td>39</td><td>28</td><td>v Spain (W/Cup)</td><td>0</td><td>0–1</td></tr>
<tr><td>1952–53</td><td>16</td><td>5</td><td></td><td></td><td></td><td></td><td>16</td><td>5</td><td>v Wales</td><td>1</td><td>4–2</td></tr>
<tr><td>1953–54</td><td>39</td><td>16</td><td>5</td><td>2</td><td></td><td></td><td>44</td><td>18</td><td></td><td colspan="2">1950–51</td></tr>
<tr><td>1954–55</td><td>38</td><td>19</td><td>10</td><td>2</td><td></td><td></td><td>48</td><td>21</td><td>v Argentina</td><td>1</td><td>2–1</td></tr>
<tr><td>1955–56</td><td>38</td><td>19</td><td>4</td><td>2</td><td></td><td></td><td>42</td><td>21</td><td>v Portugal</td><td>2</td><td>5–2</td></tr>
<tr><td>1956–57</td><td>32</td><td>12</td><td>1</td><td></td><td></td><td></td><td>33</td><td>12</td><td>v France</td><td>0</td><td>2–2</td></tr>
<tr><td></td><td></td><td></td><td></td><td></td><td></td><td></td><td></td><td></td><td></td><td colspan="2">1955–56</td></tr>
<tr><td></td><td>353</td><td>177</td><td>44</td><td>23</td><td>95</td><td>38</td><td>492</td><td>238</td><td>v Denmark</td><td>0</td><td>5–1</td></tr>
</table>

CHAPTER NINETEEN

I wish I was just starting, quite honestly

John Edward Thompson (Jet) Milburn died of lung cancer on 9 October 1988. He was sixty-four years old, and had been a heavy cigarette smoker since he was a boy. Four days later there was something akin to a state funeral as thousands of mourners lined the route taken by the cortege from his house in Ashington to St Nicholas Cathedral in Newcastle. Traffic was halted and grown men, heads bowed, wept as the black cars inched their way into the city. His body was later cremated and his ashes sprinkled on the centre-circle at St James's Park where, with genuine modesty, he had experience adulation from the age of nineteen.

In what was a moving, if somewhat spectacular send-off, mourner Jack Charlton, looking around at the milling crowds, commented: 'Knowing Wor Jackie, if he'd guessed it was going to be like this, he wouldn't have turned up.' And although the idea tickled him at the time, he probably wouldn't have attended the opening night of the musical 'Wor Jackie' either, which had its premiere at Ashington in May 1989 in front of his family and many of his friends.

In memory of a loyal employee, the Newcastle board renamed its new West Stand the 'Milburn Stand', and the *Newcastle Evening Chronicle* is currently running a campaign to have a full-size bronze statue of Milburn erected in the heart of the city, in Northumberland Street.

Tributes to Jackie Milburn could fill at least one more volume of any biography.

Linfield FC: 'As a footballer, Jackie Milburn was something special and his remarkable skills have left an endearing mark on the memories of a legion of fans in this province, particularly those with Linfield allegiances.'

Ipswich Town: 'It was with great sadness that everyone heard of the death of former manager Jackie Milburn. He faced a difficult task at Portman Road in following Sir Alf, and the pressures of managership were causing his health to suffer when he tendered his resignation. Many were sorry that he had not been successful, since there were few people in the game who were so genuine, modest and pleasant. Perhaps Jackie Milburn's fault was that he was a little too nice.'

Malcolm Macdonald: 'Sadly, now that Jackie's gone, what is going to be missed most of all is Jackie standing in the foyer of St James's Park, able to advise current players and players of the future. And for that, Newcastle United – and the players of Newcastle United over the years – will miss out tremendously on the greatest unpaid coach that I've ever known.'

Bryan Robson: 'I was very privileged and, indeed, honoured, to be involved in his testimonial – a memory that will be with me always. As for "Wor Jackie", his name will live forever when mine has faded with the passing of time.'

Tom Finney: 'Jackie was with me a lot as room-mate in our England travels. He was the fastest thing in football, and won world-wide admiration. But for all that, he was strangely insecure with no confidence in his own ability. I will always have a great regard for Jackie: he was a super lad!'

Bobby Charlton: 'Jack and I once went to the Wallaw cinema in Ashington to see a newsreel of one of Jackie's England games. We were late and had to sit through Moira Shearer in *Red Shoes* until it was repeated.'

Albert Stubbins: 'Whatever he was doing, Jackie had the capacity to impress people that he was a special kind of man. I was very proud to be associated with Jackie Milburn.'

Joe Harvey: 'It was great having him in your team, because he scored every bloody week! You can't get better than that! But he was more than just a great player – he was a lovely man.'

Chris Waddle: 'The legend will live on. I'll never forget how thrilled I was when he told me that I deserved to wear the Newcastle number-nine shirt.'

Bob Stokoe: 'I had the pleasure of playing with him on many occasions and, being a defender, had a close-up of him at full stretch, scoring some wonderful goals. He was the most exciting thing I've ever seen on a football field.'

Jack Fairbrother: 'When Milburn struck, not a player could get near him. He was unbeatable, and his match-winning goals were gems.'

Stan Matthews: 'He had that rare gift of being able to make himself popular with players and officials.'

Cardinal Basil Hume: 'He was not only a footballer, but a great gentleman, and a person who won instant respect. There was a quality of goodness about him which inspired others.'

Way back in 1953, the *Evening Chronicle* ran a competition to find out if the Geordie fans thought Milburn a better winger than centre-forward. Even from the scores of letters which were sent in, it was impossible to arrive at anything conclusive; when it came to Jackie Milburn, nothing was ever quite black and white.

But on the question of why Jackie was idolised by the folk of the North-East, many would side with Arthur Appleton:

He is a legend because of what he did when the crowds were great, when you got fifty or sixty thousand a match, and you had this man who could change a game; who could explode into action; who looked lovely running forward and who could shoot. You had one of the most dramatic and spectacular players in the game. And that – with so many people seeing him – is the basis of him being remembered.

And as the redundant miners shed their pit boots and tiptoe into the 1990s, what of the town of Ashington? If the Methodist ministers came back, they would see a great change. The pit heaps have given way to country parks, and the cesspits to surfing lakes. All that remain as reminders of 'Satan's citadel' are a pair of rusty pit-winding wheels breaking the skyline above the museum of Woodhorn colliery. Monuments of the past, they have become Ashington's own twin towers, overlooking the distant green of the football fields of Hirst Welfare.

No longer 'cinema and club conscious', the town has closed all its pictures houses – the last images flickered across the five cinema screens almost ten years ago – and of the original twenty-two working men's clubs many have gone with only a handful of those that remain still viable.

But the 'crack' never changes, as the old-timers sit playing dominoes in the West End Club: football and Newcastle United! And although St James's Park looks vastly different with its Harvey's Bar and Milburn Stand, the accolades of the success-starved fans are *still* reserved for the prolific goalscoring number nine, but now it is the mighty Mickey Quinn who blasts a pathway to new glories.

But it's all in the game to a long-suffering Newcastle United supporter like Geordie, a character in the 'Wor Jackie' musical. Leave him with his memories and he's a happy man. 'Jackie Milburn! He's your Venerable Bede in a black 'n' white strip, St Cuthbert in an England cap, and St Aidan in a pair of size six football boots, all rolled into one. He's bonnier than Bobby Shaftoe and bigger than the Lambton Worm. Whey – the man's a legend!'

And the last word . . .

Being out on the field there, the people who watched, they wanted to be in your position – simple as that. And I was delighted! But I'll tell you what: I wouldn't have been half the player without the encouragement of me own local people here. They made me what I am.

Well, football's a wonderful thing here. You've got to be born here to appreciate this. I was fortunate to get to play for this team; it's what I always wanted. And hey, I wish I was just starting, quite honestly!

JACKIE MILBURN
1924–1988

He used his feet to blast away the shackles
and the walls came tumbling down.

INDEX

arrival at Newcastle United, 22
Simpson, Ronnie, 52, 76, 108
Sinclair, John, 78–9
Slater, W. J., 66
Smith, Norman, 18, 59, 61, 110
Smith, Ted, 43
Smith, Tot, 21
South Africa, tour of, 85, 87, 92–4
sprinting, professional, 13–14
Stableforth, A. B., 85
Stobbart, George, 22, 23, 26
Stokoe, Bob, 22, 99, 103, 107, 108, 159
Stubbins, Albert, 18, 20, 21, 22, 88, 107–8
Sun, 153
Swinburne, Tom, 19–20, 22

Tait, Alec, 80, 129
Taylor, Ernie, 22, 38, 65, 75
Taylor, Wilf, 15–16, 135
televising of football, 88–9, 94
This is Your Life, 160
Thompson, Tommy, 38
tours,
    Canada, 35–6
    Europe 1951, 72–3
    Germany, 125

South Africa, 85, 87, 92–4
Trinder, Tommy, 128

Waddle, Chris, 162
wages, 123
    early 1950s, 62
    1953, 102
    maximum, 1948, 25
    Milburn's first full-time professional,
        21
Watson, Willie, 55
Wayman, Charlie, 19, 22, 23, 24, 109
Welfare Rangers, 12
Wembley Waltz, 112
White, Len, 100
Whitehead, Bobby, 79
Whittit, Arthur, 145
Whitty, John, 65
Winterbottom, Walter, 40, 46, 47, 61–2
World Cup,
    1950, 49–50
    1954, 108
Wright, Billy, 32
Wright, Dougie, 19, 22

Yiewsley Football Club, 145